D0906171

The Technology Trap

Survival in a Man-Made Environment

Leo J. Moser

Nelson-Hall nh Chicago

Library of Congress Cataloging in Publication Data

Moser, Leo John.
  Technology trap.

  Bibliography: p.
  1. Man—Influence of environment. 2. Man—Influence
on nature. 3. Human ecology. 4. Technology and
civilization. I. Title.
GF51.M63   301.31   78-26034
ISBN 0-88229-419-9 (cloth)
ISBN 0-88229-669-8 (paper)
Copyright © 1979 by Leo J. Moser

Manufactured in the United States of America

10   9   8   7   6   5   4   3   2   1

To my wife, Helen
And with appreciation to
Mark, Ann, Carol, and Robert
for their patience.

Contents

Preface ix

Part one—Introduction

1 Conqueror in Peril 3

Part two—Man: Creature of Environment

2 The Legacy of Past Environments 13
3 The Unique Nature of Our Species 25
4 The Intimacy of Mind and Environment 53
5 Limits of the Human Scale 72
6 The Fig Leaf of Culture 84

Part three—The Technological Trap Is Set

7 Primitive Technologies and New Environments 103
8 Ecology by Artifice 125
9 Man Meets Machine 138
10 Folded, Spindled, and Mutilated 149
11 How the Trap Could Spring 171

Part four—Can We Escape the Trap?

12 Can We Remake Man? 195
13 Down with Technology! 209
14 Environment as Art-Form 218

Part five—Conclusion

15 How to Survive though Civilized 237

Notes 247

Glossary 259

Index 273

Preface

A generation or so ago, an overriding faith in "human progress" was still one of the basic credos of the average citizen. New technologies and industries, like aviation, plastics, and telecommunications, were rapidly developing. The more ancient sciences, like medicine, chemistry, and biology, were being transformed by new insights and techniques. Chronic problems could, of course, be identified in the human world—hunger, disease, and illiteracy were still rampant in many areas—but the advances of science promised to provide all the needed answers. Every new solution supplied more energy for human use. Most seemed to give the species greater control over its destiny. The major flaw in this rosy picture was acknowledged to be the threat of war. But if war could be avoided or its effects contained, most people felt that future generations had every right to expect a better and better world in which to live.

In the last decades, however, we have seen the mood change dramatically. Many now openly dispute the virtues of modern technology and some see in it grave threats to human survival. Noted scientists describe *Homo sapiens* as an "endangered species," one put into jeopardy by a world of its own creation. Biologists and ecologists see the species wallowing in increasing pollution and irresponsibly expanding populations toward the breaking point. Economists remind us that our techno-industrial society is heavily dependent on sources of energy that are not renewable. Political scientists describe the dehumanization of mass-man by the few who have the power to manipulate the many. In short, our world of technology is often treated as if it were a quietly ticking bomb, and human "progress" seen as a march toward extinction.

Unfortunately, all too many facts can be marshalled to support such pessimistic theses. I believe, however, that many have thus far missed the real dimension of our problem. The reams of paper expended during the last few years on the topic of our relation to our environment have tended to center on the threat to our bodies created by modern technology and the things it pours forth. I feel that the real threat is posed in the psychological, cultural, and social realm. Sociologists like Jacques Ellul have opened the discussion of the impact of technology on modern society, but there are many other disciplines that could contribute to our understanding of the total problem but from which little has been heard in any systematic form. The reason that modern technology seems to threaten our minds and personalities has never been adequately analyzed.

Throughout human history, we have rather effectively dealt with physical threats that have been posed by our environment —particularly since the advent of what we usually call "civilization." Human inventiveness has proved more than an equal match for the physical challenges of hostile environments. Using new tools and new technologies, human beings have penetrated into more and more inhospitable environments—into the deserts, out on the seas, up the mountain slopes, far above the Arctic Circle, and even into the near-vacuums of space.

But how about our record in meeting psychological, cultural, or social challenges? Much less impressive. Little evidence of any linear progression. Proud civilizations have decayed into near chaos. Wars have continued to be waged with undiminished brutality and with increasing loss of life. Our opulent urban cultures have led not to any heaven-on-earth within our cities but to new frictions and to a weakening of an essential element in human social life: the sense of community or belonging.

With all our psychologists and psychiatrists, there is no reason to assume that we have today any less mental illness than the people of two thousand years ago. We may well have more. Fear and suspicion remain the primary emotions in the relationship between nations and cultures. It is not an impressive record.

In this work, I will be concerned with both the human environment and the nature of mankind. But my effort will be to interrelate the two in a new and, it is to be hoped, a more thoughtful way. The most important factor in this relationship, as I see it, is the structure that we call the human intelligence. The major threat to our species is the fact that our intelligence has given us unprecedented power and mastery over the world around us—power that we are not sure how to use. There is growing concern that we have created, in modern technology, a Frankenstein monster that will ultimately enslave and dehumanize the race that created it. The host of philosophic problems related to the rise of technology has only now begun to attract systematic attention. An example would be the work of Carl Mitcham & Robert Mackey, *Bibliography of the Philosophy of Technology* (Chicago: University of Chicago Press, 1973).

With humanity, it is the mind that is the crucial factor. It is our minds that will lead us either to survival or extinction. This book, in discussing our relationship to our environment, will differ from most recent works on environmental affairs in that it will put the emphasis on the many roles played by the human mind in our relationships to the world about us. It will also attempt to define and to organize into a consistent matrix many of the words we tend to use in discussing this topic. Others will have to be coined. For this reason, this book is best read in the order presented. If you wish, however, to jump immediately to a particular chapter in order to sample my views, I recommend that you use the glossary supplied in the back of the book when you come across any word that seems to have a special connotation in this work.

As a subject, ecology obviously has much to contribute, not only to the biological sciences and to the way that we deal with chemistry, engineering, and other aspects of modern technological society, but also to the social sciences, including psychology and philosophy. A fully developed "ecology of the human mind" would be vastly more complex than any other aspect of human ecology. It is strange indeed that so little attention has been given the role of the human mind in the ecological equation. Perhaps we stand too close to our own minds to see that they also have their own inner landscapes.

In the book at hand, I will attempt, then, to direct addi-

tional attention to the need to take the whole person into account in our environmental studies—our patterns of thought as
well as our technological processes, our psychological needs as
well as our chemical tolerances, our ways of analysis as well as
our industrial wastes. I will try to show more clearly the mutual
relationship between mind and environment and to demonstrate
that, just as the human mind has affected environment, it was
the challenges of past environments that formed the contours
of the human mind. Most important, I will attempt to show that
this mutual relationship is a continuing one—a relationship that
we cannot ignore if we are to survive.

Part One

Introduction

1
Conqueror in Peril

Our species, which has gained unprecedented control over all other forms of life on earth, which has even developed the technological skills needed to travel to the moon, finds its survival more seriously threatened than ever before. We know, in a general sense, the kind of factors that led the dinosaur and the dodo toward extinction. As we will see in the pages to follow, the point can be made that the human race is on a trajectory that could well lead it to the same fate. If our species is to survive, it will take conscious effort and greater understanding of the situation in which we find ourselves.

Many of the steps that so often lead to the disappearance of a species have already been taken. We can see in our recent history patterns that so often accompanied the extinction of other forms of life: those that show a gradual breakdown in the natural relationship between the organism and its environment. A species typically disappears when it either loses its original environment or when new elements are added to that environment with which it cannot cope. A noted student of the evolutionary process, George Gaylord Simpson, in a chapter on the extinction of species, concludes that the true cause of such extinction "seems to be a change in the life situation, the organism-environment integration, requiring in the organisms concerned an adaptive change which they are unable to make."[1]

Such dislocations are already happening to our species. The only difference is that the changes we face are primarily self-initiated; they are the cumulative result of past human brain activity. As I hope will appear from discussion in the chapters to follow, this may not be as significant a distinction as it may at first seem.

There has been, I will admit, general recognition in recent years of many of the physical problems that we face in maintaining an environment that will allow our species to survive. The need to come to grips with overpopulation, to conserve natural resources, to protect wildlife, and to eliminate the pollution brought about by growing industrial complexes are very important issues; and I do not wish by any means to underestimate their significance. They are very much a part of the total problem facing our species today. Nevertheless, I feel that there are factors of even greater weight that have often been overlooked: the psychological, social, and intellectual implications of living in a strange industrial world.

Certain of the symptoms that our new technologies created have become the subject of sociological concern, but their roots in the distortion of environmental relationships have often been either overlooked or only touched on in passing. Concern over the direction of evolution of our societies is by no means new. Images of a more glorious past were conjured up in some of the most ancient literature: the Garden of Eden, the Golden Age in Mediterranean mythology, the era of the sage-kings in the Confucian tradition. Bitter commentary about the effect of the industrial revolution is as old as the revolution. We see it in the eighteenth-century theories of Rousseau and in the nineteenth-century novels of Dickens. Recent writers like Kafka, Orwell, Ellul, and Marcuse have alerted us to the dangers inherent in the new systems of regimentation made possible by the techniques of the second industrial revolution. The list of identified symptoms of a growing social malaise becomes longer and longer with every passing year.

Some of the symptoms of distress that we see in our technological society today have origins that go back for millennia, and we have almost come to think of them as part of the human condition. After all, even the agriculture and city life of the ancient world was far from natural to our species. Other symptoms we associate more with the nineteenth and twentieth centuries: for example, the social disorganization of the new industrial cities, the attack on rationality as a norm of human behavior with the subsequent attempt to find alternative norms in one or another simplistic ideology, and group frustrations that spread to entire national populations—frustrations that have helped to set the base for World Wars I and II and a number of lesser wars in our century. Still other symptoms seem more specifically the problems of the present generation: for example, the increasingly apparent intellectual disorientation of contemporary society, a sense of anomie among many young people, a sharply rising crime rate in the cities, and intergroup fears and suspicions that have encouraged nations to develop nuclear weapons. All these problems—more and more—have deep roots in the changing relationship of humanity and environment. They can be prevented from becoming threats to human survival, I believe, only as we find ways to readjust that relationship.

Self-initiated changes in our environment have left us badly out of harmony with ourselves and the world around us. That outer world no longer seems to reflect our inner needs, whether we are thinking of our more basic drives, our artistic sensitivities, or our intellectual natures. We are out of patience with our world. It annoys us; it frustrates us; yet we do not seem to know how to reform it. There are those who believe we will have to reform it. There are those who believe we will have to wreck it; "Only from the ashes of the present world can we hope to create a newer and better one," they say. Others suggest that we will not have to bother to destroy our present system, for it is locked into a pattern of inevitable self-destruction. Too many patterns of modern growth—whether we are looking at population, the rate of innovation, or countless other variables—show rates of exponential expansion that seem to foretell the destruction of the system itself.[2]

In addition to what we think of as the environment, the outer world, the human has as well an inner world—the world of the mind. This inner world was, of course, forged by *Homo sapiens* and its progenitors during the long course of successive adaptations that make up the evolutionary history of the human race. Once established, the inner world of a species is not, however, easily changed. As humans have gained superficial power over the world about them, they have tended to remake that world in accordance with the immediate drives and limited pre-conceptions of their inner world. Like looking at your own re-flection in a very closely-held and flexible mirror, the process can lead to significant distortions. The disparity between the outer and inner worlds of our species has sharpened greatly with each passing year. What we need now is a broader perspective. We must stand back and look at where we really stand. We must realize, too, that much of what we see is reflection rather than reality, and we must take that factor into due account.

The inner world of our senses and intelligence evolved into the form we experience today during a period when our progenitors lived by hunting and gathering amid grassland and savanna, acting and reacting in an environment and on a scale that I will refer to here as the *middle realm*. In our *inner* natures we remain the subjects of that middle realm, virtual prisoners within its confines. On the other hand, by reorgan-izing our material surroundings and our way of life, we have so radically changed our *outer* world that we have in essence exiled ourselves from anything approaching our natural environment.

Half prisoner and half exile, techno-industrial man finds his life torn by a strange ambiguity. To meet this threat, we must first realize more clearly our limitations as subjects of the middle realm. Second, we must consciously begin to look for ways whereby we can assure that the intellectual, social, and physical contours of our outer world does less violence to the inner needs of individuals.

The concept of the middle realm, as I will use it in the chapters to follow, is much more than a new term for the an-cient or more "natural" human environment. It does more than describe the range and scale of our activities as a species. It is key to our understanding of those behavioral and conceptual patterns that have been long internalized by our species. It speaks of those structures that we usually call our minds.

The old environment—that in which our species origi-nally evolved—seems now to be a thing of the past. Today only a handful of isolated tribesmen lead their lives amid anything approaching that ancient world. But, as we will see, that aban-doned environment does live on in a very significant way. It lives within us as part of our *inner world*. For all our technology, we remain subjects of that former world. Our joys, our understandings—our very natures—are closely tied to life as it was lived in that bygone environment. We can avoid recognition of this fact only at considerable peril to the continued existence of our species. A central purpose of this book is to show how the human environment of the past—the original *middle realm*—forged our intellectual powers in their present molds, and to describe the present dilemma of reconciling our former natures with present needs and future hopes.

Even though the basic facts of evolution have been generally acknowledged for many years, intellectuals have continued into this century to characterize mankind as being basically different from the other animals in degree of adaptability. Sometimes mankind is described as if totally "plastic"—that is, as if ours were a species uniquely able to adjust at will, unconfined by any set patterns of behavior. Those who argue this view ask: Haven't groups like the Eskimos and Lapps learned to live efficiently in the frozen Arctic wastes? Don't peoples like the Quechua and Aymara show a remarkable adjustment to life on the Andean altiplano? Haven't desert tribes like the Tuareg accommodated to the glaring sun of the central Sahara? Doesn't all this show the unlimited adaptability of human beings?

Many of our philosophers will concede that "animals" are governed by genetically determined behavior patterns, but imply that we are free of any of the same compulsions. "Man is a substantial emigrant on a pilgrimage of being, and it is accordingly meaningless to set limits on what he is capable of being. . . ." declared Ortega y Gasset. "Man in a word has no nature, what he has is . . . history."[3]

To a great extent, this denial of a human nature is the context in which the modern existentialists have viewed what they considered the enigma facing modern man. A few anthropologists and—until a decade or two ago—many students of the behavior of animals under laboratory conditions were advancing similar views, although not necessarily in the same philosophic context. In fact, I believe that the real story will be seen in the chapters below to be quite otherwise—that ours will be seen to be a severely circumscribed species, just like those species that we distinguish sharply from ourselves by the term "animal."[4]

"Mankind naturally and generally loves to be flattered," wrote Benjamin Franklin in one of his early philosophic essays. "Whatever soothes our pride, and tends to exalt our species above the rest of the creation, we are pleased with and easily believe, when ungrateful truths shall be with the utmost indignation rejected. . . . But, (to use a piece of common sense) our geese are but geese though we may think them swans: and truth will be truth though it sometimes proves mortifying and distasteful."[5]

If we are to consider human behavior in the light of that of other species, we must avoid several pitfalls. To begin with, the observation of a behavioral or perceptual pattern in one species has little relevance to the probability of its existence in another species. One species often contradicts another. Only if two species are exceedingly close in terms of origins, environments, and ways of life is there likely to be any significant correlation; and even then there may not be. *Homo sapiens* has no living relative near enough to serve in this way. About all that can be proved by the isolation of an innate behavioral pattern in another species is that genetic mechanisms are *capable* of transmitting such a behavioral pattern. If a pattern similar to an innate pattern observed in a nonhuman species is observed in some ethnic group, it may either reflect an innate human pattern or a learned pattern developed within the culture involved. Which it is likely to be will depend upon whether the same pattern can be found among all human cultures and in all human individuals who are not physically defective.

Men, monkeys, and mice are all very different. Scientific information about the behavioral patterns of nonhuman species can be of value in understanding human nature only when it is treated as if a parable of sorts or as indicating a line of research to be followed with human subjects. Major problems exist when scientists use information on other species to make generalizations about humankind. First, our scientists are all human beings, and are compelled to use uniquely human systems of thought in their work; the danger is that they may be looking into the mirror of their own minds rather than only into such instruments as microscopes or telescopes. Second, the gap between *Homo sapiens* and other species is a rather unusual one, obscured as it is by the overpowering importance of the role of human cultures. Third, it is difficult to observe humans today in anything approaching what must have been our original ecological niche. Fourth, our nearest relatives, the larger primates, form a rather scattered group of genera with varying social and other behavioral norms, and consequently tell us less than we would like to know about how what-was-to-become-man lived as our species was formed. Fifth, we are interested parties in any comparison of ourselves to other species.

If we are to get at the basic problems underlying the plight of contemporary society, we must, like Franklin, be willing to study the nature of our species objectively. I share the belief—perhaps it should be called the faith—of those who feel that getting at the truth, no matter whether it is immediately flattering to the human ego or not, is in the long run of overriding value. We should not even hide the most unthinkable of thoughts, such as the likelihood of an early extinction of our species, if that is where we are led. Only by knowing ourselves as we are have we any hope of becoming what we would like to be. Only by recognizing our limitations have we any hope of overcoming or at least minimizing them. In this knowledge, not in self-delusion, lies the hope for human survival.

To start this process, I will in the next chapter survey the degree to which our species remains the creature of past environmental adjustments. At times the range of our discussion will seemingly move rather far afield from contemporary problems, but I believe that later chapters will show that this discussion not only has great bearing on the problems that we face today, but is in fact the only way in which we can properly understand them.

Part Two

Man:
Creature of
Environment

2
The Legacy of Past Environments

The contours of our bodies and our minds are the result of countless generations of comparatively successful decisions, all taken in interaction with very specific environments. This process began when certain compounds first assumed that degree of complexity and responsiveness that we would today call "life"; it continues today. Over the billions of years there were many changes of environment. That-which-was-to-become-man gradually changed, but each of those changes came about within an ecosystem, and each helped our precursors to relate themselves better to the world in which they found themselves.

No stage was a new start. To meet each new environmental challenge, what-was-to-become-man had to begin with a structure and abilities that already reflected previous adaptations. Only by a process of successive adjustments to new environmental demands and opportunities did the human mind of today develop. To understand the inner nature of that mind, it is necessary, therefore, to review the stages through which our precursors passed and to see how the effects of life in each successive environment were internalized into structures that our species retains even today.

FROM THE SEA TO THE LAND

Life originated, of course, in the sea; and for three quarters of the history of life on earth, the life-forms ancestral to us—and all other life-forms—remained there. Only during the Silurian, some 400 million years back, did the first animals venture ashore from the tidal pools. These were, however, arthropods,

nearer to today's insects than to the line of development that
was to lead to man. It took perhaps another 100 million years
or so before the arthropods were joined on land by vertebrates,
forms superficially similar to the lungfish of today. This new
line was eventually to produce, however, all the various amphibians, reptiles, birds, and mammals.

But the strange new land-dwelling species did not leave the
sea totally behind. The first were semi-aquatic. Even today sala-
manders, frogs, and other amphibians must normally return to
the water to reproduce. More important and more enduring than
the external link with the mother sea, however, was an internal
link. During the Devonian era, as the new vertebrate species
abandoned the sea as their external environment, they maintained a replica of that sea as part of their internal systems. It
could be said that the new organisms overcame the problems of
a land environment by recreating a bit of the old sea and carrying it about within them. The body fluids circulating within the
tissues of land vertebrates are believed to be close in chemical
composition to the Devonian seas: salty but not so much as the
seas have since become.

You and I are no exception. The proportions of the various chemical salts of sodium, potassium, and calcium that circu-
late within our bodies are reminiscent of that Devonian sea. Our
need for a comparatively heavy input of calcium and its use as
the basis of our bone structure, are further momentoes of the
ancient oceans, which were much richer than present day seas
in that element. Human reproduction also shows the link to the
sea. Sperm is injected in a liquid medium to find an egg that is
floating in a similar medium. Somewhat like the amphibian, we
spend our first days of life, in a sense, in the sea. But this is now
an internal sea—a micro-environment created and maintained
for that purpose within our mothers. Only with birth does our
skin experience the touch of dry air. Even as adults we remain
80 percent water.

The way in which our bodies have internalized the ancient
environment of the seas can be seen as an interesting model of
the way in which the human mind was to be gradually developed by the internalization of the successive environments

through which what-was-to-become-man passed. In a very general sense, it can perhaps also provide a model for the way in which this generation can alleviate the dangers that will face us in the environmental adjustments that must be made to our technological world. But let us return to the subject of sea vertebrates.

It is hard to say how much of our way of looking at the world about us constitutes a heritage that goes all the way back to our ocean-dwelling ancestors. Probably many of the most general features of our sensory patterns were first set within a watery environment during the development of the early vertebrates. Our eyes surely have much more in common with those typical of fish than with those of nonvertebrate terrestrial species like the insects. Even the basic contours of the bones and digits of our five-fingered hands can be seen in the skeletal structure of the powerful lobe-fins of certain Devonian fishes like the Crossopterygians. In early vertebrate evolution a reproduction pattern was also set whereby each individual vertebrate is at least potentially a breeder in a population about half male and half female. The strength of this ancient tradition has prevented the social organization of any vertebrate species from mirroring that of many social insects, where the majority of the individuals in a colony may not participate in the sexual process.

The land forms that descended from the early lungfish sought out a wide variety of ecological niches; and their sensory and perceptual patterns have varied widely. Some vertebrate forms—for example, certain cave dwellers and underground creatures—lost most if not all of their ability to see, since it was not needed in their specialized environments. The birds took to the air, although some species of birds then returned to exploit the surface of the seas.

Sweeping changes of environment can lead to great variety in the sensory and perceptual patterns of an evolutionary line over the ages.[1] Humankind was no exception to the effects of this phenomenon. Our precursors greatly changed their environment several times after leaving the seas. Each ecological change in turn had its multifaceted impact on future development.

The Curious Mammal

About 150 million years ago, a new and more efficient type of land vertebrate began to evolve: the mammal. The implications were vast indeed, the mammary gland being only a most superficial symbol of the real significance of what it is to be a mammal. Most basic was the creation of a new physiological system that could maintain a more or less constant internal body temperature, regardless of external environmental conditions. Reptiles and amphibians were necessarily sluggish during the night or colder weather and therefore had variable rates of response that imposed a natural limit on how far they could use learning. The new mammals were not so limited. They could much more rapidly and precisely control their motor activities; and at the same time, the relatively constant level of their bodily activity allowed them to use their memory of past experience as a more reliable guide to future action than the memories of variable-temperatured species could ever be.

The warm-blooded way of life, along with the development of an insulating cover of fur, also helped open the cooler areas of the earth to vertebrate land animals and allowed them more effectively to exploit the cool hours of the night. The pattern of live birth evolved by the mammals made them even more independent of the temperature of their environment, since the egg no longer had to be subject to climatic conditions but could develop within an area that was artificially maintained by the mother at the proper "tropical" temperature. Just as the chemical composition of our lymph reflects the composition of the ancient seas, the temperature level maintained within mammalian bodies probably reflects to some degree the daytime temperature of that ancient tropical zone in which the mammals first evolved.

Since the mammals were able to gain greater value from remembered experience than had earlier species, they grew to crave experience and to seek it actively. Curiosity is most characteristic of young mammals, who are, of course, in the most immediate need of gaining as much experience as they can from the environment in as short a period as possible. This need for experience and interaction also accounts for the playfulness of young mammals, a characteristic that is not shared with young reptiles or amphibians. It also accounts for the exploratory, adventurous nature of much of the activity of any mammal, regardless of age. Despite later cerebral development, *Homo* remains a very typical mammal.

Greater intelligence was also made possible and profitable by the new way of life. "If we were to attempt to define a mammal briefly," concludes a survey of vertebrate evolution, "it could perhaps be done in two words—activity and intelligence."[2]

Key to the high level of mammalian activity is, of course, the high and constant metabolism mentioned above, a pattern shared only with the birds. Key to the development of new and high intelligence in the mammals was the nursing habit, a behavioral pattern that ties the younger generation to the older for an extended period of time. The time during which the mother mammal suckles her young creates a natural training period, one in which learning can easily be transmitted from one generation to the next. The nursing habit has, indeed, been called "the world's first educational institution."[3]

As a group, the new mammals were successful; and differing lines moved toward a variety of environments. One, the cetaceans, which include the whales, porpoises, and the like, even successfully reentered the seas. The mammalian precursors of our species moved, however, into a new and stranger environment: the trees. The early primate line could not have led to anything like *Homo sapiens* without first abandoning the ground. Inhabitants of the trees, even animals as distinct from each other as the monkey and the squirrel, are forced to face somewhat similar problems—problems that make them different from the inhabitants of the ground level. Let us consider some of these.

LIFE IN THE TREES

I will begin with a question. Would you be willing to keep an uncaged monkey in your living room? Most people, I fear, would not be pleased with the prospect. The underlying reason is what is important. We keep a dog or cat in an object-filled

living room and, although it might occasionally knock over a
vase or so, it normally would show little interest in the objects
themselves. A cat can successfully maneuver even the most
crowded mantelpiece, avoiding all the objects there with dis-
interest and disdain.

Now imagine a monkey or chimpanzee perched on your
mantelpiece. It would pick up objects, turn them over, perhaps
throw them. Flowers might be taken out of the vase, strewn over
the room, the water in the vase poured out on the floor. "Monkeys are too destructive to keep in the house," we might be
tempted to conclude. But what we see here is in fact not destructiveness *per se*, but rather a tendency to manipulate—a tendency born in turn of the primate ability to "see" objects as such
and to be interested in them as such. In the forest this kind of
curiosity would not be destructive but instead productive.

We are sufficiently unlike our dogs and cats that they do
not invade our world of objects but can instead coexist with it.
We have in common with the monkey the shared experience of
forest life and the forest-dweller's mind that was the evolutionary result. His inner world has many of the same basic contours as ours. He lives in the same world with us to that extent.
For a monkey to enter your living room therefore constitutes an
invasion of your human world.

What is the forest like as an environment? To begin with,
it is a very complex one. In one classic ecological study of a
tropical rain forest, it was demonstrated that one forest could
be split into some seven distinct environments, beginning with
the ground level and moving up to the tree tops about 125 feet
above. Each level had its own pattern of sunlight, temperature,
air movement, and humidity; and each supported some species
of plants and animals that did not stray to other levels. Only the
taller trees and a few other species occupied more than one or
two layers; the rest lived in permanent isolation from those
species that occupied distinctly different levels.[4] Forest levels
have been compared to those of the sea by the biologist Marston
Bates, who found that to study a species of mosquito that was
believed associated with the spread of yellow fever in the
Colombian rain forest, it was necessary to build a platform

laboratory in the trees at the 38-meter level—for unless a tree was felled, the mosquitoes in question seldom left that strata of the forest canopy.[5] The more advanced primates apparently developed in tropical forests that were somewhat like present-day rain forests. Even today, except for four species (*Homo sapiens*, the Japanese monkey, the South African baboon, and the North African monkey), all of the numerous and varied primate species remain tropical.

THE WORLD OF THE HAND AND THE EYE

The shrew-like creatures from which the primate stock originally sprang were highly dependent on their sense of smell. It was probably by odor that these nocturnal creatures located the insects that were their primary diet. The move into the trees, however, made possible a generally vegetarian diet; and, for most of the higher primates, it led to eventual departure from the nocturnal way of life. This development had much to do with the tendency for vision to overtake smell in importance to the developing primates.

The primate tendency to rely less on the sense of smell can be illustrated by returning to that object-filled room through which the cat and dog had moved without trouble. But this time let us place bits of meat or fish in or under each of the vases and other small objects. A dog or cat would soon reduce the room to a condition about as chaotic as if we had let a monkey in. Thus, only by adding the dimension of smell would the cat or dog become interested in overturning a vase, but even then it would not do so for the vase itself but rather to find, for example, the bit of pungent fish below.

Life in the forest required very discriminating vision. Movement through trees demanded sophisticated perception of space in all three dimensions. The eyes of the primates are among the largest of those of any mammalian order, particularly in proportion to body size. Primate eyes also face forward in order to provide better depth perception. The combination of stereoscopic vision and the ability to manipulate objects made the sensory world of the primates a much more complex one than that of most species. It was in this way that primates came to see their environment more in terms of individual, shaped objects than in terms of mere pattern and movement. But this was not all: the primates also added the dimension of color to their inner world.

Among the higher vertebrates, only the primates and certain birds developed a sophisticated color sense. (Our dogs—and even the bulls that some people mistakenly believe are enraged by the red cloak of the matador—are in fact color blind.) This primate development presumably reflects the need for greater visual discrimination in the shady and light-flecked world of the forest. There seems little doubt but that the high quality of human vision resulted primarily because our progenitors were once forced to adapt to life in a shadowy and multidimensional forest environment.

Along with the sensory equipment that enabled the primate to distinguish more clearly among various objects went the evolution of the primate hand. As an instrument to manipulate objects, it had few equals. It is key to all our technologies. For the dog, a single organ, the mouth, must serve for making sounds, for eating, for defense, and for carrying objects. For the monkey, however, the two hands take most of this pressure off the mouth area, and leave it freer for chattering and other expressive activity. They also allow the monkey to rotate an object through his sensory fields for closer examination. If most of the *Carnivora* can be said to live in a world of the mouth and the nose, the primates live in a world of the hand and the eye. Much of what we have come to call intelligence has to do with the identification and manipulation of "objects." Consequently, it is not surprising that we find primate intelligence to be of a higher order.[6]

A hesitant tendency toward upright posture probably began long ago in primate history, and many species of monkey sit upright when feeding or resting. This was probably also true of the evolving apes. As primates evolved larger brains, their body size also tended to increase. Soon there were types that could not easily run along the tops of branches, holding on with their feet. Among some lines of the primates, an alternative means of moving about was gradually substituted: arm-overarm swinging, or brachiation. Exploitation of swinging through the trees as a technique led to longer arms, changes in the wrist and elbow, and a torso that was wider than it was thick. Many anthropologists believe that our progenitors went through this stage, although they never became as specialized in the skills of brachiation as the modern-day gibbons.

Whether it took the form of brachiation or not, efficient movement through the trees may well have set the pattern for mankind's later tendency to use tools. Rapid movement among trees obviously involves the routine use of tree branches for locomotion in ways that somewhat anticipate the use of tools. At the minimum, a tree-dweller must be able to estimate accurately the swing characteristics of different forms and shapes of branches, the leverage effect to be gained, their ability to hold weight, and many other complex factors. This adds up to the kind of intelligence that would set the stage for using tools.

During the period when the above mentioned bodily changes were in process, even more important changes were going on inside the primate brain. Sharp primate eyes required an increase in the size and complexity of the relevant parts of the primate brain, particularly the so-called *visual cortex,* located toward the rear of the cerebral cortex. Life in the trees not only forced the primates to rely increasingly on good vision and spatial perception, but brachiation in particular forced them to improve their sense of timing and to develop a very delicate sense of balance and muscular control. Both affector and sensory systems underwent rapid improvement as the primates evolved. A new and improved neural system gradually appeared in the primates in which the corticospinal fibers bypassed the internucial cells and made a direct connection with the motor neurons. In the other direction, the lemniscal system, which had already appeared in earlier mammals, was further developed among the primates and allowed for a more direct system of nerve fibers linking the peripheral sensory cells and the cerebral cortex.

These improved pathways for both sensory and motor activity permitted more precise controls during interaction with the environment and were probably very important in the success of the primates as they evolved. Behavioral patterns could become more flexible and this could allow for a greater reliance on learning to guide action, rather than on set sequences of automatic response. Ever since early research by the Yerkes Laboratory in Florida, we have known that the higher primates depend on learning for many responses that are unlearned in other species. Inexperienced chimpanzees must even learn how to copulate. Without training or observation, they apparently do not know what to do.[7]

TERRITORIALITY AMONG THE PRIMATES

Something should perhaps be said here about territoriality among the primates. Like certain fish and birds, many species of mammal tend to establish well-defined territories, which they will defend against others of their species. Other mammals do not. Still others appear to have several concentric circles of territory that are defended in differing ways from differing threats. The pattern is complex among primates as well. While some of the Asiatic apes, the gibbons, show clear patterns of territoriality,[8] most of the primates whose behavior is otherwise most comparable to *Homo* (the savanna monkeys of the genera *Cercopithecus* and *Macaca,* the baboons of the genera *Papio* and *Theropithecus,* the chimpanzee and the gorilla) seem to show a lack of easily defined territorial behavior.[9] All these forage through ill-defined ranges; and the areas in which individual bands operate overlap extensively. Gorillas live in small groups that pass each other in the wild with no clear evidence of avoidance, much less hostility.[10] Chimpanzees form open social groups that often interchange members and occupy common ranges.[11]

What does this prove about the "territoriality" of our progenitors as they passed through the pre-hominid primate stage? What does it prove about people today? Nothing definitive, I fear. It only shows that we cannot assert on the basis of comparative animal behavior that man must have a strong territorial instinct. Robert Ardrey was simply wrong in *African Genesis* when he implied that "territoriality" is a universal "vertebrate instinct."[12] It is by no means a universal primate characteristic, as Ardrey himself admitted in the same book when describing the gorilla.[13] He reconciled these statements by concluding that the gorilla must therefore be an "evolutionary failure," a tragic species that had lost its way and its will to survive and was now in the twilight of its evolutionary history. In his *Territorial Imperative,* published five years after *African Genesis,* Ardrey admitted that on the basis of recent research the chimpanzee also appeared to lack the expected "territoriality." The chimpanzee's good nature he then characterized as "a very small candle on a very dark night," and Ardrey was compelled to damn the chimpanzee as "an evolutionary failure" as well.[14]

We should not try to remake facts to fit theory. If we want to talk about man's territoriality, we will have to look at the evidence in man. Until we can show evidence of a universal instinct of territoriality in man, we must consider that much of any "territoriality" may be learned behavior.

LEARNING AMONG THE PRIMATES

No matter how much we accept as innate behavior in the higher primates, it is clear that the role of learning in behavior was expanded as the primate order developed. A greater ability to learn also made it possible for primates to employ imagination and symbolism at levels far beyond those that could be attained by other orders. A variety of experiments have shown that apes and monkeys can learn to manipulate symbols. Chimpanzees, for example, quickly learn the relative value of differently colored poker chips that they can use in a vending machine to get food. With plastic symbols as "words" a chimpanzee has even been trained to form simple "sentence patterns" by placing them in pre-arranged order.[15]

The higher primates were probably very adept at learning from each other. There is no question but that a skill perfected by one chimpanzee can be passed on to others of its kind who have the chance to observe it in action. In the English language there is even a verb "to ape," meaning to mimic or copy the actions of another. Out of such abilities comes the possibility of transmitting complex, learned patterns of action—the necessary basis for the development of technological skills. Much of this is the ongoing result of the high challenge of adaptation to arboreal life so successfully met by the early primates.

But for all that life amid the trees did to mold the intellectual development of what-was-to-become-man, nothing similar to man could have evolved if the stock had remained in the forest. What was required was yet another basic change in environment—the move from the trees to the forest floor and ultimately out onto the savanna.

3
The Unique Nature
of Our Species

"From ape to Adam" goes the stereotype for the stages of development to be covered by this chapter. The period that elapsed between the time when a common ancestor of present-day apes and humans still roamed the earth and the time of the emergence of *Homo sapiens* is not yet fully understood, but it was surely a complex one in evolutionary and ecological terms.

It is essential that we look in some detail at what we know or can reasonably reconstruct of this period, since it was then that the unique features that characterize our species were developed—such features as: erect posture, language, tool-making, and a more conscious and deliberate approach toward dealing with the environment generally. An understanding of these features of the life of our species is key to dealing with the problems facing our techno-industrial world.

In the views of some anthropologists, the earliest representatives of the "family of man," the hominids, may have split off from the line of early apes, represented by such fossil types as *Dryopithecus,* about 25 million years ago.[1] Others would place the branching closer to ten million years back. In either case, the hominid line has a long history, even if one not yet fully reconstructed. Fossil finds of early hominids reflect the very uneven pattern of excavation thus far. If our species survives a couple hundred more years under conditions that allow for scientific research on roughly the present scale, we are likely to be able to reconstruct the basic outlines of this development in some detail and with a high level of assurance of accuracy. Until then we will probably remain ignorant of significant factors in the past life of our species.

As it stands now, the earliest candidate for status as a hominid is represented by a series of finds in East Africa,

Eastern Europe, and the Indian subcontinent, generally classified together as *Ramapithecus*.[2] Since the remains of *Ramapithecus* thus far located are primarily jaws and teeth, speculation on its ecology remains tentative. It appears to have lived
outside tropical forest zones, however, and tooth wear suggests
a life of foraging on the edge of forests, perhaps relying primarily on tough foodstuffs like roots and nuts. Some anthropologists still hypothesize *Ramapithecus* as a predominantly
arboreal species that came to the ground only to feed.[3] The reduction in the size of the ramapithecine canine teeth, and of the
jaw generally, implies that its hands may already have taken
over the defensive/offensive and the crushing/breaking roles
played by the teeth and jaws of other primates.

The most recent ramapithecine remains are considered to
be about ten million years old; and that leaves an almost five-
million-year gap before we pick up the earliest well-established
remains of *Australopithecus*, the next hominid genus of major
significance in the effort to trace human evolution. Forms of
Australopithecus are much better known and their way of life
much easier to speculate about.[4] More significant to our interest here, the australopithecines were clearly tool-makers. The
more recent view of the genus *Australopithecus* is, however, that
it was not ancestral to mankind but was instead only a closely
related genus of hominid. This view is reinforced by the fact that
the more recent australopithecines, of little over a million years
ago, seem to have been contemporaries of other hominids much
closer to *Homo sapiens*.

With so tentative a reconstruction of hominid origins, it is
not surprising that much of what passes for knowledge of the
past is based on reconstructions from the present. Some of our
present reconstructions are bound to be modified as more fossil
material becomes available.

THE GROUND AS ENVIRONMENT: CARNIVOROUS HABITS

Despite those motion pictures of Tarzan swinging gracefully
from tree to tree, the anatomy of *Homo sapiens* is not well designed for living in the trees. Adaption to life above ground level
in the forest was a phase in our evolution that our progenitors
abandoned long ago. Trees are now more often considered an

obstacle to human travel than an aid. We have been burning and chopping them for generations.

Descent from the trees was a highly significant step. As much as life in the forest contributed to that which remains our heritage, we could not be what we are today in either our physical or mental nature if our remote ancestors had not abandoned the forest environment for the ground and a very different way of living. Although it was in the trees that the primates became typical primates, it was in the open country that hominids evolved toward *Homo sapiens*.

The hominid period was marked by significant, although gradual changes in the climates of Asia, Africa, and Europe. These changes created new local environments with new opportunities for exploitation—new ecological niches to be occupied. Our species is the result of a series of successful adaptations to such opportunities, one of which led to a descent from the trees. Other primates, like the baboons, took a similar step to the ground and out into the open; but the baboons established a quadrupedal rather than an upright way of life, running more like dogs than human beings. This had many implications for their later development.

In their new and perhaps more arid environment, our primarily vegetarian ancestors gradually became omnivores; that is to say, they ate whatever was available, whether of animal or vegetable origin. Nesting birds, their eggs, and slow-moving animals were probably the first game.

The new eating habits had major repercussions for the pattern of hominid interaction with the environment. Carnivores and omnivores typically have more complex behavioral patterns than herbivores. The purpose of much of the sensory system of a herbivore is to avoid potential predators. Its senses are primarily an alarm system. To stalk prey successfully, on the other hand, involves a considerably more active and imaginative approach. For a carnivore, intelligence is an important requirement.

Meat-eating, particularly when larger animals are the prey, also encourages the sharing of food. As a consequence, it tends to lead to more complex social development. The amorphous herd gives way to the disciplined pack. In cooperative efforts, a certain modicum of intercommunication among the hunters also becomes all-important. All these tendencies toward inceased social organization were presumably strengthened among the hominids by the new eating habits.[5]

As hunters, the early hominids presumably set a pattern different from most other carnivores, for the nature of their sensory sysems dictated that they hunt by sight and therefore by day. Carnivores like the big cats locate their prey more by scent and normally confine their hunting to night, morning, or dusk hours. The visual abilities of the hominids, although evolved in the trees, seem to have adapted well to life on the open plain. The muscles of the human eye, for example, do well at scanning the horizon; they move the eye from left to right much more rapidly and efficiently than they move it up and down. Until our modern age of air raids and rocketry, danger to as large a creature as a hominid almost always moved across the horizon.

The ability of the hunting primates to see in terms of "objects" and to perceive color gave them advantages the *Carnivora* did not have. Many birds and small mammals like hares have innate escape patterns that lead to their "freezing in place" under certain conditions of the chase. These patterns had presumably been evolved when they were successful in dealing with most potential predators. Human hunters can often still see such prey, however, and in some cases can simply walk over and pick up the immobilized animal.[6]

HOMINID AGGRESSIVENESS?

Recent discussion of the importance of the change of the early hominids away from a more strictly vegetarian and toward a truly omnivorous diet, has led some to conclude that our species, as a "carnivore," therefore has a particularly bloody background, and that we are consequently predestined by our nature to violent, even homicidal tendencies. One of the first examples of such a conclusion was a study by the anthropologist Raymond Dart, made after his analysis of *Australopithecus* finds; but the more popular version of this thesis was that in *African Genesis,* published by the playwright Robert Ardrey.[7]

Ardrey's thesis on "territoriality" has already been mentioned in chapter 2.

Although the significance of the change in eating habits was very great and may have helped to cut the hominid line off more sharply from its immediate ancestral stock, since it enabled it to occupy a separate ecological niche, the conclusions about consequent depravity seem very hard to justify. Under normal conditions, people spend much more of their time working with each other than opposing each other. If you doubt this, go along any street where you can see a variety of human activities, count the cases you see of cooperation, and compare that number with the number of cases you find of conflict.

In fact, the break with the past in eating habits had not been a total one. The hominids obviously continued to eat vegetable materials to the degree available. Moreover, many species of primate, albeit those more distantly related to our species, rely heavily on animal products—typically insects. Even many of the "higher primates" supplement their diets with animal foods; and the most advanced of the living apes, the chimpanzee, will kill an occasional small animal when the opportunity presents itself.[8] Nor has our species "turned carnivore." Even "hunting societies" characteristically obtain the larger share of their food from gathered vegetable materials. Among the Bushmen of the Kalahari, usually described as a "hunting society," gathering activities account for up to 80 percent of all foodstuffs by weight.[9] Only rare human groups, like the fishing and hunting Eskimos (who rely heavily on sea mammals) and the agricultural Masai (who rely on the milk and blood of their cattle) eat significantly less vegetable products than animal products.

Even if we were to consider our species as a "carnivore," there is little evidence that would indicate that the carnivore is any more "aggressive" by nature than the herbivore. It has been claimed that one of the most dangerous animals for a human being to meet in the wild is the boar. One thinks also of the rhinoceros and the moose. All are vegetarians. In this vein, it is also interesting to note that the hunting culture that is perhaps the most strictly carnivorous of all, that of the Eskimos, shows less of a tradition of warfare than perhaps any other human culture studied. Even the evidence of occasional cannibalism among hominids need not be interpreted as establishing a pattern of aggressiveness; in contemporary preliterate groups, cannibalism is often ceremonial, a way in which one person can gain the powers of another, and usually does not imply killings within the group as the result of the angry confrontations of persons motivated by aggressiveness.

In our discussion of the impact of technology, a specific point made by the ethologist Konrad Lorenz in his book, *On Aggression,* merits our attention. The problem that disturbs Lorenz is not so much the idea of human territoriality or the aggressive instincts of humans (both of which he incidently accepts) but the fact that we lack innate inhibitions that prevent us from killing our own kind. Lorenz describes pre-man as a basically harmless omnivore, lacking the natural weapons needed to kill a large animal. All of a sudden, with toolmaking, artificial weapons are available, and this uninhibited "dove" has acquired the "beak of a raven."[10] Human beings now find themselves able to kill one another easily. Natural aggressiveness, Lorenz asserts, which had been of value because it ensured the dispersal of individuals and the optimum use of resources, becomes a potential threat. Competition within the group, instead of leading to the creation of a natural social hierarchy and ensuring that only the fittest breed, now can become antisocial and dangerous to all.

As much as I respect Lorenz as a zoologist, I cannot quite agree with his thesis. Neither tool-use nor tool-making was any sudden discovery by our present species. Both predate even our genus. An early hominid with a sharp stick or a large rock was already fully "armed" to kill his brother, if he were inclined to do so. Since that stage, we have evolved many complex and unprecedented new behavioral patterns, and there was time enough to have evolved inhibitions against killing our own kind. The reason that innate mechanisms were not called for was, in my opinion, the fact that social controls were already in effect that did the job reasonably well. Our problem then becomes to maintain, in the current techno-industrial age, social controls that are no less effective.

Moreover, without a major redefinition of terms, I am not willing to accept Lorenz's concepts of either the natural aggressiveness or territoriality of mankind. Much of his insight is based on the behavior of other species—species that did not experience the same twistings and turnings in their ecological history as what-was-to-become-man. Nor am I clear whether Lorenz considers "aggression" to be an independent drive that somehow *causes* certain human behavior, or whether he uses the term merely as a convenient label for several behavior patterns which show certain common characteristics. The materials that Lorenz cites include examples of territorial defense, sexual selection and dominance, the establishment of social precedence, and even what we might call "self-assertiveness." It makes considerable difference whether we use the term "aggression" only as a convenient umbrella to cover all these various tendencies or whether we consider it as an underlying mechanism—a force that is not to be denied and which finds inevitable expression in our behavior.

Even if we accept something called "aggression" as part of the human equation, are there not other parts of that equation that could cancel out its dangerous implications? Couldn't we make an equally strong case for other, somewhat contradictory, factors—say, the "necessity for social acceptance"— and establish that they play a similar role in driving human actions? If aggression is not a "force" but only a "tendency" in human behavior, isn't it only one of a long list of such tendencies? In addition to a "tendency toward aggression," it seems to me that we would also list many other "tendencies": to laugh, to weep, to cooperate, to refuse to cooperate (or stubbornness), to show off (or ostentation), to be shy (or modesty), and hundreds of other, often contradictory, tendencies. We could even produce evidence for a "tendency toward submission," in direct contrast to that of aggression!

Once "aggression" is accepted as only one of a variety of behavioral factors in the human equation, who is to say how significant the aggressive factor would be in any specific situation? Obviously the circumstances and cultural training would play a major role in determining when and how each is expressed. And might not what has been called our "natural aggressiveness" be better analyzed as but one manifestation of a more general factor we might call "self-assertiveness," a factor that while it does characterize our species, need not carry the same sociopolitical implications as a loaded term like "aggressiveness?"

But let us return to our review of the bodily development of that strange new creature, the hominid.

POSTURE AND THE MIND

"Man is the featherless biped," went an ancient Greek description of man. This definition, although intentionally facetious, does serve to underline the strangeness to the mammalian tradition of our posture and our gait—another heritage of the new hominid way of life on the open ground.[11] A variety of bodily changes was brought about by the more erect posture. One was the foot. Except for the all-important, but hidden, brain, the foot has been called one of the few really specialized organs evolved by man, one perhaps specialized for running during the hunt.

Our adjustment to a fully upright posture is far from complete, as is shown by a variety of ills and discomforts that humans still tend to suffer as part of the cost of this innovation. In our modern technological world a great portion of mankind suffers from "foot trouble," whether the malady is fallen arches or a simple tendency for the feet to feel cold due to poor circulation. In our techno-industrial society, people complain of "back trouble" of countless varieties and of hernias and hemorrhoids, both caused by the weight of the internal organs on bodily structures that are not strong enough to support them without the proper muscular tone. They suffer from varicose veins in the legs and from a variety of minor ills that also relate to our not yet perfect adaptation to an erect posture.

Along with the speed made possible by the development of the human foot, there apparently came a serious problem of overheating during exertion. Quite unlike most carnivores, the early hominids were daytime hunters, exerting themselves during the heat of the day. Two developments presumably came about to help resolve this problem: the hominid stock developed an unusual capacity for cooling by perspiration and at the same time shed most of its body hair. Human sweat glands are capable of putting out over two quarts of sweat an hour. Apes, by comparison, perspire very little. There is still considerable debate on when and why our progenitors lost much of their body hair and developed new patterns of cooling.[12] It is also not clear why we shed such copious tears when we weep; other species do not. There is much of our nature about which we remain ignorant.

Development of an upright posture was very important to the hominid's intellectual development. Not only were the hands freed for the manipulation of objects in the environment, but the horizons of sensory interest were widened. The Greek word for man, *anthropos,* is believed to be derived from an expression meaning "he who looks upward." Ability to communicate may also have been encouraged by upright posture. Arms free for gestures, the new two-legged creatures confronted each other face to face. Their freed arms could give silent signals during the hunt, signals that would be visible at some distance. Food could be more easily carried back to family members.

Erect posture is also key to effective use of tools, for it frees the hands to carry objects and allows them to become more sensitive and precise in their actions. Highly sensitive hands would only be a source of pain if they had to be used for as heavy a function as bearing part of the body weight while running over rocky ground.

Many of the bodily changes that took place during hominid evolution evidence a process called neoteny, that is, the retention in the adult form of characteristics that were earlier found only in the fetal or youthful stage. The hominids, and particularly *Homo sapiens*, show many features that are more characteristic of newborn or young apes than adult ones. The "pedomorphic" or childlike features include, for example, flatness of the face, a small jaw, roundness of the head, absence of brow ridges, relative hairlessness, thin nails, and nonrotation of the big toe. The skull of a newborn ape has a surprisingly human shape compared to that of an adult of the same species.

More important, however, are the behavioral traits that we have more in common with young apes than mature ones: high educability, great curiosity, and an attitude of playfulness. These traits, although "infantile" in many species, characterize the average human being well into adulthood. Incidentally, the toy has played a very major role in technological development. Children enjoy gadgets. Gunpowder was used as an amusement for hundreds of years in China before it was made into a weapon. Although the pre-Columbian peoples of the Americas made no economic use of the wheel for carts or other purposes, there were wheeled pull-toys for children in Mexico a thousand years ago. One anthropologist who has paid special attention to technological matters has speculated that fire was probably played with by our ancestors long before they tried to put it to any specific purpose.[13]

NATURAL OBJECTS AS TOOLS

Human beings are, of course, by no means alone in *using* tools. Several species of animals have developed patterns of tool use. For example, a kind of finch in the Galapagos, the *Cactospize,* digs insects out of the bark of trees with the spine of a cactus. The sea otter often carries a stone to break the hard shells of certain shellfish. The female burrowing wasp, *Ammophila,* uses a small pebble to pound down the soil over the nest where she has laid her eggs. But most of these cases involve set patterns and all rely on the use of a readily available object. They are not examples of tool-making. Only the chimpanzee has provided many examples of what could be called the tendency to design tools to fit specific needs, and these examples represent only the most hesitant beginnings.

The tools first used by the early hominids were probably unaltered objects found in their environment. Lewis Mumford has written an article stressing the fact that the first stage of technology involved finding, not making: collecting, rather than systematic hunting. In response to all the references to "Man the Maker," or *Homo faber,* Mumford entitled his article "Man the Finder."[14] In fact, however, it is likely to have been the early hominids whose technology was only based on what could be found, not species we would classify as *Homo.*

When they began their pattern of life on the forest floor and nearby savanna, the early hominids may well have tended to cling to the edge of forested areas, and perhaps to retreat to the trees when danger arose. Like a small child clutching a familiar blanket for the sense of security it provides, the early hominids may have tended to carry "mementos of the forest" with them as they ventured out into the open; they may have sometimes carried tree branches along for comfort, camouflage, and defensive display, and only later for planned, offensive action. Although this can only be speculation, I feel that some of the first weapons and tools to appear on the savanna may well have had this humble origin. In a sense, the fetish may be older than the tool.

In obtaining game, it is likely that the early hominid used available, unmodified sticks and rocks for probing, throwing, and the like. The present-day chimpanzee shows these patterns of behavior from time to time in the wild. An ape will often throw rocks and sticks during "display behavior" in the natural environment.[15] The anthropologist John Pfeiffer is willing to speculate that the hominid of twenty-five million years ago "probably used tools such as digging sticks and clubs."[16] But I find this acceptable only if we are thinking of patterns of tool use not much beyond those now observed in the chimpanzee.

Evidence for use by early hominids of unmodified objects as tools will always remain indirect. Accumulations of non-native rocks around ancient campsites is one example of such evidence. Equally important, though even more indirect, is what the fossil record has to show of the development of the hominid hand. "Man thinks because he has a hand," reasoned Aristotle; and it is even clearer to modern science that our perceptual systems and brains are designed to provide certain inputs that take on value only if we assume an ability of our effectors to take subtle, manipulative, actions in response.

The Old World monkeys and the apes had already created the opposable thumb by developing the joint between the carpal and metacarpal. The human thumb is even more mobile; its fleshy tip can touch, with varying degrees of pressure, any other fingertip. Hominid metacarpals and phalanges long ago began to straighten out; in the apes they are curved as an adaptation to brachiation or knuckle walking.

Your hand can be used for two basic types of grip. One, the type you would use in holding a hammer, the "power grip," is used by virtually all primates. The other, the type you might use with a screwdriver or pencil, the "precision grip," relies more specifically on thumb pressure against the other finger-tips. This "precision grip" is most highly developed in the human line.[17]

Fossil hand bones of *Australopithecus* are somewhat inter-mediate between those of the modern apes and *Homo,* indicat-ing that the change in the capability of the hand began during the earliest hominid period.[18] This tends to support the specu-lation that even the early hominids were much more engaged in manipulating objects than any of the existing ape species. Along with tooth and jaw reduction, it tends to collaborate theories of very early hominid use of unmodified objects as tools.

The Birth of Creative Technology

Benjamin Franklin is believed to be the first to have defined our species as the "tool-making animal." Surely it is the conscious manufacture of tools, rather than the use of natural objects as tools, that sets off *Homo sapiens* among the animals. But tool-making is apparently older than our species.

The oldest manufactured tools yet discovered are those found at Koobi Fora, a site east of Lake Turkana in Kenya. These are choppers and flake tools, as well as cobbles, dating back 2,600,000 years.[19] The species of hominid responsible is not yet established. Tools were probably systematically manu-factured of softer materials, such as tree branches, long before they were made of stone; but only the latter material had much chance of lasting from so early a period.

Tool-making as a concept need not only apply to the manufacture of hand tools and weapons, but can be usefully expanded to cover the making of all artifacts of a practical nature. Clothing, shelters, hearths, and the like, would certainly be considered the results of the tool-making tradition. One of the oldest excavated living floors, from Bed I at Olduvai Gorge, Tanzania, dated about 1,800,000 years ago, shows not only stone tools in association with australopithecine remains, but also a circle of rocks that seems to have been a foundation for some sort of shelter.[20]

Many of the animal bones found in conjunction with *Australopithecus* may in fact have been used as tools, and some may even have been redesigned for use as tools. Bones, horns, and animal teeth were obviously capable of such exploitation, and are prominently used in later cultures.[21]

Certain groups of *Australopithecus* seem to have become quite adept at tool-making. Some paleo-anthropologists have described these early tool-making species of East Africa as no longer australopithecines but as properly belonging to the genus *Homo* and have named them "Homo habilis." For our purposes here, the exact terminology is not as important as the general realization that complex tool-making cultures can already be traced back as far as the lower Pleistocene, some two million years ago. With their better tools, these more advanced forms, whether we consider them species of *Australopithecus* or *Homo,* had begun to hunt the larger animals of the East African plains, apparently first stalking aged or injured specimens.[22]

The facts of hominid evolution make it clear that technology is not something that modern man has recently created. Archeological finds show that the tool-making tradition is very likely much older than the genus *Homo* and that its further development was probably a key factor in the success of our species in exploiting the opportunities of hunting the larger mammals. Without technologies, *Homo sapiens* could not have evolved. Nor could earlier forms of *Homo.* Perhaps *Australopithecus* was no less dependent on technologies for its survival as a genus during the four-million-year period that we can trace its existence.

The great breakthrough had been the *idea* of manufacturing tools. The various forms of technology, such as clothing, shelters, fire, and the like, were natural extensions of the basic concept of expropriating bits and pieces from the environment to manipulate or redesign them to serve human ends. Stereoscopic vision, the opposable thumb, and upright posture all played a role in making this possible. But it was specifically the human brain that allowed for the great subtlety of conscious design that has led to our current levels of technology.

What we have seen of the origins of technology here con-

tradict the theory of writers like Jacques Ellul, which treat
technology as some type of extraneous force. On the contrary,
the impetus of technology comes from within our nature. It is
nothing alien.

I would agree with Ellul that a basic characteristic of technology is artificiality, but would not go on to conclude that it is
therefore "opposed to nature," that technology necessarily "destroys, eliminates, or subordinates the natural world,"
or that the worlds of nature and technology "obey different imperatives, different directives, and different laws which have
nothing in common."[23] To the contrary, it seems obvious to me
that the world of technology is grafted onto the natural world,
being based on the redesign and reordering of elements already
in the environment natural to our species. Moreover, that redesign and reordering of the outer world was carried out in
accord with perceptual patterns and conceptual abilities that
were already part of our "inner nature." Many of the ways that
humans characteristically analyze and synthesize data from the
environment probably were established during the millions of
years represented by the early hominid period. This does not
mean that certain forms of technology may not distort natural
relationships or that technology may not ultimately prove fatal
to our species. It does, however, mean that we are not dealing
with a basic dualism. To create a new Manichaeanism in which
technology is cast as a *diabolus ex machina* does not help us to
understand the problems of the contemporary world.

The views of Martin Heidegger on the nature of technology
are more to the point. Heidegger views technology as firmly
grounded in the structure of man's being, not as something
apart. Technology mediates between man and nature in ordinary experience; most specifically it plays a major role in the
way that man encounters entities and experiences himself as the
originator and recipient of ongoing action in his environment.[24] Heidegger's emphasis on entities is, perhaps, a reflection of his existentialist concern for the concept of being. In
fact, the human tendency to think and "see" in terms of entities is only one of the many systems of analysis and/or syn-
thesis by which we naturally interpret and interrelate with the
world about us—all of which form the phylogenetic structures

which have made our technologies possible. These systems are to a great measure the heritage of the remarkable developments of the hominid period.

For simplicity, I will use the term *analysis-systems* to refer to the series of patterns that all human groups use for organizing their perceptions and planning their actions within their environment. (Strictly speaking, some might better be called *synthesis-systems*.) These analysis-systems include such considerations as: time, space, motion, entities, categories, causation, and the like. We usually think about them as if they were features of the objective, *outer* world, but the way in which we deal with each reflects instead the *inner* contours of our perceptual and intellectual capabilities. These analysis-systems define what we might call "the ecology of the human mind"—how the structures of our brains reflect the success of our progenitors in dealing with their environments. They are also fundamental to our ability to talk about our environment and to plan joint actions within that environment.

THE DAWN OF SYMBOL-MAKING

T. S. Eliot declared, "Man is a spirit and symbols are his meat." Exactly when our precursors began to use symbols can hardly be documented; but with a more analytic approach toward the environment, the symbolic approach became possible. Some anthropologists have proposed that the use of tools and the use of language require very similar biologically determined abilities and that if we find evidence of a hunting or fishing technology, we should be able to assume that the community involved was actively using a language.[25] There is much to recommend the idea, as we will see in later chapters.

The human ability to use language is based on physiological structures, not only those of the organs of speech but, more significantly, those of the brain. The order of development of these skills during the early hominid period is largely unknown. It is not difficult to assert, however, that the new symbol-making capabilities were developed during interaction with the environment and that they reflected skills that hominids were successful in using to deal with that environment.

At about the same time that language began to appear,

there was developing another dramatic difference between the hominid brain and what had been the pattern in all earlier species: hemispheric dominance, or "lateralization," within the cerebral cortex. Instead of the two sides of the brain operating in much the same way, which is still the case with the apes, an asymmetrical pattern began to develop. Usually it was the left side that seemed to accrue the new control functions and to become the dominant hemisphere. Given the way the motor activities of the body are orientated in the brain, this led naturally to the pattern of action we call right-handedness. On the walls of ancient caves we see the traced outlines of left hands, showing that it was the active right hand that was doing the tracing.

Part of what was involved was clearly the development of new pathways in the brain. With a monkey, such as a macaque, the visual and auditory areas of the brain are quite separate and have relatively few direct connections with each other. In the human brain there are many direct routes between the two areas, so it is naturally easier to associate a visual image with a spoken sound. As a matter of fact, the human brain also links the visual and auditory areas closely with the tactile nerve system, a very large proportion of which serves the hands. Since the connecting fibers in the brain are so numerous, what we would call a special "switching station" was evolved during the hominid period.[29] This structure, which is about the size of a half dollar, lies on the cortex below the temple on the individual's dominant side.

The process of lateralization seems firmly bound up with our ability to carry on those symbolic activities that we call language. This is most dramatically shown in cases of brain damage, where loss or injury of the crucial portions of the left hemisphere commonly modifies or destroys the victim's ability to speak or understand—provided, of course, he or she is right-handed. (For the left-handed, it is usually the right hemisphere that is critical to speech.) Significantly, the pattern of hemispheric dominance does not show up at birth, but appears during the maturational process, in pace with the development of manual dexterity and the use of language.

Symbolic activity will be discussed more fully in later chapters. At this point, it is sufficient to note that: 1) symbol-making activity is dependent on specific brain structures evolved over a very long period; 2) symbol-making began much earlier than our species, probably much earlier than our genus; and 3) symbol-making seems closely associated with the other mental abilities that form the basis for human technology.

THE GENUS HOMO

What had been hypothesized about the age of our genus has been put into some disarray since the 1972 discovery near Kenya's Lake Turkana (formerly Lake Rudolph) by Richard Leakey of a 2,800,000-year-old skull that he classifies as belonging to the genus *Homo*. If such classification is accepted, the age of mankind must be much greater than previously thought and the australopithecines will definitely have to be considered a more primitive form of hominid that had lived on long after our genus was well established.

But timing is not the only problem created by this find. It is a rule of ecology that two species do not inhabit the same ecological niche for long; one replaces the other. If *Homo* and *Australopithecus* coexisted for over a million years in East Africa, they presumably pursued somewhat different ways of life. Thus, what we thought we could extrapolate about the probable ecology of our ancestors from the australopithecine record is thrown into question. Only more finds will sort this out.

If we overlook the find just mentioned (and the proposal that certain forms that many consider to be australopithecines be classified as "Homo habilis"), the earliest well dated fossil finds of our genus are those made in Java. Originally described as *Pithecanthropus erectus*, "Java man" is now almost universally categorized as *Homo erectus*.[27]

About 750,000 years ago, *Homo erectus* was already a widespread species. Very similar forms are represented by finds in Asia, Africa, and Europe. The brain size of the new species shows another cycle of expansion. Later forms have half-again the cranial capacity of earlier forms. Much of this brain enlargement may have had to do with the intellectual and planning needs of hunting, the widening use of language, and the concomitant need for improvement of memory capacity.

With the evolution of a larger race with a comparatively

larger and more complex brain, the larger mammals could be more easily hunted. Some forms of the australopithecines seem to have preyed on big game, but with the appearance of the genus *Homo,* antelopes, elephants, hippopotami, and buffalo all fell within the range of hominid attack. Hunting, particularly for big game, was a task that demanded both intelligence and the ability of the larger social group to cooperate in a common endeavor. Many human capacities for problem-solving were surely developed in this context.[28]

Among the sites occupied by *Homo erectus* were the caves at Choukoutien near Peking. These showed the use of fire and of manufactured stone tools of both the flake and chopper type. Worked bits of bone were evident as well. About three quarters of the animal bones that presumably represented Peking Man's prey were from deer. Also present were bones of the mammoth, sheep, camel, bison, water buffalo, ostrich, and otter. Fruit seeds were also found within the caves. Peking Man is estimated to have lived a half million years ago.

Human use of fire apparently long predated Peking Man. Hearths have been discovered in caves in France that date back at least 750,000 years. The actual beginnings of the use of fire may well antedate by a considerable margin any evidence yet found—or that will ever be found for that matter. It is only the rather rare site, such as those in caves, that are likely to provide unambiguous evidence of the systematic use of fire as a human technology.

In the higher hunting period, the drive for information was intensified. Geographical information came to be of great value. The location of distant supplies of water had to be remembered. Habits of various species of game had to be well learned, including their patterns of reaction when under attack.

Sharp powers of perception were essential. Those conceptual powers we often call intellect were almost surely expanded. Some of this is probably reflected in the gradually increasing brain size that can be traced in the fossil record.[29] Some probably involved additional changes in the internal workings of the brain, deep structural patterns that the fossil record is not ever likely to fully reveal.

Hunting the larger animals also required an ability to work

toward a distant goal. Planning in time had to become a necessity. Most of the nonhuman primates are unable to concentrate on a single objective for more than a quarter of an hour at a time, surely not more than half an hour. On the other hand, a carnivore, let's say a wolf, can easily stalk his prey for hours at a time, if not for days. A longer attention span was surely one more way that the higher hominids were very different from their immediate precursors.[30]

Technology developed at an increasing pace. By the time of *Homo erectus,* fire played a major role in human activity. A wide variety of weapons were in use, including bolas—stones linked by leather tongs and used to entangle game. The mental life of the species must have had very much in common with that of *Homo sapiens,* although the individual probably averaged somewhat lower in general intelligence.

REPRODUCTION AND DEVELOPMENT

Pregnancy and birth posed problems of adaptation for the evolving hominids. The history of successive australopithecine forms shows a gradual increase in size. Early forms were only about four feet tall and perhaps sixty pounds in weight, later forms nearer five feet and one hundred pounds. Brain and head size expanded at least proportionately. The same pattern of size increase may well have been true of the hominid line ancestral to *Homo.* Larger animals tend to have longer gestation periods. The elephant has a gestation period of about twenty months; and the newborn elephant calf is well developed and able to keep up with the moving herd. Gestation could not, however, lengthen among the hominids. A baby with too large a head could not be born through the rather narrow opening of a pelvis designed for upright posture. Hominid young consequently had to be born into the world at increasingly "premature" stages. After the period of gestation within the womb, uterogestation, there had to be what might be called a secondary period of gestation, a period of very special care outside the womb that has been called "exterogestation."

In *Homo sapiens,* this period of exterogestation is at least as long as uterogestation; nine months after birth the human infant can hardly get about on its own at all, only at a crawl.

This increasing "prematurity" of hominid birth had implications far beyond those that related to pregnancy and birth. Out of lengthening dependency on the part of hominid young there came new social needs and novel educational opportunities.

The helpless human infant is much more dependent on its mother than the young of other primate species. It can not survive if its mother does not carry it about for over a year. In contrast, a newborn baboon needs help only a day or two; after that it is strong enough to cling to its mother's body hair. Since only a bipedal mother would have arms free enough to take on such a burden, we can assume that the present pattern of exterogestation required the prior development of an upright posture.

As a result of this strange developmental stage, humans came to have many behavioral characteristics that were shared by no other species. Some of these characteristics may be ominous for the future. The psychotherapist Anthony Storr, who views mankind as a particularly aggressive species, believes so.[31] Using concepts similar to those of Lorenz and conclusions drawn from psychoanalytic theory and practice, Storr sees the human condition as a particularly vulnerable one precisely because our long period of abject dependency as infants and children. The concomitant feelings of humiliation and disregard that all children experience, in Storr's opinion, generate impulses of hate and revenge. These create in humans a vindictive spirit that surpasses the aggressive tendencies to be found in other species. This, Storr feels, is why only humans will behave cruelly to the weak and defeated, something other species do not do.

On the face of it, I see some explanatory value in this thesis. Surely all humans go through a long and often painful apprenticeship before they can take care of themselves. To what extent this could account for some of the nastiest aspects of human behavior will have to be established by future research. This long apprenticeship is, of course, also our best hope for conditioning within mankind, by means of the learning process, the sort of restraints that we need for living together peacefully.

NEW SEXUAL PATTERNS

During the hominid period there had been sharp changes in the sexual nature of what-was-to-become-man. *Homo* contrasts with the other primates, including the higher apes, in a variety of ways in this regard.

Sexual contact in the hominid presumably took place in a context of social communication. The human female is no longer sexually available or attractive to the male only during periods of estrus or "heat," as is the case with all mammals, even the apes. At some point in hominid development, the hormonal approach to sex began to be replaced by a new pattern that was much more cerebral. Estrus disappeared entirely, some postulate, because it ran counter to the evolving pattern of periodic male absence on hunting expeditions; sexual ties would be stronger if sexual availability and attraction were reasonably constant. However, there may have been other, as yet undiscovered, reasons for the change.

But there were other departures. Sexual features that attracted the evolving male hominid were no longer those visible from the rear, as is the case with the other primates; note the "sexual skin" of the chimpanzee, for example. They included instead a whole set of new features that could be seen only from the front: rounded breasts, the areolae (pigmented areas of sensitive skin surrounding the nipples), pubic hair, smooth facial skin (absence of beard), fuller lips, etc. Obviously the ancient invitation to mount from the rear had been replaced by sexual features that implied face-to-face contact—a pattern that also reflected greater cerebral control over the sex act and increased abilities to communicate emotion when face-to-face. The fact that male and female voices are almost totally distinct may be another indication that oral communication was much involved in sexual relationships.

Two other sexual changes during the hominid period may reflect the same tendencies toward cerebral control in a social context. One is the female orgasm, a pattern of response not found in the ape or other primates. Although it is perhaps not accurate to say that nothing at all resembling a female orgasm is to be found in any other species, it is surely differently developed in *Homo*. The other change involved the male: the loss of the small bone or cartilage found in the penis of many mammals, including all monkeys and apes. This stiffening bone, called the *os penis* or *baculum,* apparently disappeared during the hominid period. Some speculate that the loss may have been part of general evolution toward more deliberate, slower, and more gentle copulation.

The traditional Freudian psychologists might dispute how successful our species has been in evolving a brain-controlled pattern of sexuality to replace that which was purely hormone-controlled. It is clear, however, that a major revolution was involved, one in which we may still find ourselves.

Hunting as a way of life probably had its impact on the sexual dimorphism in the evolving hominids. Males were somewhat larger; they were able to run faster; they were stronger; they ranged farther. Patterns of sexual dimorphism vary among the primates. The male gorilla is very much larger than the female. On the other hand, the male and female chimpanzee do not show much contrast by human standards. Several human features that mark our species as quite different from the apes also play a role in our patterns of sexual dimorphism: in the female, prominent breasts, rounded buttocks, broader hips; in the male, longer legs, beards, occasional balding in maturity.

The distortions of sexual roles caused by the artificial world of "civilization" have probably obscured the original distinctions between male and female human beings. We have only begun to study such matters objectively. It is very important that we learn more about this subject if we are to hope to understand the multifaceted problems of our adjustments to the techno-industrial world. Since the days of Freud, we have been aware that many of the problems plaguing us in our adjustments have heavy sexual overtones. Whatever the causes, sexuality is, for both human sexes, a much different and more pervasive force than it appears to be among the other primates.

Homo Sapiens ON THE SCENE

We do not know how old our species is. Since scientific judgment is often divided on where one species ends and another begins, this is not surprising. With *Homo sapiens* the record is much less distinct than usual. Recent finds have raised the possibility that our genus, if not our species, is considerably older than scientists had believed only a decade or so ago.

What we do know, however, is that some 200,000 years ago the first widespread fossils begin to appear of what anthropologists today universally classify as *Homo sapiens*. Many of those fossil finds were in Europe, where the so-called Neanderthal variety of *Homo sapiens* long held ground. A major difference between *Homo erectus* and Neanderthal Man was an increase in brain size.

Neanderthal groups obviously possessed a complex culture. They made a varied kit of stone tools that are usually described as the Mousterian tradition. Since they lived in Europe during the time of the Last Glaciation, at least some Neanderthal groups must have developed effective fur wardrobes. A common tool was a flint scraper that would have served well in preparing pelts.

The Neanderthal type disappears from the European fossil record perhaps 35,000 years ago. In its place there appears, by 25,000 B.C., evidence of a fully modern population. There are those who consider that the Neanderthal variety of *Homo sapiens* was simply a developmental stage that led to the modern variety; this is disputed by others, who see the Neanderthals as an offshoot who were later displaced by our precursors. Technological development shows considerable continuity from one stage to the other, with only a gradual increase in the sophistication of tools.[32]

Not too long after the appearance of the modern form of *Homo sapiens,* we find signs that human beings had even crossed the area that is now the Bering Sea and were on their way to occupation of the Americas, an area never previously inhabited by any hominid species. Except for minor changes, like the retreat, and in some cases the absorption, of old subvarieties or "races" and the expansion of others, there has apparently been little change in the human gene pool since. There is no question but that *Homo sapiens* has always been dependent on technological skills and traditions. When the modern species can first be identified, the record of systematic tool-making by earlier forms of hominids was already at least two million years long.

Our species did not come into existence and then "invent" tool-making. Instead, *Homo sapiens* was born of a line of creatures who, while very different in many ways from our present species, were already well committed to the technological approach and who probably could not have survived without culturally transmitted technologies. Our technological abilities were evolved *while using technologies*.

ECOLOGY AND THE INDIVIDUAL

As we have seen, our species came into existence as the result of a long series of adjustments to new environments. Although we do not yet know all we would like to know about the hominid period, it was surely a period in which many new and unprecedented adaptations were made. Some involved surface anatomy, but the more important involved creating new decision-making roles for the brain. All these adaptations were the result of how successfully individual hominids had interacted in the face of environmental challenges and opportunities.

Not only can the total ecological relationship of a species be analyzed as the sum total of the relationships of all individuals within the species, but it can be further broken down in terms of several zones of interaction that face each individual. Different people react differently to changing environmental factors in terms of the degree of closeness of those factors to their immediate concerns.

I believe it will be useful to introduce at this point the concept that there are distinct zones of personal action and social interaction that surround the individual. These zones will be taken as a series of concentric environments, centered on the individual, much like the layers of an onion. Each will include all those zones within.

Beginning at the core, I believe that we can usefully identify five natural and rather distinct layers. *Zone one* is the area immediately touching the skin; it includes the air available to breathe, and objects readily touched by the extremities. Humans, like all animal forms, are highly motivated by zone one considerations. They will struggle mightily for air, to avoid excessive heat, or to prevent pain from environmental factors. *Zone two* is an area within about two or three meters of the individual, that area in which normal conversation would take place. It is here that not only most social and symbol-making activity takes place, but most tool-making as well. *Zone three* is the maximum area of social interaction. It reaches out a couple hundred feet under most circumstances, depending on environmental factors, to include an area as far as the voice will carry or one person can recognize another's face. *Zone four* extends as far as one can see or otherwise gather information from any one location. It would encompass the immediate range during the hunt. *Zone five* is a very irregular and varying area made up of all the Zone four areas which a person experiences during his lifetime. It originally covered the hunting and gathering area of the individual's tribe or ethnic group; now the zone is extended in size as a result of greater mobility, but it still represents "the world as the individual directly experiences it."

When a woman stops to take a rock out of her shoe, she is thinking in terms of Zone one considerations. When a shopkeeper tries to make a sale to a customer, both are dealing in the Zone two frame. When you enter a classroom or auditorium for a lecture, you are in Zone three. A man cheering on his team in a football stadium is reacting to Zone four considerations. A public speaker who says "pollution has gotten significantly worse in the last fifteen years" is talking in terms of Zone five.

Beyond these five natural zones there are two that we often think about today, but which are conceptual constructs. We do not experience them in the same direct way. These are: *Zone six,* the biosphere, all of the surface of the earth, the oceans, and atmosphere; and *Zone seven,* the universe, as far out as observable or conceivable.

The first five of these zones have, I believe, general but natural limits based on the nature of human interaction with the environment and other folk. Within those limits, the exact boundary of some of the zones can differ as the result of the cultural traditions of the individual, probably in turn reflecting the environmental features in which the culture in question developed.[33] The distinction between zones six and seven is a modern innovation, since it requires separating Earth from beyond-Earth, a concept only elaborated after discoveries such as those of Copernicus and the explorers who first sailed around the world.

I believe that the boundaries of the first five zones were built into hominid behavior patterns long ago and were already well established when early *Homo* was still a hunter-gatherer.

I believe that they remain in effect in many subtle ways in even our modern techno-industrial world. They are, in practice, "ecological zones for the individual" that still map out differing ways in which the individual human being integrates into the "outer world." Any detailed study of whether "territoriality" exists in mankind as an innate or learned trait should take into account the fact that the various zones mentioned above are dealt with in distinct ways by human beings.

Many of the problems facing techno-industrial society can be better understood if we remember that the individual's priority of attention will almost always lead to the considerations of the smaller zone being given precedence over the larger in the decision-making process. This principle, which I will call "inner zone primacy," has major implications for the course of human events, since the actions of the species are in fact only the sum of all the actions of individual human beings. The principle will come up again in later chapters.

Is Ours a Specialized Species?

Having traced the evolutionary history of *Homo sapiens* in ecological terms, we will want to take a final look at the result and consider just how specialized the new species was when it first emerged.

It has been popular, even among some anthropologists, to describe ours as a generally "unspecialized" species, often noting in passing that this is one of our biologic strengths. The evolutionary record shows that species with highly specialized ways of life or highly specialized organs face certain risks that may lead to their extinction. For example, environmental changes that would cause the disappearance of the grasses in a certain area would lead to the extinction of all those species in the area that were adapted specifically and solely to a diet of grass. Although there is some controversy among students of evolution, the fantastic antlers of some past species of stags like *Megaloceros* or the "Irish elk," the giantism of the South American sloth, and the massive teeth of the saber-tooth tiger have all been cited as lines of specialization that, when carried too far, contributed to extinction.

But, conclude some anthropologists, overspecialization is

a danger that we do not face. We have all five digits on each extremity. We have retained much of the general body shape of the early mammals. We maintain, albeit at lower levels in some cases, each of the basic sensory systems of the land vertebrates. We move in a wide variety of environments. No, they say, our precursors did not lose their sight like the mole, turn their hands and forearms into wings like the bat, or undergo any other change of so basic a nature; ours is not a highly specialized species.

As we have seen, the factor that this approach overlooks is the most obvious: the human brain. Otherwise we do remain pretty well an unspecialized form of mammal. It is true that we have our upright posture and the rather strange foot that goes along with it, but these developments do not compare in complexity or implications to those that went into forming the human brain.

The brain of *Homo sapiens* is probably as highly specialized an organ as can be found in any species. During the hominid period, its role was elaborated and its functions were extended beyond all precedent. We have seen that even the expression of sexuality is largely a brain function in *Homo sapiens*; the man or woman with something else on his or her mind does not make a very ardent lover.

It surely took a very long time for the human brain to evolve the various features that separate it so distinctly from the brain of the ape—a fact that may argue in favor of some of the longer estimates of the time covered by the hominid period. By comparison, the rather strange events of the last ten thousand years represent only a short interlude. Nevertheless, they are putting to test whether the human brain can cope with its own successes.

The question then arises: Is our species dangerously "overspecialized" because of its cerebral development? Will, perhaps, the final use of our tools be for self-destruction? The answer will probably be soon in coming, speaking in evolutionary terms. But it is not easy for us to arrive at an answer here. Return to earth in another ten thousand years. By that time the answer should be apparent. As a matter of fact, the next five hundred years, perhaps even the next fifty, may tell the story.

Many of the large mammals that early hominids hunted (for example, the mastodon, the woolly rhinoceros of Southern Europe, the North American horse, the South American giant sloth) may well be extinct as the result of hominid technology, their too-successful hunting methods. Much of present-day wildlife faces the same fate from more recent developments in human technology. In the final analysis, the last species to face extinction as the result of human inventiveness could be *Homo sapiens* itself.

How then can we hope to maintain a stable ecological relationship with our present environment? What would be the nature of that relationship? Can we hope to attain perfect harmony with the world around us? Can we survive with less? These questions will be discussed in the next chapter.

4
The Intimacy of Mind and Environment

We have looked at how our species developed through ages of contact with differing environments. Let's now look at how people presently interact with the world around them. We will need great insight if we are to understand the problems posed by modern technology. We will start with a psychological experiment.

Imagine that you are lying relaxed on a comfortable bed in a small room. Translucent glasses prevent you from seeing anything but diffused light. All you can hear is a monotonous hum from a nearby machine. Your hands are restrained by gloves that will not allow you to touch anything. Your legs cannot even touch each other.

How long could you take it? How long could you tolerate such a monotonous sameness, deprived of all meaningful sensation? Not very long, showed early experiments undertaken at McGill University with an eye to the implications of sensory deprivation for space travelers.

At first, the twenty-odd male college students who were subjects of the experiment found they could fight the boredom with sleep; but this worked only for a day or so. They then became increasingly bored (even though they were allowed to get up to eat and to go to the toilet). Some of the students could stand this routine only for the second day. The longest period that any could tolerate it was only five days. Toward the end, the subjects suffered visual and auditory hallucinations. It was as if their minds were forced to imagine incoming information to fill an intolerable lack of input. Even more important, it was found that, upon emerging, they could not think in a systematic fashion. Their perceptions were impaired and their tested intelligence had temporarily deteriorated.[1]

Many similar studies in sensory deprivation have been conducted since. In more severe tests, subjects were floated in a tank of warm water; their hands were covered by a kind of glove that even prevented contact between fingers; white noise and dim neutral light were all they could hear or see. Most subjects could tolerate only a few waking hours of so extreme an isolation from interaction with an environment.

This tells us an important story. The very health of a human being seems to demand a flow of sensory information. We see that the mind is designed to respond actively to continuous information from an environment. Deprive someone of all reciprocal relations with an environment, and you run the risk of destroying that person. Despite the complexities of the inner world that our species has evolved over countless millennia, each of us still requires continued contact with a world external to our own consciousness. As a consequence of these studies, astronauts have been given as active as possible a schedule of activities during their confined flights.

The fact that sensory deprivation can lead to a degree of social withdrawal may account for its use in pacifying troublesome criminals. Although some may react violently to solitary confinement at first, this reaction tends to give way to passivity and to result in a more docile prisoner, albeit one less and less prepared to reenter normal social relationships, within the prison or without. Prolonged physical isolation and inactivity in a completely segregated area can lead to "confinement psychosis," a psychotic reaction that is often marked by hallucinations and delusions similar to those induced by certain of the above-mentioned scientific experiments in sensory deprivation. In prison parlance, the prisoner goes "stir crazy."

As a species, we not only need information *per se,* but we need certain specific kinds of information in order to live. The exact content of needed information may vary from culture to culture; an inhabitant of modern industrial Australia needs different facts than did the aborigine who lived in the same area several hundred years before. Even within the same culture, a farmer and a fisherman are likely to gather differing facts from observing the same weather conditions. Nevertheless, there remain certain consistencies in the basic kinds of information that all persons seek out. We are not the passive receivers of sense data. On the contrary, we actively seek the information that we feel we need or might need for action. We not only see, we look; we not only hear, we listen. The turning of our head, the focusing of our eyes, our movement from place to place—these all are part and parcel of our active search for more and better information. Motor activity, even the seemingly random motor activity of a fidgeting child, plays a major role in gathering information on the environment. Actions that seem to be the result of idle curiosity, as well as those actions that we usually call play, are examples of this tendency.[2]

The relationship of any living thing to its environment must be an active one. We see this even with microorganisms. Among the mammals, exploratory behavior takes up a particularly large amount of the individual's time and effort. Some of this exploratory behavior can be described as "specific exploration." For example, the organism feels disturbed because it doesn't have enough information to make a specific decision and so it searches for the needed information. But this does not account for all exploratory behavior. Often an animal seems to be after what it feels is the optimum degree of variety, novelty, and complexity in its input of sensory data, without particular regard for how it will use that data. This pattern of activity, common in mammals, has been called *diversive exploration*. It is as if the sense organs and mind demanded a certain level of complexity of input for good health and proper activity.

As a consequence, humans have characteristically decorated the world about them, adding new stimuli for the senses. The Aurignacians covered the clay walls of their caves with meandering finger marks. Early hunters decorated their spears and spear-throwers with images or geometric designs. Primitive tribesmen painted and tatooed their own naked bodies, thus creating more complex sensory images of themselves. Today we still tend to cover with decoration the simple functional forms of the things we make, from the murals on the walls of great public buildings to the designs on candy wrappers. The only explanation can be that there is something in our nature that enjoys, and seeks out or creates, a richness of sensory experience.

SENSORY OVERLOAD

At the other end of the spectrum from sensory deprivation, it
is, however, possible to overburden our senses. This is usually
called *sensory overload*. The modern technological world throws
at us a wealth of sensory data of a complexity unknown to
primitives: streams of headlights and taillights on the evening
highways, telephone directories, blinking neon signs, statistical
charts and graphs in learned journals, the people flashing by us
as our train pulls out of a subway station, singing commercials
on automobile radios, and countless other impressions that
would have been incomprehensible in the simple cultural environment of early *Homo sapiens*. Modern media, like radio and
television, also pour information toward us from all parts of the
globe, challenging our ability to make an integrated whole out
of their impressionistic complexity. News broadcasts and head-
lines collect for us the tragedies and conflicts of the most distant
nations. Airplanes roar overhead, crashing the sound barrier.
We travel from major city to major city in an hour or two, often
having to accommodate in the process to differing regional ways
of doing things. The simple lines of modern architecture, the
unadorned shapes of contemporary sculpture, and the monotonous beat of some present-day music can all be looked upon as
reactions to the chaos and complexity of the industrial world in
which we live. They provide us with a new simplicity, one that
gives a kind of momentary relief in a world threatened by
sensory overload.

Normally, the problem of too varied a sensory input is
solved by our ignoring the irrelevant information and paying
attention only to the needed data. This type of control can act
at all levels. A receptor cell can respond only to those chemical
or physical changes that it is designed to detect. It is necessarily
indifferent to other stimuli. No creature of any complexity can
respond to all of the stimuli that are registered by its sensory
system at a given time. In the human, the central nervous system must thus give a very specific order of priority to the wealth
of redundant data that it receives, for the various senses have
been evolved to be used within certain patterns of balance. This
fact has been used in dentistry in a device known as an audiac:

the patient puts on earphones and turns up the volume of noise to a higher and higher level until he or she can no longer feel the pain of the dental work. The overload of one sensory system thus can numb the others.

In the modern technological world, however, it is not easy to ignore all irrelevant or distracting information. Since the patterns of that world are all so new, it is by no means easy to separate what is important from what is not. If we were to ignore too much of the new industrial world about us, we would quickly find it difficult to participate in that world at all. Remember that your ability to sort out one red light in a maze of flashing neon may mean the difference between life and death when you try to cross a busy city street.

CONTROL AND FEEDBACK

But if we are to establish the proper balance with the external world about us, how are we to do it? How does an organism normally relate itself to a changing environment? Can we hope to perfect our relationship to the strange new man-made world in which we find ourselves?

Almost all our actions, except perhaps the simple knee-jerk type of reflex, require us to adjust in some controlled way to changes in our environment. By analogy with certain mechanical principles, this type of interaction is usually called a *feedback* system. Review of the nature of feedback can, I believe, help us to understand the interplay of ecological factors in our lives.

The thermostat of a kitchen oven provides a simple example of the principles of feedback. The two basic elements required for the system are: (1) an *indicator,* some sort of receiver that can relate the current state of affairs to an established goal, and that can quantify any corrective action that might be required to meet that goal; and (2) a *control,* a mechanism that is capable of regulating in some way the output of the system. In the example of a gas oven, the indicator is a thermostat, while the control mechanism would be a valve on the gas line. In this example, part of the system's output—that is, heat that the oven has generated—is picked up by the indicator (the thermostat) and this information is fed back to the control (the gas valve) of the oven in order to regulate future output of heat. Thus, when the measured temperature reaches a certain point, the gas is automatically turned down. Living organisms use many similar control mechanisms. In the case of a dog chasing a cat, the dog's sense organs act as indicator, his muscular system as control. As he sees the cat veer to the right, he adjusts his own bodily movement in that direction.

When the information that is fed back by the indicator sets off an action to reverse or limit the prior action of the system, we have what is called *negative feedback*. The oven gets too hot, the gas is turned down. Negative feedback controls act to stabilize a system; they keep it directed toward the goals for which it is set. In the example of the oven, the controls maintain a stable temperature.

There can be, however, systems that work in the opposite way. These are called *positive feedback* systems. Such a system reinforces rather than moderates any sensed change. For example, the thermostat, finding the oven temperature above what it was set for, would turn the gas up even higher! Any system that would escalate a situation in this way would obviously be very unstable, even self-destructive. No oven could be effective if so organized. Yet positive feedback systems do exist under certain circumstances. The accelerating pace of the modern world, in which each new scientific discovery or technological innovation seems to lead to several more, has the basic characteristics of positive feedback.

Timing plays a major role in any feedback system. Because it takes time to adjust to a change, either too great or too little sensitivity to change can endanger the stability of any self-guided system—whether an oven or a culture. The temporal horizon of the human being is also much more extended than that of other species. A rat can sustain a delayed reaction about four minutes, a cat for seven hours, a chimpanzee for two days.[3] People will work toward a consistent goal for periods of decades. This extension of the possible time lapse between stimulus and response makes human feedback systems unique.

The cultural patterns elaborated by our species allow vastly increased possibilities for long delayed responses and permit the concurrent use of a rich overlay of reinforcing systems. For our species, the symbol plays a major role not only in the way that we perceive the world about us—in the "indicator" function— but also in the way we control and regulate our relations with our environment and with one another. Thus, Congress may hold hearings on the effects of present legislation, and later use the information gained in order to draft needed amendments to the laws on the books.

Tools and other cultural artifacts play a major role, both as indicators and as controls, in our interrelation with our environment. Our cultural and historical memories, whether written or unwritten, allow a longer time lapse in the process of feedback than enjoyed by any other species. A doctor, for example, may prescribe a medicine as the result of basic research that had been conducted years before. An architect will make decisions on the basis of data that was collected a generation earlier on the strength of materials. In other species, feedback is primarily a process internal to the individual organism. For our species, external indicators, external records, external tools and devices replace or augment our unaided senses, memory, and muscles. An action that we take is more likely to be conscious rather than unconscious, and to be based on a body of learning transmittted from generation to generation by cultural means rather than based on raw sensory data that the individual concerned has personally gathered.

Our very consciousness of our own goals and desires—of our relationship to the outer world—plays the role of an "indicator" in a feedback system. The conscious process gives us a running means for testing out our own actions. For this reason, we must expect to make conscious efforts to solve the many problems we face in adjusting to the new world of modern technology. Otherwise, we may find ourselves subject to that ultimate of all negative controls in biological development: extinction as a species.

THE FUNCTIONAL CIRCLE

What can we learn about how other organisms adjust to the world about them that may be of value in our efforts to meet our own current problems?

Consider the life cycle of the butterfly, its transformation

from egg to larva, then to pupa and finally to flying adult. Consider the way of life of the termite, isolated deep in its own dark
world. Or consider the world of the dolphin, hunting in packs
in mid-ocean. All these life forms lead very different lives, move
within very different environments; all are very different from
us in the way in which they relate themselves to their world. The
difference is not, however, only one of external environment.
In one sense, we cohabit the same external world with all these
creatures. But this does not make us like any one of them
or any of them much like a human being. Although the beaver
and termite may attack the same tree, the worlds that they perceive are hardly tangent. Each sees its environment in its own
way, in a pattern that its species has evolved for the kind of life
that it has made its own.

That an animal's knowledge of the "outside world" is a
subjective reflection of its adjustment to the kind of environment that its species has chosen as its own was first pointed out
early in this century by Jacob von Uexküll.[4] According to the
theories of von Uexküll, any organism, in order to survive, had
to be fully integrated into its environment; that is, the organism's receptor system (which gathers needed sensory data on
its environment) and its effector system (which carries out its
actions) must be in equilibrium. These two systems, he felt,
form a single, interrelated whole. Von Uexküll called this the
functional circle of the organism. Each species lives and acts
within its own circle, and its inner life must remain a mystery
to all other species.

These concepts remain of value to us today in our efforts
to understand the problems facing mankind as a species. To
guide the actions that it must take in response to changes in its
environment, any animal must collect information about those
changes. The more complex the behavior patterns of a species,
the more data it must gather for safe decision-making. The
senses of each species are designed to gather only the kind of
information that it needs for the kind of actions that it is liable
to take. Since the kinds of decisions that must be made will vary
from species to species, the kinds of information needed will
also vary.

Marston Bates, a scientist who spent four years in charge

of a laboratory in Albania studying one species of mosquito and eight years in charge of another laboratory in the rain forests of Colombia studying another species, has confessed that he did not make much progress in his attempts to look at the world from the mosquito's point of view.[5] Presumably the mosquitos had even less of an appreciation for the nature—much less the inner motives—of Dr. Bates.

Our relationship to our environment can also be quantified. The information content of any message, including the input of the receptor nerves of a sense organ, can be measured by analyzing the degree to which it narrows down the range of otherwise possible alternatives. When we make decisions, the smallest number of alternatives to choose from is, of course, two. Examples of this would include the "on" and "off" positions of a light switch, or any question that we might answer with yes or no. The minimum possible amount of information is one of these two-way alternatives, called a *binary unit* or one *bit* of information. Great numbers of bits are needed to describe any complex transmission. For example, the music recorded on a single inch of magnetic tape would take some ten thousand binary digits for a full description, although you might not really need all for normal, high fidelity. Similarly, a good television channel is capable of carrying about twenty million bits a second, although a million bits a second would get most of the program over to you.

As interacting organisms, we need not only a sufficient volume of information about our environment, but need certain kinds of information more than others. Our senses are very selective; like the selective indicator of any feedback system, they pick only certain frequencies of sound and only certain light waves and ignore the rest. There is an obvious reason for this.

Normally, a species does not waste effort and so does not collect information on matters beyond its capacity to respond. When responsive action is not possible, facts can be of no interest. Only when a specific kind of information is valuable for making decisions is an organism likely to evolve the senses required to collect that information. In countless generations of pine trees, for example, there has been no progress toward evolving a sense of vision, or even the type of nervous system that might precede it. A tree has no need to see as long as it is committed to an immobile life based on photosynthesis. Its green needles may show a certain sensitivity to the sunlight that they require, but the pine tree does not need to look out at the world around it; for if it did, and saw a forest fire or a lumber jack coming, it could not pick up its roots and flee. The passive and the helpless need no facts.

The same selective factors operate in respect to the patterns of similarity and distinction that we use in organizing our sense data into more complex understandings. The intelligence of an animal, like its systems for gathering sensory information, are tools forged to fulfill specific biologic purposes in terms of its total ecological adjustment, its way of life. "Every organism," declared von Uexküll, "is a melody which sings itself."

We can see, then, that the nervous system of any animal involves a circular flow of impulses: information coming from the sense organs to the brain area, and motor impulses traveling back out to the organs of action. The equilibrium between the receptor system and the effector system keeps the organism in a very special type of balance with its environment. Negative feedback systems keep the organism in a stable relationship with the world about it. The nature of this relationship varies somewhat with each species, but all these relationships have in common the fact that they are designed to allow individual members of the species to continue to exist and to reproduce themselves. When such equilibrium is impossible—whether because of changes in the environment or the genetic breakdown of the species itself—the species can no longer survive. If we are to survive in our new, man-made environment, it will be necessary that we establish equilibrium with it.

Among the more complex animals, patterns of interaction with the environment increasingly vary from one individual to another. Over time, they vary as immediate environmental conditions change. This is particularly true with people. Medical studies in the prison environment tend to show that the prisoners, too, maintain a degree of balance between the input of sensory data from their environment and their output in terms of levels of activity.⁶ Thus, a prisoner put in solitary confinement will not typically react by becoming more active. Rather than rage and storm about, the confinee will instead "withdraw into a shell," to a level of inactivity in which output better matches the lowered level of sensory input.

How well a person can adapt to difficult situations is surely related to that general psychological factor that we usually call motivation. Human activity, perhaps even more than that of other animal species, demands a sense of purpose. All animals—even all organisms—are goal-seekers. Adaptation and adjustment to the environment are not passive activities but take place in a context of goal-seeking, the maximization of gains for both the individual and the species.

We are unique in the way that conscious processes determine how we pursue so many of our goals. This purposive or telic aspect of our nature would seem on first thought to provide us with a guarantee against suffering from the effects of our own technologies. Surely all technological innovations are made in order to serve human goals; when they do not, we should be able to reject them for other lines of action that better serve our ends. The reason that this does not always work out is, however, nothing more complex than what I termed "inner-zone primacy" in chapter 3. Each human individual will normally give priority of attention in decision-making to those factors impinging on his or her own innermost zones of interaction with the environment, and there is no guarantee that the sum of such actions will answer the needs of the species in its general relationship to the environment. The sum of a lot of little "good decisions" can add up to one big, "bad decision"!

The problem that upsets goal-seeking is, of course, the ancient one of ignorance. We do not have enough information about our total environment or even about the subtle interrelationships of our known world in order to predict the impact of all actions we take. The danger is that a line of technology will serve certain immediate purposes of those who have devised it, but will turn out on the larger scale or over the longer term to have second-order consequences that are destructive of human purposes. And, most worrisome, in some cases the process is not reversible once the change has been introduced. In essence, we need to expand our consciousness of the effects of our actions.

All our evidence points to the fact that the activity level and pattern of life of any successful organism must be in constant balance with the effective forces of its environment. Von Uexküll went so far as to declare that each organism was not simply "adjusted to" its environment but was fully "integrated into" it.

Can we, in today's world, hope to maintain the essential balance, to integrate ourselves successfully into the techno-industrial world about us? Before answering this question, let's look at the nature of adaptation.

THE IMPERFECTION OF ALL ADAPTATION

The closest you are likely to come to eating a fossil is when you have an oyster. The oyster, among all species that are familiar to the average person, has probably changed the least over the longest period. Oysters of two hundred million years ago were very much like those of today, but there were not always oysters nor will there always be. We cannot take a very old person as proof that some people are immortal. All life demands change. Between differing species there are only differing rates of that change.

The adaptation of a species is not permanent or absolute. If it were, plant or animal species would never become extinct; and it is a matter of fact that the overwhelming number of species of life that have evolved on planet Earth have already become extinct. It is not just environmental change but also successively better adaptations on the part of other species that cause many species to disappear, and thus cede their ecological niches to newcomers. What may appear a remarkable form of adaptation from one point of view, may be found in retrospect, however, to have been a dangerous "overspecialization," one that contributed to the extinction of the species.

An organ does not have to be perfect to be highly valuable to the survival of a species. Even that amazing instrument the human eye has a blind spot and severe limitations of range. Moreover, successful adaptation in one aspect of life may give a species a comparative advantage in survival and thus allow the species to carry along other nonadaptive features. Erect posture was originally an adaptation of great significance in our evolutionary history, but it gave rise to many secondary problems. Minor structural changes that could make our arches, backs, and abdomens stronger may never come. The type of pressure-controlling valves that are to be found in the vessels that run between our ribs (vessels that became horizontal when our ancestors became upright) would be of great value in preventing varicose veins of our overdeveloped legs. They are not, however, going to migrate.

In fact, there is a great deal of evidence to show that the adaptation of any organism to its environment is imperfect. In stressing this, I must differ from von Uexküll. Not only do all environments necessarily vary somewhat over time, but organisms are by their nature constantly changing. At the very minimum, animals move within environments which are never absolutely uniform from place to place. If new locations were not likely to differ in some way from the old, animals would never have developed mobility to begin with. It is best to think of animals as in the process of "adapting" rather than as being "adapted."

The full functional circle of any animal involves small adjustments that slightly change its relationship to its environment. That relationship is a dynamic one characterized as much by uneasiness as by simple equilibrium. In a philosophical pamphlet published when he was only nineteen, Benjamin Franklin asserted the primary role of uneasiness or discontent in all biological activity:

> Thus is uneasiness the first spring and cause of all action, for till we are uneasy in rest, we can have no desire to move, and without desire of moving there can be no voluntary motion. . . . I might here observe, how necessary a thing in the order and design of the universe this pain or uneasiness is, and how beautiful in its place. . . . This may appear odd at first view, but a little consideration will make it evident; for it is impossible to assign any other cause for the voluntary motion of an animal than its uneasiness . . .[7]

The constant need for change, adjustment, and readjustment is even more characteristic of our species than of less complex organisms. This is probably true even if we do not take into consideration our characteristic use of culture as a means of adapting to a variety of environments, a topic we will discuss in future chapters. "The more complex an organism," the great scientist, Sir Charles Sherrington reminded us, "the more points of contact it has with the environment of shifting relationships."[8]

When we return with these considerations in mind to von Uexküll's concept of the functional circle of organism and environment, it becomes necessary to modify his model slightly and to replace the idea of a perfect circle with our more dynamic model: a circle that does not quite come back upon itself. This new, dynamic circle can be envisioned as a spiraling action, with a bit of a wobble to its course. The irregularity is so small, however, that it can be seen as less than a true circle only by long and careful analysis. But like the elliptic shape of the earth, this deviation from geometrical regularity is both significant and revealing. It is, in fact, this irregularity in the shape of the functional circle that accounts for all movement in biological evolution.

In some species, for example the small sea shell *Lingula,* a form of life that has existed without major change for almost twice as long as the oyster (i.e., 400,000,000 years), the functional circle must be very close to a true circle. In other species, indeed in whole classes like the present-day mammals or birds, functional circles evidence a wide variety of deviant shapes. All of this brings us to the question of just how near perfect *Homo sapiens* is likely to be in its adjustment to the environment.

Since our species is one of the most complex on Earth and, according to our standards at least, by far the most intelligent, it is tempting to assume that we represent ultimate intelligence and that our adjustment to the environment can therefore claim some sort of objective validity—that we see the world as it really is. In terms of the antiquity of life, however, ours has been the most intelligent life-form on earth for a very short time. The brightest reptile of a hundred million years ago did not fully mirror in its mind the world around it. It was probably quite unaware of much of what we would call reality—the passage of time for example. We would show great vanity to assert that our world could not be envisioned in any basically different way by the dominant species of a hundred million years from now. These are very philosophic considerations, and not the sort that can be easily analyzed. They do, however, help remind that we must struggle against a natural tendency to see the world in a subjective way peculiar to our species.

Modern genetic studies also lead to the conclusion that the odds are indescribably small that the adaptation of our species to our kind of environment is the best possible, even given the complexity of *Homo sapiens* as a species as a limiting factor. Using the concept of the "genetic landscape," a statistical continuum that shows the various possible "adaptive peaks" that a species might occupy, the chance that our species occupies the highest such peak has been roughly computed by the biologist Garrett Hardin.[9] Without going into all the statistical computations made, it will suffice to say that Hardin, making the most conservative assumptions, comes up with the likelihood that we occupy the highest or even one of the highest possible adaptive peaks at not much better than one chance in 10^{2950}. The odds would be much worse if we should consider the possibility of species that would be more complex in structure than we are.

Now, 10^{2950} is a number that is so large that we are first tempted to call it "astronomical." But, in fact, nothing in astonomy can even begin to compare with it; the total number of electrons in the known universe was once computed to be only of the order of 10^{87}. If Hardin's computations are anywhere near correct, we must assume that there is no real chance that mankind has made anything near the very best of all possible adjustments to our natural environment.

My purpose in noting the extreme unlikelihood that the human adjustment is anywhere near a perfect one is not to shed light on the problems of our bodily adaptations, like digestion, respiration, or locomotion. It is to make us think about our perceptual, intellectual, and other psychological adaptations. We find it easy to identify failings in the structure of our teeth, musculature, or feet; and we can easily complain about our continued possession of an appendix that seems to serve little use

but as a dangerous locus for infection. It is not so easy to identify our mental limitations, however, since our very thinking
must be conducted within these limitations. All our science and
all our technology has not altered that basic fact.

THE LAWS OF IGNORANCE

It follows from the nature of organisms, and from the considerations underlined above, that no organism can make its action
decisions in the light of all possible information on its total-
environment. To be able to do so, an organism would have to
be omniscient. In fact, however, all goal-seeking activities of
organisms are undertaken in the light of limited information.
The sensory data collected by each organism reflects, of course,
the kind of information most valuable to the type of decisions
it must make. Since it takes energy to gain information, there
is a necessary economy involved in selecting that input which
will be most valuable in terms of output.

Since no organism could collect all of the potentially available information on its immediate environment and many lack
certain very valuable information, it is accurate to say that all
biological activity takes place in a context of ignorance. There
are, however, acceptable and unacceptable levels of ignorance.
No organism can be totally ignorant and long survive. Information gathering is essential even to plant life at the cellular level.

Ignorance of the nature of ignorance is widespread. Perhaps it will be useful to outline some of its basic laws as they
relate to human activity. (1) *The ignorance factor*: some ignorance is involved in all human actions, since we can never be
aware of all aspects of our total-environment or of all of the
possible second-order consequences of our acts. (2) *The negative nature of ignorance*: ignorance is not an external force; it
never "compels" us to take any unwise action; it is only the
absence of information. (3) *The limits of ignorance*: to have
survived as a species, we cannot be totally ignorant of any aspect of our environment crucial to survival; factors essential to
any species for its decisions must be knowable in some sense.
(4) *Acceptable levels of ignorance*: effective and safe human
decision-making requires an adequate ratio between available

information and the significance and scale of the decision involved.

Our problem with technology today can be seen primarily as the result of violations of the fourth law of ignorance listed above. The decision-information ratio normal to *Homo sapiens* has been violated as a result of the scale of our society, the subsequent rate of innovation, and the newness and complexity of our modern environment. We simply do not have enough information about consequences to be making certain types of decisions at the rate we are making them.

Especially dangerous, however, is the fact that certain decisions are irreversible. Some genies cannot be put back in their bottles once released. The need to identify the second-order consequences of all irreversible decisions is the highest priority in our struggle to minimize the dangers of human ignorance. We will return to this problem in the pages to come.

INNER AND OUTER ENVIRONMENTS

From this discussion of the problems involved in the interaction of any species with the world about it, and our earlier review of the ecological changes through which what-was-to-become-man passed, we see that there are two directions from which we can view the relationship of a species to its environment. First, we can treat the environment as if it were something external and objective, the place a species lives, a place from which the species can move if newer and more advantageous possibilities should open nearby. Second, we can look on the environment through the eyes of the species itself, limited by its areas of ignorance, enlightened by its selective sensory system. Now, it is no longer a place but *the* place—a subjective world that is known only as the evolution of the species has prepared it to be understood. The contours of this world were formulated, of course, by countless generations of feedback from the more objective environment. Since each species has had, however, different needs and therefore different sensory and perceptual systems, the nature of that feedback has varied greatly from species to species.

It will be useful to talk about, and at times to contrast

these two sides of our interrelationships with the world—what
I will call the "outer" and "inner" environments of our species.
In the English language this usage creates a problem, since the
phrase "inner environment" conjures up a somewhat paradoxi-
cal image. It happens, however, that the German language has
two neatly paired, contrasting terms that have been used for the
outer and inner world of animal species. *Umwelt,* the "surrounding world," is a German term that is very often simply
translated by the English term "environment." *Innenwelt,* the
"inner world," is less commonly used in German, but a quite
clear and proper term. It is, however, without an exact English
equivalent. As a consequence, when I want to put the idea of
the *Innenwelt* into English terms, I must use circumlocutions
like the "inner environment" or "inner world."

As I wish to use them, however, the two concepts of *Umwelt* and *Innenwelt* are closely related, the two sides of a coin
as it were. They designate the two sides of the functional circle.
Although this is a relationship that may be lost sight of when the
more cumbersome English terms are used, I hope that you will
keep this pairing in mind as I use the concepts. From time to
time, when I feel it is important to make a clearer contrast, I
will use the German terms.

Umwelt, as I use it, will cover only the environment "as
perceived" by the species in question. It will not encompass all
of the *total-environment,* which is a term that I will use when
I want to refer to both the perceived and unperceived elements
of the environment. Ultrasonic waves that cannot be heard and
infrared "light" that cannot be seen have always been part of
the total-environment of our species, although it is only with
the advent of modern science that we have become aware of
their existence.

The two concepts, *Umwelt* and *Innenwelt,* and their interrelationships, will help us in understanding the problems facing
humanity today. It is generally recognized, for example, that the
problem of our adaptation to the new world of science and technology has both its external and internal aspects. Physically, we
face adjustment to a new world in which we are squeezed into
congested cities, forced to breathe polluted air, and separated
forever from the old environment of field and forest. This is the

crisis of our *Umwelt,* what is usually called the "environmental problem" of the contemporary world.

But as we have seen, this cannot be the whole problem. Intellectually, we must also face adjustment to new scientific concepts that have redefined the social world about us and seem to exclude our purposes from any real significance therein. The individual faces a technological world in which machines seem to pace all activities and mass media swamp the senses; change seems to remain the only invariable. In the terms introduced above, this may be called the crisis of our *Innenwelt.* It has created much of the contemporary feeling of alienation, since many in our society already sense that the contours of our new outer world no longer have much relationship to the needs of the old world, still locked within us.

5
Limits of the Human Scale

Over two thousand years ago, the Chinese philosopher Chuang Chou looked at our relationship to the environment and asked: "If a man sleeps in a damp place, he will wake up half dead with backache; but is this true of the eel? If a man tries to live in the trees, he will tremble in constant fear; but does the monkey? Of the three—eel, monkey, and man—who knows the right place to live?" Later on, Chuang Chou came up with the even more penetrating question: "How are we to know what we call nature is not man, or that what we call man is not nature?" These questions, raised so long ago, underline a major theme of this book: As members of the species *Homo sapiens*, we are prepared to survive in only a specifically human type of world, and we can understand and cope with that world only through those powers already evolved by our species.

As we have seen in the immediately preceding chapters, our evolutionary past as imprinted upon our genetic present creates for us a specifically human world—the environment as understood by man. What seems to us to be simply the "outside world" is not an absolute. It is not a neutral or purely objective world, since many of its characteristics are not shared with the sensory worlds of other species that we know about and probably would not be shared by a species more complex than ours. The functional circle of mankind may be quite a large one, but it too has its perimeters.

The Human Data System

We have seen that our senses, like those of what we call the lower animals, provide us with certain very specific types of encoded information, data that we are well prepared to use in dealing with the world surrounding us. Our senses do not, however, automatically convey a true and objective image of all of reality. Our human world, to use the words of von Uexküll, "cannot claim to be any more real than the animal's world."[1] As with other species, our senses form a basic link in the total system under which we deal with our environment—as does the remainder of our bodily anatomy, including the internal structure of our brains. Our senses belong only to us, not to our environment. They represent our outreach for information that we need to survive and are not in any way an objective input provided us by an objective reality. They do not report on all of the total-environment.

We have already mentioned many factors that have contributed to forming the human world. In some cases, our anatomy bears the imprint not only of the early human environment, but also, as we discussed above, of worlds long abandoned by what-was-to-become-man. The details of our sensory world are to a great extent a legacy of the primate stage, during which members of our ancestral stock created for themselves a vision-centered, three-dimensional, colored world of "things" to be manipulated. Our way of theorizing about that world was established during the period of cerebral expansion that took place in the hominid line. Thus, our nature as a species was firmly established long before any human cultural group had departed from the pattern of life followed by early *Homo* on the ancient plains.

Every species must carve for itself an ecological niche, and this requires an act of definition, the establishment of biological norms. A simple example can be seen in the fact that each species has its optimum environmental temperature and tends to seek it out. In the laboratory, we can demonstrate this by the use of the so-called "temperature organ," a long box that is warmed at one end and cooled at the other. When we put a group of small animals of a particular species, for example, a hundred ants, into the temperature organ, we will find that they soon tend to group at the point in the box which corresponds to the optimum temperature of their species.[2] All species tend to act in this way toward environmental variables. We are no exception.

Our sensory equipment has well-established limitations,

like that of any species. Our ears can hear sounds within a given frequency range; our eyes can see only certain wave lengths of light. Beyond these sensory limitations there are additional limits to our capacity for awareness, for control, and for discrimination. We have also our well-established norms for complexity, speed, scale, and variety. On each such continuum there is a medium point that we tend to seek, one that is for us "normal." For this reason, in this book I refer to the world that is normal for man as the *middle realm*. To deviate from its norms in either direction brings increasing physical discomfort and intellectual disorientation, just as movement in either direction would cause discomfort to the ants in a "temperature organ." What we see here is that the human mind, like the human body, must live in ecological balance with the world about it.

THE HUMAN SCALE

A major limiting factor that has contributed to creating the human world is, of course, the size of our bodies—our place in the scale of things. Our world of action is necessarily different from that of creatures of other sizes, even though they may inhabit the same geographic environment that we inhabit. To a man and an ant together at sea level on the same beach, the sand and the wind will not only be quite different phenomena because of scale, but the differentials of surface tension and air resistance will also make the basic physics of their worlds quite different. The ant can fall or be blown for a distance equal to a hundred or more times his length and not even be stunned; our bodies could never survive such an impact. The elastic surface of water allows certain insects to travel over it using surface tension alone, but this possibility simply does not exist for us. You need only to watch an ant for a few minutes in order to realize that most of its activities could not be conducted at our scale.

Julian Huxley, in an essay on the comparative size of organisms, concluded not only that the human body is roughly halfway between the smallest and largest forms of terrestrial life—a filterable virus and a California redwood—but also that we are almost exactly halfway between an atom and a star in size.[3] Although an individual human body would come only about two-fifths of the way up the cosmic scale from the weight of an electron to that which Huxley estimated for the entire universe, the total bulk of all humanity would stand near the middle of this continuum as well.

But we must be cautious here; I'm afraid that our apparent middle position in "the scheme of things" may very well be nothing more than an expression of the limits of our powers of observation and understanding. It appears reasonable to assume that it is about as difficult for us to extend our understanding to the limits of the very small (to the microcosm) as to extend it to the limits of the very large (to the macrocosm). If this be the case, we should not be surprised, when we average the two, if we come back to ourselves. Nevertheless, for convenience' sake, I have called the world of things at the human scale the *middle realm*. Whether it is truly intermediate in terms of any objective scale may be impossible for us ever to say in any definite sense; but for us it seems the *middle realm*, and it must remain so.

THE SIMPLE AND THE COMPLEX

Our limits often require that we simplify the complexity of the world around us to a level that more closely fits our abilities. A human being can consciously keep track of only a certain number of details or variables at a time. Even though our capacity in this respect is probably well above that of the other terrestrial species, there can be no question but that we continuously simplify the complexities of our environment so that we can cope with it better. Language forces this simplification upon us, since all symbolic activity is based on the selection of a finite number of somewhat arbitrarily chosen categories under which we can classify the infinite variety of our experience. All artistic traditions show the human tendency to select and simplify—to stylize—the perceived complexities of the world around us.

Science also demonstrates how necessary it is for us to simplify our environment in order to understand it. A full chemical description of the contents of a room, molecule by molecule, would require volumes too bulky to squeeze into the room; a subatomic description would be even more cumber-

some. We could not comprehend, much less use, such a mass
of description. What we need for action on the human scale is
information at the human scale of complexity, information that
accords with the norms of our middle realm. Too much monotony in our environment is also contrary to our nature and, if
carried too far, as in solitary confinement, can destroy the individual. Too much confusion is equally dangerous to our well
being, a problem that can become acute under the conditions
of modern technological society. We seek optimum points between chaotic complexity and boring monotony, just as a group
of ants will seek out the temperature appropriate to its species
when put in the "temperature organ."

Let's look now at the issue of complexity. Most of the systems of analysis elaborated in human culture, no matter where,
rely on no more than seven variables. If more seem to exist, the
anthropologist who is studying the culture in question will
typically decide that he has not yet completed his job of analysis, and that some of the supposedly individual factors are in
reality combinations of others. Even our social organizations
show this. For example, if the number of totemic clans within
a tribal group is significantly larger than seven, we will usually
find that certain clans are traditionally grouped together into
larger unities. There are about thirty different clans in the Torres Islands, for example, but they are in turn classified into two
basic moieties on the basis of whether the totemic animal of the
clan is a terrestrial or marine species. Similar patterns were
found in many American Indian tribes, in Africa, and elsewhere. In India, the numerous caste and caste-like relationships
prevailing in traditional society were capable of being generalized into four basic categories, plus the so-called "untouch-
ables," who were without caste.

This is not to say, of course, that we never make and use
lists of similar terms that run to more than seven items. Lists of
considerable length tend to deal, however, with the less crucial
aspects of our environment and society. Moreover, as I indicated above, long lists of similar entities could usually be
grouped according to hierarchies, which would subdivide the
list into smaller groupings. Our natural propensity toward
"manageable numbers" may not even end here. There is some

evidence that the *number of levels* in any hierarchical classification system also tends to be limited, by much the same human factors, to a number of levels no greater than seven or eight. Thus, the traditional zoologist, while he added intermediate categories from time to time, relied primarily on a six-level hierarchy of phylum, class, order, family, genus, and species within which to organize his subject matter.

If there do tend to be norms that govern our construction of hierarchies, this might explain why the various common-use vocabularies of most languages seem to be about the same length. Claude Lévi-Strauss has raised a question pertinent to this issue in his discussion of the number of species that are given names in primitive societies. "In the present state of knowledge, the figure of two thousand appears to correspond well, in order of magnitude, to a sort of threshold corresponding roughly to the capacity of memory and power of definition of ethnozoologies or ethnobotanies relying on oral tradition." He went on to ask: "It would be interesting to know if this threshold has any significant properties from the point of view of Information Theory."[4] Recent studies of folk taxonomies around the world confirm the tendency for identified generic taxa to be limited to about the same number in all cultures, "regardless of the richness of the environment in which the particular people live."[5]

There are, of course, natural limits to the capacities of our minds to process sensory information. The psychologist George Miller has stated that our capacity to make distinctions as well as our capacity for immediate recall of symbolic material tends to run to "seven items, plus or minus two"—depending on the nature of the symbols used.[6]

Miller went on to call "seven, plus or minus two" a "magical number" in man's information system. Speaking of the narrow range in our tendency to make distinctions, he stated: "There seems to be some limitation built into us either by learning or by the design of our nervous systems, a limit that keeps our channel capacities in this general range." Miller considered that it would be safe to conclude on the basis of present evidence that our species has "a finite and rather small capacity for making such unidimensional judgements and that this capacity does not vary a great deal from one simple sensory attribute to another."[7]

I personally consider that seven is closer to the upper limit and that Miller's maximum of nine (seven plus two) is too high. Studies of the human short-term memory system show the *chunk* capacity to be in the range of five to seven. Perhaps "six, plus or minus two" would be a more realistic "magical number."[8] But this is a minor difference.

More research needs to be done on the size of the vocabularies in common use among the peoples of the world. My impression, however, is that most languages, whether used by "primitive" or "civilized" peoples, run to something between thirty and forty thousand active, spoken words. The average person may, in turn, use only about half of these words on any regular basis. Of course, much will also depend on exactly how the concept of a "word" is to be defined; for example, whether two rather distinct meanings given to the same root are treated as one or two "words," whether adding a regular suffix creates a new word, and the like. Most practical dictionaries of spoken language tend toward thirty or forty thousand words, regardless of the language involved.[9]

Of course, many dictionaries contain a much larger corpus of words than just indicated. One of the most complete dictionaries of the English language, the unabridged Merriam-Webster, contains about 600,000 entries and has additional lists of geographic terms and proper names. This total approaches the magnitude of seven to the seventh power (823,543). We must recognize, however, that no one speaks, writes, or even reads in terms of the full vocabulary of the unabridged Merriam-Webster. Nor does any human language appear to contain so long a list of active vocabulary items. Obviously, "seven to the seventh place" presents too large a number of elements to constitute a practical system of analysis for a human being. This need not, however, contradict the general concept that seven is a rough but significant number in analysis, since it is very unlikely that all points of subdivision in any hierarchy would be filled with a full seven members. In fact, at some points in a typical hierarchy, no subdivision will exist, just as some genera of animals will have only one species. At other points, there will be only two subcategories, and the like. A six-level hierarchy that averaged six members at each point of subdivision would come to 46,656 entries at its base. This would bring us very close to the thirty or forty thousand scale that seems more or less characteristic of the full vocabulary of our spoken languages.

The above generalization about hierarchies, I would be the first to admit, is most simplistic in nature—more of a parable in numbers than scientific fact. Obviously, the vocabularies of languages are not organized into formal hierarchies with any degree of precision. Anyone who has worked with *Roget's Thesaurus* will realize this. I do, however, believe that beneath the above numerical generalities we can see additional evidence that the human mind works within very real norms.

In my opinion, the numerical boundaries that we have been discussing reflect natural limitations on our abilities to handle complexity in our environment, rather than simply representing limitations on our memory. This is an important point. Many persons learn three or more languages from childhood; any normal child seems quite capable of doing so. Under ideal circumstances, the average young person can master a half dozen spoken languages; it is need and opportunity rather than any special ability that is the controlling factor. These persons obviously can remember and can freely use a total number of words far exceeding 40,000, and they can do so without difficulty. Although it does not seem possible for one person to command all 600,000 entries in the Merriam-Webster, there are probably many practical linguists—especially in central Europe —who do remember and use a total number of words in various languages that exceed that sum. The limiting factor, therefore, does not appear to be the human memory but rather our ability to keep track of subtle analytical distinctions *within a single system of categories.*

Not only our intellectual life but also our social life shows the impact of some of the same limitations of scale. A scientific study of "small social groups" of human beings showed that instability becomes noticeable when the group reaches five, with a tendency for a subgroup of two to pair off against a subgroup of three and then to put pressure on one of the three to be rejected from the group. As the size of a group is expanded to

include eight individuals, the study concludes, "another critical
level" is reached and many of the characteristics of smaller
groups decrease.[10] Anyone walking through a large cocktail
party or reception can notice some of these same size-limitation
factors at work.

THE PACE OF HUMAN LIFE

Now, I'd like to turn from the issue of complexity to touch
briefly on that of pace. Like other species, man also operates
at certain rates in time. This is true even of modern technological man. Our sensory limitations illustrate this. Anyone who has
seen a time-lapse motion picture of growing plants realizes how
different our environment would appear if we viewed it at a
different speed. Species vary in metabolism and in their speed
of reaction. Like the blurring spokes of a turning wheel, some
actions in our environment are too fast for us to be aware of
without using special scientific instruments. Others, like the
growth of plants, are too slow. A visitor from outer space might
be puzzled by our motion pictures, for he might very well see
them for what they really are: a series of still photographs. For
us, however, they seem to display action. In these various ways,
we see that our *Innenwelt* sets boundaries of pace for our perceptions of the *Umwelt*.

By technological means we have greatly increased the pace
of modern life. The impact represents more than the availability
of new and faster machines. Studies of persons randomly observed walking demonstrate that people tend to walk faster in
direct relationship to the size of the community they are in. The
larger the town, the greater the hustle. It is not just that our
transportation systems move us faster, we orient ourselves in
time differently. In modern technological societies, the unit of
time that is perceived as significant to the individual is much
smaller than is the case in traditional societies. A nomadic
tribesman would never worry because he was ten minutes late.

Despite the cultural factor, the limits on the pace at which
human beings can operate remain very real. As the limit is approached, stress is clearly evident. The "super-heroes" of the
comic strips and television, from Superman to Bionic Woman,
have commonly had as part of their battery of powers the ability

to operate at a pace well beyond that which is normal to the human race.

ORDER AND SYMMETRY: MAN AS PATTERN MAKER

Children have enjoyed kaleidoscopes for generations. Little wonder. One of the strongest drives of our species is the effort to make patterns out of the jumbled world in which we find ourselves. All ethnic groups seem to look for repetitive themes, two-way contrasts, and symmetrical patterns in the world about them. This drive to find order appears related to our desire to be better able to predict and therefore to control happenings in the world about us. But it seems to go beyond these considerations and to be reflected also in our aesthetic natures.

Even here, however, the human tendency to try to find a middle ground is apparent. Too much uniformity, too much symmetry, becomes boring. People shun monotony of form almost as vehemently as they shun disorder in their environment. As has been shown by the anthropologist Anthony F. C. Wallace in his essay "On Being Just Complicated Enough," we have clear norms for the complexity of our culturally institutionalized activities.[11] Wallace saw limits in taxonomical systems that were approached at the two-to-the-sixth-power of complexity. He viewed these as based on the nature of man, not as cultural considerations, concluding that "psychologically speaking it seems likely that the primitive hunter and the urban technician live in cognitive worlds of approximately equal complexity and crowdedness."[12]

To the extent that we find what we are willing to accept as a satisfactory and satisfying degree of symmetry within a body of fact, we tend to lose interest in it. It is no longer a challenge, and we are forced to combat boredom by moving further into new bodies of data. This fact has done a great deal to encourage the gradual expansion of the area of human knowledge.

TRANSCENDING THE MIDDLE-REALM?

All concepts that we create to interpret the nature of our universe—our concepts about space, time, substance, motion, among many others—represent superstructures built upon unlearned perceptual patterns and thought processes that our species has evolved to deal with practical, mundane problems. These unlearned analysis-systems play as great a role in the concepts of modern science as they do in the myths of the Maori or the parables of the early Greek philosophers.

The paradoxes that logicians find in concepts like infinity and eternity are surely not paradoxes of nature, but reflect instead failings in human comprehension: the limitations of our analysis-systems. In terms of survival as a species, mankind has thus far never needed to comprehend many aspects of the total-environment, and has consequently not evolved a mind capable of dealing with them without serious problems. Some of our problems in understanding the world about us are obviously created when we uncritically extend the limited analysis-systems that we use to comprehend our everyday environment to situations and circumstances beyond the range of past human experience and need for understanding.

Pascal recognized this general problem. "Let us then know our limits," he said, "we are something, but we are not all. . . . In the order of intelligible things, our intelligence holds the same position as our body holds in the vast extent of nature. Restricted in every way, this middle state between two extremes is common to all our weaknesses."[13]

It is precisely because of this feature of all our intellectual activity that I will use the term *middle realm* to describe that which is the characteristically human environment. And I wish to imply by the term much more than a half-way position on the continuum of size or speed or degree of complexity. For us, the middle realm remains in all ways the true norm, the median point, the center ground on which we must stand to do our thinking. This is true because our brains were evolved in that realm to solve the problems of that realm.

This intermediacy can be seen in every feature of our inner world that can be put on a continuum. It can be seen in all the analysis-systems that we use to make sense of the world around us—not only in our perceptions of space, the passage of time, or the speed of objects in motion, but also in our natural understandings of the concrete and the abstract, of continuity and change, of large numbers or small fractions, of multiplicity and uniformity, of original causes and final purposes. In all these matters, we find it easier to function at intermediate levels, more difficult to accept or understand concepts that carry us too far in either direction.

Like the first human beings, we live in this middle realm, this world-as-we-understand-it, and we have inherited both a sensory and a reactive system designed for life within its scale of size, complexity, and speed. We operate best, we think best, within its limitations. Taken as a whole, these limitations constitute a major part of what I would call the *ecology of the human mind*. If we find ourselves in a state of tension with our surroundings today, it is because of our tendency to ignore our natural limitations or to try to overcome them by cultural innovation of an unplanned, uncoordinated nature.

We have talked thus far primarily of the phylogenetic nature of *Homo sapiens* as a species, and of the limitations which that nature places upon our physical, social, and intellectual development. The problems which confront this modern technological age are, of course, reflections of our culture-building propensities. This feature is what we will examine in the next section.

6
The Fig Leaf of Culture

No human being ever faces the environment in his or her natural, naked state. Our species is very different from others, primarily in that our "functional circle" contains so many more interposed stages and processes. Between our perceptions and our actions lie many layers of cultural clothing and artifice.

By the time that our present species, *Homo sapiens,* first entered the scene, the pattern was well established. Cultural activity mediated between man and environment. The hunt for the larger mammals had to be planned beforehand. Tools and weapons were prepared for the individual hunting foray; strategy was probably discussed. From the cave paintings of southern France and Spain, we are led to suspect that good omens were sought and ceremonies enacted to assure the success of the hunt. After the kill, the game was skinned, carved up with tools, and then cooked. Cooking represented a sort of intermediary digestive process, one that rendered edible that which people were ill-prepared by nature to eat raw. Cooking was of special value because the teeth, jaws, and digestion of early man had more in common with those of a vegetarian ape than those of a carnivore like the dog or tiger. Food processing related not only to the fruit of the hunt, of course, but also to the plant foods gathered by early peoples. Grinding, boiling, baking, and other processing rendered more digestible the harder grains, several key root crops, and a variety of other foodstuffs.

The processing of food is only one of the countless ways our species reworks its environment in order to take fuller advantage of it. To a degree unlike any other species, man also interposes an intermediary world of learned behavior between the process of gathering sensory data and his response to that data.

Our mediating cultural world thus has two directions of thrust: inward and outward. One relates more to our perceptor system, the other to our affectors. Together they make an integral whole.

The first thrust is inward; we build a new world of concepts with our minds, one that acts upon our *Innenwelt* or inner world. Thus our cultural world affects the way in which we think about and even perceive the physical world around us. The mediating process that is involved we can call *perceptor-mediation.* Its value is to make the incoming sensory data more readily useful to us. Thus it represents a kind of *input-facilitation* system.

The second thrust is outward: by cultural means we act upon or modify our *Umwelt,* the things that we perceive around us. For example, the tools and technical skills of a culture establish the patterns and set the limits on how members of that culture can react to or alter their environment. This mediation process we can classify as *effector-mediation.* Its goal is to increase our effectiveness in dealing with the external features of the environment. Thus it represents a kind of *output-facilitation.*

We see our world through a screen of symbols—what Humboldt, and more recently Weisgerber, called the *sprachliche Zwischenwelt,*[1] somewhat similar to what I have called *perceptor-mediation.* We also act on our world through the intermediacy of man-made instruments and processes, my concept of *effector-mediation.* I believe it useful, therefore, to expand Weisgerber's concept of a *Zwischenwelt* to include more than just the linguistic aspect and to apply it to all phases of human culture that we use to deal with our environment. The German term *Zwischenwelt,* which could be translated as "the world between," makes a useful contrast to the concepts of *Umwelt* and *Innenwelt.* So, with another round of apologies to the reader, I intend to introduce a third German word into our discussion. I will use the term *Zwischenwelt* to stand for the entire *mediating world* of culture that our species has created, all that stands between our naked bodies and untrained minds and the world about us. As will be seen below, it is through this intermediary world, this *Zwischenwelt,* that human beings have accumulated so much more information about their world than any other species; and only by its mediacy have they learned to manipulate and transform the world about them in manners thus far unprecedented on this planet.

Although the development of language and the creation of tools can be treated in terms of the functional circle as two contrasting directions of the expansion of the human *Zwischenwelt,* I believe it is useful to treat the *Zwischenwelt* as a simple, united matrix. I feel that the concept of *the basic unity of tool and symbol* will be valuable in understanding our ecological interactions with our environment.

No other evolutionary line on planet Earth has yet developed to anything near a comparable degree this type of mediating environment. It is a new element that is important primarily to the human ecosystem. Our precursors had, however, been developing along this line for a long time. Complex hominid tool-making cultures have already been dated back some two million years, to the australopithecine era in East Africa. Our archeologists cannot, of course, dig up clear traces of linguistic or other conceptual activity as they can excavate tools and campsites, yet it does not seem unreasonable to assume that many of the same cortical structures may be required for both activities. Perhaps some day our studies of the human brain will teach us more about the relationship between tool-making and the symbolic process. At the present, all I can say is that it seems that there is likely to be a direct relationship. "Systematic making of tools," concludes one study of tool-making, "implies a marked capacity for conceptual thought."[2] The idea that the two skills require very similar genetically determined abilities has also been formally advanced by students of human communication.[3]

But recognition of a relationship between the two sides of the *Zwischenwelt* need not lead us to assume that language and tool-making skills emerged at simultaneous rates. One may have led the way for the other. In the child, linguistic skills and the ability to manipulate and use objects develop concurrently and in accord with relatively well-established schedules. If anything, the child seems to develop a rather impressive degree of language ability before he or she evidences much in the way of motor development. For example, at eighteen months an infant still has difficulty stacking five blocks on top of each other, but may already be able to use forty different words. At thirty months, the typical child can build a tower only about six blocks high, but can make proper sentences of two to five words. Considering the abilities of other species, the symbolic side of the child's development seems to be by far the greater intellectual accomplishment. In *The Myth of the Machine,* Lewis Mumford develops in some detail the thesis that symbolic activity preceded and is more basic than tool-making in the human line, and that only the durability of artifacts has created the opposite impression.[4] Perhaps, however, this problem resembles the old story of the chicken and the egg.

Our language abilities are, of course, closely associated with our tendency to categorize objects and to make generalizations on the basis of the perceptual data that we gather. These abilities in turn create a new conceptual world, one that is separately built by each cultural group, but upon common perceptual and intellectual abilities. "The environment man makes for himself," the anthropologist Montagu reminds us, "is created through his symbol-using ability, his capacity for abstraction."[5]

People of all cultures show a strong tendency to "see" their environment symbolically and to remember it in symbolic terms. Language seems to flow almost as much from this intellectual tendency as from the need or desire to communicate. Symbolic activity forms part of a great range of human activities: religious symbolism, festivals, dances, graphic arts, music, mythic concepts, and a score of other features common to all human cultures. The graphic arts in particular demonstrate the close interrelation of the abilities we use in tool-making with those involved in symbol-making.

Symbolic processes appear to have a physiological basis. Patients who have suffered from brain damage, for example, often lose their ability to draw pictures at the same time that they lose their power to interpret or define isolated words. Aphasiacs may often be able to use words in concrete circumstances although they will be unable to manipulate them in any isolated or abstract manner. If we were all so limited in our conceptual activity, our species could not have risen to its present dominance among the species of earth.

As our techno-industrial world has created new concepts, we have changed the very contours of the world in which we conceive ourselves. The degree to which the actual external environment has been changed may not in fact be as significant as the psychological fact that the world now appears different to us. Our world picture is entirely new. During the same time that society was forging the contours of the modern industrial world, it was also creating a new intellectual world, one with features quite different from the middle realm in which we are by nature most comfortable.

THE TOOL AND HUMAN CULTURE

During an average day, the inhabitants of our techno-industrial world have very little direct contact with their environment other than by means of tools and related artifacts. They are awakened by alarm clocks, get out of beds, and put on clothes; they prepare breakfast using a large variety of utensils and tools. They take a bus or drive to work, sit on innumerable kinds of chairs, do their physical work with the help of various tools and machines, record their thoughts with pen or typewriter or on a computer. As they walk through life, they do so upon shoes; many even see the world about them through eyeglasses. All of these artifacts are part of our cultural *Zwischenwelt*.

When was the last time you dealt with the natural environment without the intermediacy of any tool or man-made artifact? Perhaps, if you pulled weeds in your garden this morning, you can reply "Why only this morning!" But unless you did it without wearing gloves, you will be unable to qualify—and the use of a hoe or shovel would obviously disqualify you. Think it over. You may be surprised to realize how long it has been since you dealt directly with any feature of the natural world.

Today our effectors seldom impact directly upon the environment but instead operate through a variety of effector-mediation processes which provide us a sort of leverage over the world about us. A great deal of the human adjustment to the environment, even in the early days of *Homo sapiens*, was brought about through such mediacy. The artifacts that play a role in these processes we call "tools," and include not only weapons and instruments that we manipulate with our hands but all our purposive cultural artifacts.

Such artifacts have allowed us to live in environments otherwise too hostile for our constitution: frozen tracts like those of the Arctic, or desert wastes like those of the Gobi. They have allowed hunters to catch game and fish that would have otherwise eluded them. They have allowed us to create strange new ways of life like agriculture that have brought us increasing control over a greater share of the available energy sources of the earth's surface.

No primitive tribe, no matter how remote from the centers of world civilization, has ever been found that was without a complex inventory of cultural artifacts. There can be no doubt but that the genus *Homo* and its precursors have depended on much more than their bodily equipment to deal with the world about them for a very long time. At first, these extrasomatic devices were probably very limited in effectiveness and only rarely used. Today the bulk of our artifacts dwarfs mankind itself. The inhabitants of our technological world can properly be described as living within a "technomass," an accumulation of artifacts that has grown even more rapidly in bulk than the "biomass" represented by our expanding populations.

The creation of tools is only one of a variety of cultural systems that we use in order to increase the impact of our effector system on our environment. Other systems that serve to enhance our output include technological processes and methodologies, modification of environmental features, the collection of oral or written bodies of data on past experience, and the like.

Human tool-making relies upon characteristic features of primate anatomy: the mobile hand, the opposable thumb, stereoscopic vision, and an upright sitting posture that frees the hand for manipulating objects. It also is based on features of primate mental life: the tendency to perceive the world in terms of objects, greater reliance on learning, better memory, and a penetrating curiosity about the novel or unusual. In *Homo sapiens,* tool-making is one of the most overt of the traits that characterize the species. Although several other species show tendencies to make use of certain natural objects of the environment in a tool-like manner, and many species of insects and birds innately build complex structures like webs and nests, only the primates seem to be capable of imaginative tool-making of the sort that is universal in all human groups. Even among the primates these abilities appear only rarely, and then primarily among the African apes, the forms that seem closest to the hominid line. Chimpanzees in captivity have, for example, shown their ability to fit a stick of small diameter into the socket of a thicker stick in order to make a longer tool for use in reaching food. If the smaller stick will not fit in, the chimp may even chew on it to make it smaller. Such action is, however, very rare, even among chimpanzees raised among humans.

In one case, a newly liberated orangutan was seen to react to the first snake it saw in the wild by seizing a stick from the forest floor and chasing and hitting the snake as it escaped into a hole.[6] A captive female orang named Jiggs has also been reported to have used the principle of the lever systematically in her attempts to escape her cage.[7] Gorillas, too, share many of the same tendencies. Toto, the gorilla raised to maturity by the Hoyts in their Havana garden, would appropriate any available tools—rakes, shovels, or pruning shears—as weapons of attack when enraged.[8] In one quite separate line of the primates, the New World monkey *Cebus,* some of the same tool-making capabilities seem to exist, perhaps on a level equal to the African apes. A *Cebus* has been reported, for example, to have torn pieces of newspaper and rolled them in order to make a tool to reach a desired object.

Evidence collected in the wild of primate tool-using and tool-making is scanty and generally of very recent collection; it is therefore somewhat inconclusive. Nevertheless, Jane Goodall, after observing wild chimpanzees over a two-year period in Tanzania, reported a large variety of activities that could be called tool-using and a few that might qualify as primitive stages in the tool-making tradition. For example, she noted that chimpanzees, when collecting termites to eat, would pick a blade of grass or dried twig, poke it into the hole of a termite nest, and then pull it out covered with attacking termites. After the termites were eaten, the straw was pushed back into the hole for more. As the straw became bent or worn in this process, the chimpanzee would break off the damaged end. If it were too large for a hole, he might strip it down to a narrower size.[9] Chimpanzees in their natural habitat have also been seen stripping leaves from a twig and using it to clean mud from their bodies; they have also been observed dipping water from a stream with a handful of crumpled leaves. Wild chimpanzees often throw rocks to chase away baboons, using both overarm and underarm techniques. Orangutans have also been reported to use sticks to probe ant and termite nests, and their tool-using abilities may rival those of the better known chimpanzees. All this evidence, sketchy as it is, tends to indicate that our precursors, as they entered the higher primate stage, had probably already begun to show the first signs of that type of tool-oriented behavior that has since led *Homo sapiens* to world dominance. There is, however, little hint among other primates of the scale of technology-building that has characterized mankind.

Key to all tool-making activity of the human type is the conscious ability to anticipate future events and needs. This ability occasionally seems to be shown in the actions of many of the higher primates, although on a very limited scale when compared to what is normal for human beings. Chimpanzees have been observed, for example, carrying a favorite twig for collecting termites for a half mile, from termite hill to termite hill. The flexibility of this kind of primate action contrasts sharply with the seemingly future-directed actions of insect species, such as those ants that carry cut bits of leaves into their nests to cultivate their fungus gardens, or of species of squirrels or birds that store food for winter. These latter patterns of response all appear, however, to be unreasoned, purely instinctive.

Our species has as part of its "inner environment" ways of thinking about time that are distinctively different from the way in which most other species handle that aspect of the environment. This more complex way of dealing with time, which we may share to some slight extent with the other higher primates, is crucial to the entire culture-building process. The long-term planning involved in the agricultural way of life would be impossible without it. So would be the making of tools for anything other than immediate use.

The oldest man-made tools that we know of are made of stone, and the early archeologists named the first stage of tool-making activity the Old Stone Age, or Paleolithic. Some recent archeologists suggest, however, that this phase may have been preceded by an even earlier stage during which human beings made tools of plant materials like wood, leaves, gourds, and fibers, as well as animal materials like bone, antlers, horn, sinews, tendons, hides, and teeth. Organic materials are, of course, more easily destroyed than stone artifacts and the fossil record is not a dependable guide on this point. On the basis of our observation of the other primates, it seems reasonable to me to assume that early hominids fashioned tools from branches of shrubs and trees by stripping off twigs and leaves long before they even tried to make tools of stone. The one is simply so much easier to do than the other.

Consequently, tool-using may be much more ancient in the hominid and prehominid line than our finds of stone tools indicate. One recent study sets the hypothetical data for the beginning of the unskilled use of tools by what-was-to-become-man as far back as thirteen million years ago.[10] Moreover, the conscious manufacture of tool-making tools may also be an older tradition than we previously thought. The great number of concave stone scrapers that appear in early Paleolithic times may have been designed to strip branches down to make wooden spears or digging sticks, used somewhat as the stone scrapers of present-day Australian aborigines.

Tools greatly extended the range of human bodily functions. *Homo faber,* man the maker, has even been suggested as an appropriate name for our species. But the articles fashioned by hominids did not end with the hand-tool and the weapon.

Beyond the weapons of the hunt, one of the most important extrasomatic devices created by early cultures was clothing. Making clothing was already a sophisticated art in the Aurignacian and Magdalenian cultures of Paleolithic Europe, as we see from the ivory bodkins, bone-fasteners, and bone needles they left behind. By creating an envelope of warmth around their bodies at the closest zone of their contact with the environment, humans could maintain their body temperature more easily, and were able to pursue the larger game animals into ice-age environments without having to evolve any new bodily protection such as fur-like body hair. On the occasional warm day, a hunter could shed his wrap, while the animals that were his prey were still encumbered by their protective coats. On the coldest days, human beings did not have to go into hibernation, but could instead add new layers of protection. Clothing allowed much more flexibility than the hairshedding of many mammals or the moulting of birds, and allowed human beings to maintain an even higher level of vitality under changing climatic conditions. In their ability to maintain an even temperature in the face of environmental change, they became "super mammals." They had surpassed all the other species in an ability so characteristic of mammals as a group.

Clothing served more than a heat-preserving function, however, and the basic idea may even have been first developed while all human beings remained in the warmer climes. To begin with, clothing can be useful to protect one from many things: the desert sun, drying winds, insects, or thorns. Among the Arunta of Central Australia, for example, nakedness is the rule, except for a belt of human hair around the waist that is used to carry weapons and thus free the hands for actions while on the move. Throughout the tropics today, as on our beaches, totally nonfunctional clothing is widely valued as decoration and for social role-playing purposes. As a consequence, we should never simply equate the idea of clothing with the need for added warmth.

For the occupation of colder lands, of similar importance to clothing was the development of shelters and the effective use of fire for heating. Caves are too rare a natural feature of our environment; man-made shelters were needed. Partly underground houses built in rectangular pits and roofed with logs and earth—but complete with fireplaces—were being built on the Russian steppes by the Upper Paleolithic period. In them we find a complex inventory of sophisticated stone implements: choppers, scrapers, spear heads, knives, drills, gravers, chisels, and hammers. Of bone and horn there were spear throwers, spear and harpoon tips, needles, awls, buttons, and fishhooks.

It is now generally conceded that the bow and arrow was already in use during the Upper Paleolithic period, specifically in Europe's Magdalenian culture. The Stone Age rock-paintings of southeast Spain, which may be as old as the Upper Paleolithic times, clearly show the use of bows and arrows; one appears to show honey-collecting by means of a rope ladder and the use of a handled bag or basket of some sort.

Moving through the so-called Mesolithic period and into the Neolithic, we find that the rate of tool and other cultural innovations increases rapidly. Two factors probably interacted to increase the seeming speed of innovation: larger populations and better cultural systems for retaining the results of past experience. By the Neolithic period we are clearly dealing with the beginning of a great cultural explosion, the effects of which we are still seeing in our daily lives today. Our question beyond this point is no longer one of establishing the trend or analyzing the nature of human tool-making, but in determining where it will all end.

THE SYMBOL AND HUMAN CULTURE

"It is a very inconvenient habit of kittens . . ." Alice is reported to have observed in *Through the Looking Glass*, "that, whatever you say to them they always purr. If they would only purr for 'yes,' and mew for 'no,' or any rule of that sort . . . one could keep up a conversation! But how *can* you talk with a person if they *always* say the same thing?" Lewis Carroll reports that, in response to Alice's comments, the kitten only purred, and that it was impossible to guess whether it had agreed or not.[11] Alice's problem is important to us here, for the source of her annoyance was her pet's inability to operate like a human being, i.e., its inability to create and use arbitrary symbols. A dog may take the sight of its leash as a symbol of a prospective walk, but this is quite another matter; the leash and the walk have a natural association. It is our tendency to attach arbitrary meanings to actions and sounds that make us so different from all other species.

The making of symbols is surely as significant as the making of tools in defining what it is that makes the human *Innenwelt* so different from that of other species. Language, the most complex development of this ability, is found among all races and cultures of mankind. The ability to speak a language is not primarily a matter of the development of the lips or the tongue, but of possession of the required brain structures. The "naming of things," perhaps the primary stage in language creation, is closely dependent on the human analysis-system in accordance with which we single out certain entities from the environment and then group those entities into categories. The specific categories that are carved out of the environment differ for each language, but there can be no doubt but that the formation of categories is a universal trait of mankind. It is basic also to our processes of generalization, quantification (counting), and logical deduction.

The mediation of a specific symbol system is what provides an ethnic group with much of its culturally conditioned way of perceiving the environment about it, its own perceptor-mediation system. This screen of symbols is as much part of the *Zwischenwelt* as are the tools and other artifacts of the group. The difference is that the symbols tune the receptor system; the tools give leverage to the effector system.

Theoreticians have advanced a variety of theses to explain the origin of human language. Only few generalities seem safe. Human language abilities surely evolved through gradual stages during the hominid period. An early stage may have evolved the use by our progenitors of an innate "call system" similar to that found among other species of animals. As human powers of association and memory developed, what was originally a closed system may gradually have opened to allow the creation of new, coined calls that could blend with the innate system, making more complex forms. Thus a sort of "pre-language" would have been created on top of the earlier call system of automatic groans, sighs, grunts of anger, whines, and the like.

Members of the same family or hunting band would naturally learn to associate a certain variant of a cry with a particular kind of danger, a certain whimper with a particular emotion. A good memory was essential. What began as a variation in sound without prior significance would be remembered with significance. By reproducing the sounds arbitrarily associated with it, a past emotion, a remembered experience, would naturally be conjured up. True language, with symbols strung into long utterances (sentences), could gradually evolve from this stage.

Obviously, language has long affected how people perceive the environment. One research psychologist has asserted that he feels that human language was evolved as a method of constructing reality from perceptual data and that its role in communication and directing action was a side effect.[12] In my terminology, this would be to say that language played a role in perceptor-mediation before it played a role in communication. I would be inclined to guess that the two roles were concurrent.

Very possibly, many of the characteristics of the genus *Homo* were evolved within communities that were already using something we could call pre-language. During this long period, it is likely that natural selection operated to encourage the continued development of those abilities needed for the use of true language. The primates as a group evolved under social conditions. *Homo sapiens* could only have evolved in an intensely social environment, since a human being can only be raised as a member of a group. The human infant immediately requires its mother's breast. If it is to survive, it must rely on the group's protection for at least several years. This long dependence—and the subsequent opportunities presented for training —are a heritage we share with the mammals as a class. We have, however, most significantly extended its duration.

For a child to learn to speak, he or she must go through phases of learning, each of which can take place only at a particular age. The tradition of consciously providing just that kind of learning is a very ancient one. It is older than the species *Homo sapiens* itself and is perhaps older than species like *Homo erectus* or even genera such as *Australopithecus*. From archeological evidence, we have a few hints that very early humans used symbolic ritual in their dealings with the world, a fact that many anthropologists consider increases the chance that true language already formed part of their heritage. Surely symbols and ritual remain very closely associated in existing preliterate cultures.[13]

Universal existence of language among all human groups recorded in history, regardless of time and place, tends to indicate that there may be a natural basis underlying its use. The fact that the spoken languages of the world seem to show about the same degree of complexity is further evidence for a firm phylogenetic basis for human language. All normal children seem to pass through a well-defined "babbling stage" in their development, and it may be that this reflects some natural maturational period required as a prerequisite to the later use of a language. The other primates do not appear to pass through any very similar phase. Some students of language suggest that this babbling stage in human infants may to some degree resemble an earlier stage in the evolution of human speech.[14]

After a lot of early argument on the subject, recent studies by both linguists and psychologists have led to increasingly specific evidence that the more basic features of human linguistic activity are in fact unlearned.[15] We can at least say that "We are capable of language by our very nature," and that our ability to use language is obviously tied to a series of typically human characteristics, including the human perceptual systems, the human pattern of maturation, and cerebral dominance.[16] Work on comparative mythology by the anthropologist Claude Lévi-Strauss also appears to lead to similar conclusions, since in his view all human languages reflect a universal unconscious embodied in the very structure of the human brain.

The frustrations and pressures of the strange, crowded— and at times dehumanized—life in our modern industrial complexes, as well as our ability to wage war of the destructive nature that is possible today, are all results of symbolic activity. These physical and psychological problems could not have come into existence had we not been capable of weaving matrixes of symbols. "All the great dangers threatening humanity with extinction," says the zoologist Lorenz, "are direct consequences of conceptual thought and verbal speech."[17] Without symbols there could be no technologies.

Our symbols not only bring us into closer communication with our group, but because they are learned rather than innate they also serve to separate one cultural group from another. Even what cultures talk about is sharply limited by their environmental needs and historical experiences. "You cannot talk about the ocean with a well frog," declared Chuang Chou, "for he is limited by his environment. You cannot speak of ice with a summer insect, for he is restricted by his time."[18] In a sense, we are even more restricted. We are also limited to talking only of those things which exist in our personal environment; but even among *those* things, we are limited to that fraction of the environment that has been chosen for attention by the specific language we speak.

The use of language and the creation of technical concepts are not the only systems that we use to sharpen the abilities of our receptor system in order to gain more effectively the information we need from our environment. Education is another major system that serves to enhance the value of the effective input of our organs of perception. Practical training in skills, such as that received by an apprentice, involves learning (by example and trial more than by verbal means) to make new distinctions among sensory input. The know-how of skilled craftsmen, their "feel" for how their materials are reacting to their tools, is not by any means something that can easily be expressed in symbolic (verbal) form. But it is very real, an essential part of technological culture.

Our intermediary cultural world—our *Zwischenwelt*—embraces many aspects, not only tool-making and other aspects of technology, not only symbol-making activities, like language, art, religion, and literature, but also interpersonal relations. "Culture," stated the anthropologist Herskovits, "is the man-made part of the environment."[19] A culture represents more than a collection of things and ideas; it is a whole—a living whole.

Cultures tend, however, to be very conservative, highly unsystematic, and slow to discard error. For example, palmistry is still accepted by some within Western culture. "Customs are not enacted," wrote Mark Twain, "they grow gradually up, imperceptible and unconsciously, like an oak from its seed. In the fullness of their strength they can stand up straight in front of a world of argument and reasoning, and yield not an inch."[20] There are, of course, psychosocial reasons for cultures being as tenacious as they are. As the result of a great deal of information gathering over generations, they do not quickly change in the light of any new input of data. Today we often see that technological innovation has outpaced needed psychological and social changes in our way of life.

Having looked at the basic characteristics of human culture, we are ready now to move on to see how the possibilities inherent in human culture have set the trap in which we find ourselves today. The first step in this process was the successful expansion into almost all environments on planet Earth of a variety of what we would today call traditional cultures.

Part Three

The
Technological Trap
Is Set

7
Primitive Technologies and New Environments

Human efforts at culture-making were highly successful—too successful, some may fear. But no matter how we evaluate their outcome, there can be no question but that they transformed our ways of interacting with our environment. "Culture has swamped biology," declared the biologist Marston Bates. "The human animal is there, somewhere, but so deeply encrusted with tradition, with ideas, with learned behavior, that he is hard to find."[1]

As human beings spread over the planet, the new "cultural encrustation" took many forms. Over the years, layer after layer of cultural adaptation was passed on to succeeding generations, leading to more and more specific adjustments to local environments and to better technological exploitation of more difficult environments. As a mechanism for adaption to the environment, the process of cultural transmission quickly grew to rival the genetic processes. Features of the biological *Innenwelt* soon became hard to see among the complexities of the *Zwischenwelt* represented by human culture. A cultural component can be traced in the behavior of many species, particularly primates,[2] but the significance of that component in human behavior is unprecedented.

Particularly important was the fact that culture change, slow as it appeared among primitive groups, was much more responsive to conscious guidance; and it provided a much more flexible way to adjust to environments that were themselves changing. The era in which *Homo sapiens* evolved was one of considerable climate change, a period marked by great ice ages in Europe and significant though also gradual changes of environmental conditions elsewhere. The hominids that took the best advantage of these changing conditions were likely to have been among the more flexible, less specialized examples. The creatures would have found cultural adaptation, no matter how primitive, a great help in exploiting their environments.

The curious patterns of wear on the teeth of many Neaderthals suggests that they may have been using their teeth to hold objects being worked on, perhaps even to process skins into usable leather in a way similar to that of present-day Eskimos.[3] During the later ice ages of Europe, hunting bands may well have already developed fitted clothing to meet the challenge of the environment. The construction of shelters and settlements can also be traced far back into the stone ages.[4]

"Man is a pliable animal," wrote Dostoevsky, "a being who gets accustomed to everything!"[5] Compared with other animals, *Homo sapiens* does remain very plastic in his responses. This striking fact has led some to a serious mistake— to conclude that man is totally plastic. There are two basic reasons for such an error. First, our species is really more "plastic" than most; realization of the extent of human educability is very important if you want to understand the nature of mankind. Second, being human ourselves, we are naturally more aware of the conscious process of decision-making in the life of our own species. We must remember, however, that human plasticity still falls within bounds that are set by genetic considerations, even though its range is very large.

Technological attainments like fire, tools, and clothing were essential to the spread of *Homo* into climes radically different from that in which the genus had evolved. The successes of big game hunting, discussed in chapter 3, may also have encouraged the move into colder lands. First, the hide of a large kill had to be removed in order to get to the edible part; and this literally put furs and hides that could be used for clothing into human hands. Second, migration of the ancient bison, the woolly rhinoceros, and other game may have gradually induced humans into colder lands. No matter how it came about, by the time we arrive at Paleolithic cultures like that of the Magdalenians, we find humans who could live in a quite inhospitable environment by heavy reliance on culturally transmitted technologies.

Some students of human races see in modern racial characteristics the vestiges of varied bodily adjustments to environmental conditions. They may cite the dark skin of the Negroid races as evolved in order to filter the rays of the tropical sun more effectively, and the eye fold of the Mongolian race as a protection evolved against the cold. The facts appear by no means clear, however. Occasionally such explanations turn out to be contradictory.

Several factors combined to blur the dividing lines between human races. First, all of the major racial stocks came into existence in the Old World, where they never lost geographic contact with each other. (Had hominids reached the isolation of America or Australia a million or so years ago, we might today have really distinct subspecies.) Changing climatic factors also tended to force groups to keep on the move over the millennia, even if exceedingly slowly. This served to prevent the kind of isolation that would have been necessary for the evolution of distinct, localized subspecies. As a consequence of these close contacts, no genetic change took place in any branch of *Homo sapiens* that was sufficient to prevent one localized race from inbreeding with other nearby races. Hybrid vigor, a factor long familiar to botanists, may even have tended to favor the success of mixed groups.

But most important of all, people had already adopted a pattern of adjusting to the environment by changes in their technology rather than in their anatomy.[6] This fact spelled the doom of sharply separate human races. They weren't needed! With clothing, a light colored skin will do in the tropics. With a diet naturally rich in vitamin D, the darker-skinned Eskimo could adapt to northern climes just as well as the fair-skinned Norse. Technologies of increasing complexity allowed bands of men to enter a greater variety of environments without having to make any bodily adjustments. Racial distinctions grew increasingly blurred with increased mobility. Thus, it was the overpowering effect of human cultures that prevented any tendency to create strongly divergent, specialized races that were adapted to specific environmental conditions.

In this chapter we will look into some of the adaptations made by so-called "primitive" (i.e., preliterate) cultures in order to see how technology and the symbol-making processes were used to make new environments inhabitable by human beings. As discussed in chapter 3, technology has ancient roots, with clear evidence predating the species. Evidence of symbol-making activity is, however, much harder to find. For that reason, it will be more convenient here not to try to reconstruct the cultural adaptations of preliterate human groups that existed long ago, but to look instead at similar groups that have survived long enough to be observed by modern anthropological science.[7]

A look at these preliterate cultures will shed light on probable patterns of adjustment of ancient cultures that we know only from the archeological record and help us: 1) to appreciate the diversity of adaptation that our species had already evidenced before our ancestors began to remake the environment with the agricultural revolution; and 2) to understand how the inner environment of our species was reflected in the way that humans first approached environments alien to our physical nature. The more complex patterns of technological adjustment that we usually call "civilization" will be covered in later chapters.

The fact that "primitive" societies are dying out in the contemporary world should not lead us to conclude that the social, economic, or ecological patterns they reflected were in any way defective. They flourished quite successfully for much longer than any subsequent "civilized" system has yet endured.[8]

THE DESERT

If you or I were to be stranded in the middle of a true desert in the summer without water, we would find it difficult to survive one day. Consider the problem that you would face. During the first morning hour of sun, perspiration would extract more than a quart of water from your body. By afternoon, you would have lost fifteen pounds by dehydration. Your only chance of surviving into the second day would rest on luck in finding some shade, at least partial, from the sun's rays. The most appropriate clothing would not provide much help. Even with abundant dry food and a gallon of water a day, you could still live in the open desert for only a week or so before being overtaken by extreme fatigue, cramps, fever, delirium, and death.

As part of our heritage from our seagoing ancestors, we

need water to exist. As part of our early hominid heritage, we need it in large quantities: two gallons a day is the common ration for desert conditions. We also need salt to maintain the chemical balance of our internal sea. Without a complex *Zwischenwelt,* which would include both cultural know-how and an array of artifacts, human beings simply cannot survive severe desert conditions. As a consequence, early man had to avoid lands that were too often subjected to drought. Only with cultural developments could these forbidding areas be entered. This was done by the careful engineering of available water.

It does not take what we would call a "highly developed" culture in order to exist in a desert environment. Two of the most primitive of all presently existing cultural groups inhabited desert environments: the aborigines of Central Australia and the Bushmen of the Kalahari Desert in South Africa, both of whom went naked in the sun. Although bodily acclimation and physical conditioning both played some role, the adaptation of these peoples to the desert was primarily the result of cultural skills. In the traditional patterns of groups like the aborigines and Bushmen—still remembered by the older generation—we see the human adjustment to desert life at its lowest level of cultural complexity. Little in the environment was altered by their cultural activities. Australian aborigines, for their part, did set fire to dry grass to drive out game and removed vegetation that would otherwise choke off the few water-holes in their areas. But beyond such minor changes, the aborigines continued to live in and among a natural environment, relying on hunting, fishing, and the collection of wild plant foods. Yet even here, the pattern of human culture remained an impressively complex one when we study it fully.

There are certain common characteristics in all preliterate adaptive patterns in the desert environment. Activity must be avoided during the heat of the day whenever possible, and water and other liquids must be closely conserved, often recycled. In both cultures under discussion children were not weaned until four or five years old.

The meager resources of the desert were put to intensive use by the aborigines. They ate the meat of the kangaroo, made tools and pins out of its bones, used its leg tendons as spear and axe bindings, made necklaces of its claws, and used its fat to lubricate their skins and to prevent excessive drying, often adding red ochre for decoration. Everything at all edible was eaten: snakes, lizards, honey, insect grubs, ants, seeds, and grasses. When game was short, they knew what alternative sources of food they might be able to fall back upon. In times of extreme food shortage, some aborigine groups even ate the dry earth of termite hills. Certain useful mineral salts could be gained this way and the digestive tract kept operative. High bulk, low calorie food to the extreme!

The Australian aborigines learned much about the change of seasons: they knew the typical patterns of wind direction, temperature, and humidity. Every aboriginal boy had to commit to memory the exact location and name of all springs, mud holes, and other places where water might be collected within the tribal territory. In time of drought, the tribe knew which direction to migrate where they would be likely to find seasonal pools from desert rains. The total amount of information that an aborigine needed to assimilate in order to deal with his environment successfully was not significantly less than that needed by many in modern society to attain satisfactory decision/information ratios. Without written records, the memories of tribal elders were the most precious source of vital data, a fact which assured them a major social role in leadership.

All possible sources of water had to be sought out. The aborigines of central Australia hunted out a species of large toad, *Notaden bennetti,* which fills itself with water in the rainy season and then lies dormant in the dry river beds. Aborigines had developed ways to tap the baobab and other trees for their water supply. Central Australian aborigines also knew how to put the scarcity of water to their advantage, and to catch the emu by adding *pituri,* a stupifying drug, to water set out as bait.

Naked and with only the most primitive of shelters, the Australian aborigines relied on fire or on sleeping with their dogs to keep warm when the temperature fell at night. Shelters were very simple. In good weather, the shade of a tree was ample protection at mid-day. If the day was windy, tufts of dry grass were collected to make windbreaks.

The Bushmen of the Kalahari also coped with the desert

through a *Zwischenwelt* that was relatively simple in terms of the weight of its cultural artifacts, its technomass. Their success did, however, involve a wide variety of techniques.[9] The men usually hunted in the cool of the morning or at dusk, with spears or simple bows. Arrows had bone barbs that carried a poison made from a preparation extracted from a local root or from the deadly caterpillar, the *ngwa*. When they stalked the ostrich, Bushmen covered themselves with a dust so that they would match the color of the dry grass. To get close enough for a kill they had learned to disguise themselves as ostriches. To do this, the hunter plaited a saddle of grass, to which he attached ostrich feathers, and fitted this over his shoulders to look like an ostrich body. The hunter carried a long stick to represent the head and neck of the ostrich. To be even less conspicuous, he imitated a variety of typical ostrich actions, such as feeding and preening. Experience taught him to stay downwind from the birds to avoid detection.

The Bushmen women were primarily responsible for looking after the water supplies of the group. They filled ostrich egg shells with water and buried them for later use. It was also the women who searched out the *tsama* melons and the watery *bi* root, major sources of moisture during the ten-month dry period.

At night, Kalahari Bushmen normally took shelter in a circular lean-to made of saplings set in the ground. This provided a windbreak, and also reflected back part of the heat of the campfire. They made some light clothing of animal skins. Bushmen hunters carefully saved the moisture of the large game they killed. After a kill, a bag was quickly made from the animal's stomach and into it they collected all available blood. After return to camp, they opened the larger bones to extract the marrow. In certain areas, a hollow reed with a built-in grass filter could be used to suck water out of holes dug down to the water level of dry river beds. Bushmen carefully saved urine in *tsama* rinds for later use in processes like the curing of fox skins.

Social life in the Kalahari also reflected the demands of the desert. Bushmen hunting parties would temporarily break up into single family groups in order to survive more easily among the sparse resources of the dry season. Bushmen language was rich in terminology centered on the insects, animals, and birds, and on the roots and herbs that were important to their way of life. This is no different situation that that under which the children of our machine-centered age learn a vocabulary filled with terms for automobiles and other appliances. One of the most effective perceptor-mediation processes has always been the creation of a vocabulary centered on the distinctions most needed in order to thrive successfully in the chosen environment.

During the hottest and driest months, dehydration is a real threat in the Kalahari, and Bushmen went out only in the coolest hours of the day. For the remainder of the day, they lay still in shallow pits that they dug for themselves in the shade. These pits were lined with the left-over scrapings of *bi* roots, the pulp that remained after the moisture had been extracted as well as possible. The Bushmen would also urinate on these scrapings. This added moisture to the pit and consequently helped to prevent dehydration of its occupant during the heat of the day.[10] In this way, the Bushman created within his pit a type of microenvironment that was closer to that in which man had developed, and cooler and more moist than that of the Kalahari. He altered the innermost zone of his personal environment only —to use the concept of concentric zones advanced in chapter 3. But his ability to do so meant the difference between survival and death.

At a more advanced cultural level, several ethnic groups have established themselves in desert regions by relying on a nomadic way of life dependent on herds of domesticated animals, species better adapted to the desert than human beings. The Bedouins, for example, practice no agriculture, but they do raise goats, camels, sheep, and horses. In the most arid regions, the Bedouins depend on camel milk as their basic liquid fare. Grazing can have a heavy environmental impact, and so the life of the nomadic herdsmen leaves a heavier mark upon the land than that of hunters like the Bushmen or Australian aborigines.

Bedouin clothing is effectively designed to ward off the desert heat. The veil, worn in certain desert tribes by males as well as females, has a real functional value in a dry land given to dust or sand storms. As an article of clothing, it is common in desert lands or lands influenced by the culture of the desert; the veil is very rare elsewhere. The turban performs much the same function, insulating the head from the sun's rays. The *litham* of the Tuaregs of the Sahara serves the purpose of both turban and veil. It is formed by winding the head and face with a ten-foot-long strip of cloth so that only a slit for the eyes remains open. Within his robes and under his *litham,* the Tuareg can maintain inner-zone environmental conditions that allow him to pass through some of the most inhospitable areas of planet Earth.

Peoples as advanced as the Bedouins or Tuaregs could go beyond modifying only the innermost environmental zone surrounding their bodies, and found many ways to create envelopes of modified temperature that were large enough to encompass the second zone mentioned in chapter 3, a space on the scale in which human conversations normally take place. The typical Bedouin tent is covered with fabrics made of black goat's hair and is always pitched so that it opens downwind. It effectively operates to dissipate the heat of the desert within a space large enough for normal social interaction—a great convenience for its inhabitants compared to the immobilized Bushmen in their pits.

THE FOREST

We remain strangely ambivalent toward the environment most recently abandoned by our precursors: the forest. Our poetry is full of the beauties of the woodlands; much of our mythology reflects an almost religious awe for the tree; landscape painting constantly depicts wooded scenes.

Nevertheless, when people come in close contact with the forest, first impulse is often to destroy it—to "clear" the land. This is usually explained as necessary in order to serve human ends. This tendency to clear away the trees can be observed not only in temperate lands, where vast forests have been felled to make way for agriculture, but also in the way that primitive tribesmen deal with life in the tropical rain forest. When agricultural groups plant trees for economic value, they typically plant them in rows, between which they can move freely and see at a distance. All this shows the degree to which we have turned away from the possibility of living in and among the trees.

The Lele people of southwest Zaire show this ambivalence toward the forest on which they depend. On one side, they view it with a near poetic fervor as the source of all good things: all their food (except for the peanuts raised by the women in open areas), drink, clothing, building supplies, and sacred medicines. It is inherently cleaner and better than the dusty clearing in which the village stands. The Lele will not even eat the flesh of a pig raised in the village, but trade it instead to other peoples, simply because it was not raised in the forest. But for the Lele, the forest is at the same time a place of danger. Lele women may enter it only under the proper circumstances or risk ill for the entire tribe. Nor can a male Lele enter if he has had a recent nightmare or is in mourning. The quasi-religious awe the Lele have for the forest is expressed even by the verb they use for "entering" the forest—*nyingena*—a term one would use for "plunging into" water or "going inside" a hut and which suggests entry into a new and quite separate environment.[11]

Although the latter phases of human evolution are the obvious result of a move out of the forest and onto the open ground, the dispersal of the species saw many cultures reenter the heavily forested areas of the world. The reentry was on new terms. Unlike their tree-dwelling ancestors, the new hominids now moved primarily on the forest floor, making their place of domicile in the more open places between the trees. *Homo sapiens* was no longer physically adapted to forest living at all, and only by means of cultural innovations, through development of an appropriate *Zwischenwelt,* could the old forest be exploited once again.

Although rain forests are the home of some of the most primitive hunting cultures remaining on the planet—tribes like the Pygmies of Africa or the Xingu of the Amazon basin—those cultures have nevertheless evolved a most complex repertoire of hunting techniques. The reason is that animals in the jungle are almost impossible to bring down in a chase. No human being, no matter how agile, would have much chance of catching a monkey, bird, or flying squirrel with his bare hands. Human beings are built now to move best in the open. The Tarzan myth aside, we are too big and too clumsy to move rapidly through the trees of a rain forest. Only by working out a complex new technology could human beings carry the hunt back into the forest. Techniques for doing so included not only bows and arrows but also blow guns and poison-tipped darts, nets, snares, and traps in many forms. These artifacts allowed human beings to do things beyond the abilities of their unaided effector systems.

There is much we can use in the forest. It is rich in comparison to the desert. Since *Homo sapiens* is basically omnivorous, the fruits and nuts of the forest are still available as food. In lush areas, trees provide a wide variety of readily available raw materials. As a consequence, forest-dwelling cultures have developed which make wide use of not only the fruit of trees, but also their leaves, woods, saps, and resins.

On the rivers of the rain forests, dug-out or bark canoes, nets, traps, and a wide variety of other fishing gear and associated techniques have been developed by preliterate groups, even among very primitive tribes like the Xingu of Brazil or the Wai-Wai of Guyana. For protection from the heavy rainfall, and perhaps also due to the sheer abundance of available building materials, even the most primitive jungle dwellers often have complex architectural cultures. Very large communal or ceremonial dwellings are common. The Camayura, one of the tribes of the Xingu, build communal huts of grass thatching with walls two feet thick. Inside, the women keep a fire constantly burning to assure dryness during the long rainy season. Thus within the communal hut the Camayura can maintain, at a Zone two level, environmental conditions that are far more in keeping with the environment in which their ancestors developed than is the rain forest without.

Human beings long ago found out that they could control the forest somewhat by the use of fire; and in many forested areas various techniques have been perfected that required the clearing or partial clearing of wooded lands by burning. Among the forest-dwelling Bemba of central Africa, the most important ceremony of the year was the "tree-cutting season." Clearly, the environmental impact of preliterate human communities on forest regions has been considerable.

Truly primitive, forest-dwelling cultures are rare. Perhaps they have always been. One good, current example is that of the

Pygmies of the Ituri Forest in northeastern Zaire. As distinct from the Bantu tribes of the area, these groups live in the forest itself, rather than in man-made clearings. It may even be that the Pygmies, by inventing stories about the spirits of the forest to tell their more recently arrived Bantu neighbors, actually conspire to keep the Bantus worried about venturing too deeply into the forest depths. Within the forest, the Pygmies live in hastily built hemispherical huts of mud and leaves. These are built by the women, although the males cut the saplings needed for the frames of the huts. Even these are set up, however, in naturally open spaces within the forest, since like the rest of us, the Pygmy is descended from ancestors better adapted to live in the open than among the trees.[12] Such open spaces represent the unconscious and unspoken need to seek a more natural setting for human activity at the Zone three dimension, to use the terms introduced in chapter 3.

The Pygmies of the Ituri were positive about the forest as an environment. Calling themselves "the children of the forest," they did not fear it. "We are only afraid of that which is outside the forest," was the comment of one Pygmy to the anthropologist Colin Turnbull, who spent many years among them.[13]

The Tasaday, a recently discovered band of hunter-gatherers in the Philippines, represent a Stone Age culture that was able to exist deep within a tropical rain forest. The Tasaday did not even have a word in the language for "clearing"; when they first visited one, they coined an expression "where the eye looks too far."[14] Tasaday survival in so dense a forest may, however, have been partially the result of the fact that their ancestors, fleeing a plague, had been able to locate a series of open-air caves in the hillside above much of the forest. The cave that the band invariably slept in was the highest, the one most open to the sun.[15]

It was not only in tropical jungles that human communities made cultural adjustments to life among the trees; the same was done in temperate areas. Forest peoples of the cooler regions would include the Algonguin of North America, the Ainu of northern Japan, and the early Finnish tribes of northeastern Europe. The ingenious adaptations of the woodland Indians to their forests, from their trapping skills to their many uses of birchbark, are familiar to Americans. The Daniel Boones and Davy Crocketts of the American frontier copied Indian patterns of adjustment to the forest environment. Russian culture is also heavily marked by long association with the forest, a place of refuge during much of the last thousand years or so from the nomads of the open steppes. Witness the bear as a symbol of the Russian state or the Russian predeliction for forest foods like honey, berries, and mushrooms. Over the years, however, both in North America and Eurasia, much of the temperate forest was felled to make way for the more open environment of agriculture.

The chosen environment of a culture can affect the way its members interpret the sense data they receive. Most human beings will commonly estimate a horizontal line to be longer than a vertical line of the same length. Peoples that dwell in environments that are heavily forested, and therefore visually restricted, have been scientifically established to be less susceptible to this illusion. Interestingly, urban dwellers fall between the two groups in susceptibility. This is much as one might expect from the structure of their physical environment.[16]

OCEAN ENVIRONMENTS

"The sea is naturally an inhospitable and hostile element to man," declares the geographer Perpillou. "On the coasts there are dangerous tides and storms, and the coastline itself is the continental frontier beyond which there is only the vast, barren, inaccessible, and fatal ocean."[17] These difficulties have not, however, prevented certain cultural groups from moving far out onto the seas to make a living.

Many lines of mammals have returned to life in the sea. Sea otters illustrate one degree of this readjustment—quadrupeds that still retain their ability to move freely on land. The seal and walrus have gone further, only retaining enough in the way of flippers to be able to move about on the beaches and rocks of the shore. The dolphins and whales represent the full return of mammals to the ancient environment of the sea.

Compared with these forms, no group of *Homo sapiens* has attempted any significant physical readjustment to the sea. A great deal of anatomical change would be required to succeed in such a readjustment. As human bodies are now built, only the surface of the sea is readily open to us. A person cannot normally dive any deeper than fifty or sixty feet without special breathing apparatus; the absolute record is about two-hundred feet. Even an Aqua-lung does not allow us to penetrate more than two- or three-hundred feet into the sea. In order for us to live long in the water, we would need more than a new method of breathing, our internal chemistry would have to adjust to the saltier oceans of today, and our skin would have to change in order to tolerate the constant moisture.

The human body can, however, easily stand short periods in surface waters, and the ocean is a storehouse of a vast number of edible products that are obtainable without too much difficulty from the shore. Many cultures have profitably exploited the fringes of the sea. Very early human deposits show both decorative and practical use of seashells. Peoples of many cultures have learned how to swim, although the exact strokes differ. It was, however, only with the development of new "tools" like boats and rafts that the surface away from the shore was opened to systematic human exploitation. Sailing across the surface of the seas is much more akin to life on the ancient plains than entering into the water itself. It is not surprising, then, that human exploitation of the resources of the sea has generally been conducted from surface craft.

Of the preliterate peoples who made extensive use of the sea as environment, few could compare to the Polynesians. Polynesian seagoing technology took many forms, and included single canoes, double canoes, and outriggers. Life in their chosen environment required a sophisticated handling of space relationships. To cover the great distances between islands, the Polynesians had to develop, for example, navigational techniques using the stars. Perceptor-mediation processes were very important. All aspects of the sea had to be sharply observed: patches of hanging cloud that might indicate a landfall, the seasonal movement of migratory birds, the shape of waves, the changing color of the sea. Their language reflected such distinctions. The same kind of terminology and lore also played a major role in the success of the Marshallese and other Micronesian peoples in navigating the vast expanses of the Pacific.

The Polynesians maintained a complex inventory of tools

and other devices: coconut graters, shell axes, pump drills, fish traps, angling gear, paddles, fish nets, bait containers, and the like.[18] They also developed a wide variety of techniques or procedures for dealing with the dangers of their watery world. For example, they sometimes carried a frigate bird to sea, so that it could, if necessary, be released to show the way to land.

Since little in the way of hunting was possible on most of the islands they inhabited, the Polynesians traditionally depended on simple agriculture and fishing for their food. Following the ancient patterns, it was the males who were primarily engaged in the more dangerous and far-ranging side of life—the exploitation of the seas—while the women stayed closer to the home base. Cultivated plants included the coconut, pandanus, breadfruit, banana, and a variety of root crops like the yam, sweet potato, and taro. Wild fruits of a wide variety were also collected. The coconut palm, a plant that will tolerate a saltier environment than most, was most valuable to the Polynesians, not only for food but also as a building material.

In their sea environment, the Polynesians were very successful. When they entered history they were one of the most far-flung ethnic groups on earth. For our purposes here, it is revealing to note that, although the Polynesians lived so successfully on the seas and on islands heavily covered with tropical growth, their most sacred places were artificially maintained clearings, somewhat of the nature of village greens. Here, social and religious life both had their center; open-air meetings were held and the *kava* ceremony observed. Sacred structures dedicated to the gods were often adjacent to this open area. The maintenance of such level spaces, open to the sky, were universal throughout Polynesia, in some areas formally demarked by stone walls while in others they were not.[19] Like the forest-dwelling Pygmy with his tiny clearing, the Polynesian can thus be seen to have constructed, at the Zone three level, a model of the ancient world of the open plain in the midst of a strange environment of sea and tropical forest.

THE COLD CLIMES

Perhaps it was the coming of the ice ages that first forced human beings to try to adjust to weather conditions that were sharply colder than those under which man had first evolved.

Like the sea otter, which has abandoned the shore for full-time life in the seas under the pressure of human predators, early man may have been compelled by sheer necessity to adjust to new and colder environments. Perhaps, however, the cause was a related change in the availability of game. Whatever the reason, the effect was that an ability to live in colder lands became crucial to certain human groups. A naked creature who rapidly dissipates his body heat, unaided man could never survive under arctic or semiarctic conditions. *Homo sapiens* could not easily evolve a new skin of fur to meet the latest change in surroundings. As can be established from Paleolithic sites in Europe, early technology—a *Zwischenwelt* that featured as part of its output-facilitation system the use of both fire and clothing —provided an answer.

One of the best-known contemporary groups to have made an adjustment to an extremely cold and seemingly inhospitable environment is the Eskimo. Living in the Arctic wastes, these people depend almost totally on fishing and hunting the mammals of the ocean shores, animals like the seal and the polar bear. Eskimos collect as food only very small amounts of a limited variety of Arctic plant life, such as berries and mosses. This pattern, incidently, makes the Eskimo one of the most exclusively carnivorous groups of human beings on the planet.

Eskimo clothing is complex and very well made. Originally, the Eskimo wore clothes only when outside. As soon as he entered the warmth of his well-designed shelter, the Eskimo stripped to the skin. Within his shelter, the Eskimo thus maintained a comfortable micro-environment at the Zone two level, one that allowed him temporarily the same freedom from clothing as was possible for his distant ancestor on the savanna.

Seal blubber was the principal fuel and it also provided the needed illumination under the often darkened conditions of the Arctic. When it was too bright from the snow glare, a level of brightness above the usual capacity of the human eye, the Eskimo used snow goggles with narrow slits cut in them through which the horizon could be safely scanned. It is interesting to note that, despite the inhospitable climate and the reliance on a carnivorous way of life, Eskimo culture was not characteristically aggressive. Eskimo groups did not engage in anything similar to warfare and reacted with friendliness toward strangers rather than with anxiety and suspicion. The good intentions of others were presumed and a chance to cooperate welcomed in expectation of a pleasurable exchange of services.

Great emphasis was placed on cooperation within the Eskimo group. The custom of wife sharing may have had its roots in the prevention of tensions and envy within the group. Nevertheless, antagonism and competition between individuals did exist, even in the traditional society. Resorting to violence within the group was considered dangerous to all and would result, therefore, in group condemnation. If the transgression were serious enough, the guilty person was expelled from the group. As a result of these inhibitions, interpersonal conflict was acted out by song duels, in which each contestant was forced to suffer the other's insults in the presence of all. Incidently, the most degrading of all insults, worse even than allegation of incest or intercourse with dogs, was the charge that one had stolen food from one's own children.[20]

Rather than avoiding the cold weather features of their environment, the Eskimos used their technological ingenuity to turn them to their advantage. Snow was exploited as a building material, food supplies were quick-frozen for storage, panes of specially frozen fresh-water ice became windows and skylights of dwellings. Freezing temperatures were even put to advantage during the hunt. An example was a common way of killing bears. A flexible piece of whale bone was sharpened at both ends, bent over double, and frozen into a piece of blubber. This was put out in an area frequented by bears. After the frozen piece of blubber was bolted down by a bear, it began to thaw out. The whalebone straightened and penetrated the bear's stomach lining. Eskimos then tracked the dying animal by the bloodstains it left.

Many ingenious methods and a complex collection of specific-use artifacts show that the Eskimos were considerably more "gadget-conscious" than most other primitive people. To live so specialized a life in so difficult an outer environment required a complex material *Zwischenwelt*. Upon the arrival of European explorers in their area, Eskimos showed great interest in all the things of Western culture—much as if they had been culturally "pre-adapted" to a more modern technology. During the 1870s Eskimos were frequently hired by whaling ships as donkey-engine men. Most preagricultural tribesmen would have been worse than useless in such a capacity.

One of the technologically most primitive of all examples of human adjustment to the cold climates was that of the Indian tribes south of the Strait of Magellan. The Yahgan people, southernmost of these, lived in the very rigorous climate of the coasts and islands of western Tierra del Fuego. Often the Yahgans wore as their only clothing a seal skin draped over the windward shoulder. They did, however, protect their naked skin and add somewhat to their ability to retain warmth by greasing, oiling, and painting their bodies. Their nakedness was partly compensated for by the constant use of fire. Although the Yahgans made a number of types of birchbark canoes and a variety of tools for hunting, including harpoons, the complexity of their material culture could not compare with that of the Eskimos. For food, the Yahgans collected mussels and other shellfish, sea otters, seals, penguins, and other birds, and a few plant materials. Because of their dependence on the products of the seas, the Yahgans spent more than half of their time huddled low in their canoes, a habit that some claimed tended to stunt the development of their legs. When on land, the Yahgans lived in small temporary shelters made of sticks and covered with bark, grass, and occasionally seal skins. This type of shelter was open enough to allow plenty of air for a campfire. The fact that the Yahgans used fires so continually for added warmth was the reason that their land was called "Tierra del Fuego" by the early explorers—the Land of Fire. Even Yahgan canoes were heated by fireplaces.

OTHER ENVIRONMENTS

Man is a prolific creature, and population pressure over the millennia has forced human groups to move into a wide variety of marginal areas around the world. In addition to the broad categories of desert, sea, forest, and cold climes, there are many other environments to which men have culturally adapted their ways of life: swamplands, river deltas, rugged mountainous terrain, and extremely high altitudes. Life in each of these environments required its own particular cultural innovations and adjustments, a particular type of *Zwischenwelt*. Each required a series of technologies that, while much simpler than those of the modern world, have all their basic features in common with later forms of technology.

Life at extremely high altitudes is particularly difficult for man and requires considerable cultural ingenuity. The two areas where this accommodation has been made on a large scale are Tibet and the Andean zone of South America. Regardless of the problem of temperature, life at very high altitudes puts a physical strain on the human body. Mankind probably evolved somewhere near the bottom layer of the ten-mile-deep ocean of air that blankets our planet. We still do our best at the lower attitudes. The thinner air at 5,000 feet provides only 83 percent of the pressure that exists at sea level, and it cannot do as effective a job of forcing oxygen into our lung membranes so that it can enter the blood stream. At 10,000 feet, the percentage drops to 67 percent; at 15,000 to 54 percent. The Quechua and Aymara Indians of the Andes live at these higher levels. If a person grows up under such conditions, his body will make some adjustment to the strain, but an adult immigrant will find it very difficult to live under conditions of air pressure that are so different from those under which our species evolved.[21]

In summary, we can say that, even with all the variety of possible cultural adjustments, human beings have shown continued preference for environments which at least approximate that in which the species evolved. Human population remains the most dense in those areas. Even today, with all our technology, only a comparatively small portion of humankind lives in climatic zones that differ sharply from that in which the species evolved. Like ants in a "temperature organ," about 95 percent of Earth's population is crowded into that 65 percent of the planet's land surface which has a mean annual temperature between 40°F and 80°F. The other 5 percent are scattered in marginal areas with a mean annual temperature between 32°F and 40°F or between 80°F and 86°F.

About 18 percent of Earth's land surface is totally uninhabited because of cold. This includes Antarctica, interior Greenland, and a variety of Arctic and Antarctic islands. Excess heat renders a much smaller area uninhabitable, some of the desert areas of the Sahara or Saudi Arabia for example. Most of these areas could be inhabited, however, if there were sufficient water. Even with specialized clothing it is hard for a person to be outside for more than an hour or so at temperatures below $-5°F$ or above $120°F$. To exist under such climatic conditions we must use technological means to create artificial micro-environments, and hide therein until the outside temperature becomes more moderate.

PRIMITIVE TECHNOLOGIES AND THE FUNCTIONAL CIRCLE

In the above discussion of some of the preliterate cultures which have survived into the modern world, we see that the technological approach to human adaptation to the environment is not something unique to the industrial or even to the postagricultural era. None of the cultures described could have existed where they did without complex technologies based on long experience. I believe it would be safe to conclude that our abilities to construct technologies, and perhaps strong propensities to do so, flow from neural patterns that are older than the genus *Homo*. Our sensory systems (our receptors) are well designed to be tuned to receive very specific, needed inputs. This is done by the imposition of a screen of culturally transmitted concepts and terminologies as well as by training in culturally transmittable skills that require careful, but nonverbal, discernment. On the other side of the functional circle, our organs of action (our effectors) are well designed to create and use tools in order to exploit the environment more effectively in the pursuit of human objectives.

Our technologies are based on intrinsic human abilities that are the sum of past evolution, even though a specific tool may be the result of a need to respond to an extrinsic factor, such as a change in local environmental conditions. We have seen that the role of early technology was not to provide humans with new powers to help them adapt to new environments or to change existing environments, but often served only to create small envelopes of the old environment with which humans could protect themselves from alien environmental conditions to which they could not in fact adapt. Clothing, shelters, and clearings are all examples of systems to that modest end, although each represents a wider zone of contact with the environment.

From our discussion of human tolerances for temperature, air pressure, and the like, we see that, even with our sciences and our technologies, we still remain limited in our physical ability to adjust to conditions about us. Compared to other life-forms, it is true, *Homo sapiens* has shown an ability to live within a wide variety of environments, but there still are clear limits to our physiological adaptability. We must not forget that fact.

The more primitive, preliterate cultures did not generally change very rapidly when compared to more modern cultures. Since intelligence was as high as today, why was not the rate of innovation? Shepard, in his book *The Tender Carnivore and the Sacred Game,* has proposed that the rate of tool-change may be fixed by our biology—a constant that could be expressed in terms of so many man-years per change. This would make the rate of innovation a function of population size. At ten million man-years per tool-change, he stated, the rate would be one change each twenty years in a population of 500,000 hunter-gatherers but 350 changes a year with the current world population.[22] I believe that there is some validity in this thesis, and that we would be slandering the technological abilities of pre-literate humans to assume that they were somehow less prone to come up with imaginative ideas about how to do things than we are. But I do not believe a numbers game based on population would tell the whole story, for some other very real problems stood in the way of innovation within primitive cultures. I would say that the rate of innovation was comparatively slower then because of at least four factors: 1) the relatively smaller populations, noted by Shepard, which meant fewer potential innovators; 2) the lack of systematic record-keeping of past experience, which meant that much innovation and information was simply forgotten; 3) the isolation of humanity into very small groups, which slowed communication; and 4) a warranted expectation, partly as the result of the above factors, that the future would be like the past.

Even under these circumstances, however, there was a

cumulative effect to the process of innovation. Many new methods of doing things were discovered, were remembered, and were passed on from community to community, until they became the common heritage of large populations and the basis upon which new innovations were made. Gradually the escalating pace of innovation led to a situation with some of the ominous features of a positive feedback system. But before addressing the problems of the immediate past and present, we must look at the nature of the more complex technologies that began in the Neolithic and have led to the the present situation.

8
Ecology by Artifice

Anthropologists estimate the total possessions of an Arunta tribesman in Central Australia to weigh twenty-one pounds for an adult male and about twelve for a female. All else that surrounds the Arunta is virtually unaltered nature. Techno-industrial man is today, by comparison, swallowed up by a world of crafted objects, painted walls, and concrete slabs, the technomass of his culture.

Look, if you will, about yourself right now. What proportion of your present surroundings could really be considered part of any "natural environment?" How many objects can you see that are untouched by human crafts and technologies? Seriously make the test. If you find yourself inside a room, chances are high that you will be able to see very little of the "furniture" of the ancient environment—perhaps a house plant or a green bit of tree outside your window, perhaps a rock used as a paperweight, perhaps a housefly. All else is liable to be man-made chairs, walls, rugs, doors, lamps, bookcases, and the like. Notice the number of squares and rectangles you have within your present field of vision, beginning with this page. How many straight lines or right angles did *Australopithecus,* or much more recent Cro-Magnon man, see in an average day? Even the house plant or paperweight rock that you may see is liable to have been formed in part by human hands, to be more a part of our *Zwischenwelt* than of the original environment.

Perhaps the only unchanged part of the ancient environment that you can see from where you are is at the window: a patch of blue sky marked by a fragment of cloud. But even here human hands may have reached, for all too many of our skies have been grayed by industrial pollution.

What have we done with our world?

We have remade it. Nothing less.

"Man exists in a world of his own creation," wrote the American philosopher A. B. Johnson in 1836. "He cannot step, but on ground transformed by culture; nor look, but on objects produced by art. The animals which constitute his food are unknown to nature, while trees, herbs, and fruits, are the trophies of his labor."[1] Ironically, most people today would probably consider life in 1836 close to nature, so far have we "progressed" since then.

When and how did we begin this process of almost totally remaking our environment? Culture itself does not require it. The Eskimos, for example, did not restructure the world around them; they adjusted themselves within it. They created only thin envelopes around their bodies by the clothing that encompassed them when they were out of doors, or they fashioned slightly larger envelopes by means of the shelters that protected them at night. Out beyond these inner circles, the outer features of their arctic world remained much as if humanity had never existed.

Although the cultural adjustments to varied climatic zones made by pre-agricultural groups, which we discussed in the last chapter, did not have the effect of completely remaking the environment, they did have some impact on the *Umwelt*. For example, over-hunting by humans probably led to the extinction of several species, and early use of fire apparently resulted in the permanent environmental modification of certain grasslands and forests. But despite the activities of primitive bands, the plains remained the plains, the brown desert soil was just as dry, and wild woodlands represented a typical temperate ground cover. By their cultures, including their various tools, early humans fitted themselves into their environment without doing any great violence to it.

As our ancestors accumulated more and more cultural information, however, it became increasingly easy for them to re-engineer certain features of their environment in order to meet human needs more efficiently. Using simple tools, they could clear weeds and thickets away from water holes and reeds away from fishing places; they could build bridges over streams and ravines, make clearings for habitation, cut paths through forest and bush, and protect places where valuable trees or root crops grew by removing competing plants. They may have first cultivated root plants like the taro and yam. The notion of putting a root or cutting back into the ground to let it grow is much simpler to conceive than sowing seeds.

The groundwork was gradually prepared for primitive agriculture. Dogs were domesticated while man was still only a hunter, and this relationship may have set the pattern for the early domestication of other animals like goats and sheep. In the Near East there is evidence of grazing herds of such animals as early as 8500 B.C.[2] These animals, unlike dogs, have feeding patterns that do not compete with ours. The grasses that they eat we cannot properly digest. Such species could serve human beings as very useful intermediaries; they could recycle inedible grasses into the edible materials of milk and meat. In addition, they supplied hide and hair that could be put to use in other technologies. People incorporated these species of animals, as the plant species they cultivated, into their expanding *Zwischenwelt,* treating the animals much as if they were tools or processing machines.

Quite a few primitive tribesmen still follow patterns of life similar to those which characterized the dawn of agriculture. As a matter of fact, even the most primitive cultures existent today usually practice some form of simple agriculture along with their fishing, hunting, and gathering. The Murung, who inhabit the Chittagong Hill Tracts in the hilly jungle region that forms a border between Bangladesh and Burma, are an example. They engage in a primitive type of agriculture called *jhooming,* in which they clear a piece of land by fire, dig shallow holes with dagger-like tools, and drop mixed seeds—rice, melon, tobacco, cotton, corn, and so on—in each hole. Whatever sprouts at a hole is protected by clearing away the weeds. Except for the destruction of a certain amount of groundcover, Murung agriculture has a lot in common with the food-gathering stage in its limited ecological effects.

A major incentive in the human drive to remake and reorganize the environment has always been to increase the amount of energy in human hands. In the most general sense, our landscapes have been remade primarily in order to increase the proportion of the sun's energy that can be mobilized for human purposes.

The primary sources of energy on the surface of the earth comes, of course, from the rays of the sun. Since we are not plants and cannot directly turn this solar energy into the chemical energy that we need as food, we are forced to use indirect methods. The simplest solutions are either to eat green plants that have been produced by the direct utilization of solar energy, or to eat animals that live on those plants. But there are other ways to get energy. Wood and other indigestible plant materials can, for example, be burned, in a sense liberating the warmth of the sun that had been stored in the plant fiber in the form of chemical energy.

Sources of energy that cannot be traced to the action of the sun are few, and they have been insignificant so far in human history. These include power from the tides, the exploitation of volcanic heat, and most recently nuclear power. Virtually all else can be directly or indirectly traced to solar energy, and this would include animal power, hydroelectric power, wind power, and the chemical power of foods and fuels—even the fossil fuels like coal and petroleum.

The sun's rays falling on a square centimeter of the earth's surface at a right angle produce some 1.94 gram calories of heat a minute. When we compute this for the entire surface of the earth, allowing for the angle of the rays and the average length of daylight, we get what can be called the basic solar "energy pool" available to life on earth. This energy pool is vast beyond our comprehension. In these days of concern about an "energy crisis," it is worth noting that, according to estimates, the earth receives in three days of sunlight as much energy as we could get by burning all our potential reserves of oil, coal, tars, and natural gas, along with the wood of all our forests.[3] A great deal of solar energy is, of course, reflected back into space by cloud cover or by barren wastes of rock or ice, but a sizable proportion falls on the seas, and they teem with life. Much of the rest falls on productive land, and it too supports countless forms of life. The development of agriculture was the most significant technological step that our species made to increase its share of the global energy pool.[4]

THE AGRICULTURAL PATTERN

The artificial cultivation of selected plants was a way of assuring that the sun's energy would be used in creating foods of value to humanity rather than benefiting inedible plants or falling on dry wastes. To the soil, the agriculturalist brought the proper seeds and the crucial water. He stood by to remove choking weeds. The sun did the rest.

Our female ancestors may well be responsible for this greatest of all cultural revolutions in mankind's long development, since horticulture and agriculture most likely began as the result of their observations and actions. Under the pattern of somewhat more distinct sexual roles that had resulted from the move toward big game hunting, the males were almost assuredly the ones that did most of the hunting in very early human cultures, while it was the women who gathered plant materials, with the help of the pre-adolescent children. At this point we can only guess, but I would imagine that women were observing the growth of plants and artificially cultivating them for thousands of years before the potential value of the system was fully realized.

Agriculture opened the possibility for much denser human populations. Even the most systematic hunting and collecting economy could never support more than a small fraction of the present world population.[5] This is a factor we can never forget as we look at our options for the future. We have long been locked into the trap of dependence on complex technologies such as that of agriculture.

After developing agriculture, our species was never to be the same again. The change of life-style was quite unlike that created by the descent from the trees or any of the other major ecological revolutions that what-was-to-become-man had experienced. It took place within the *Zwischenwelt* and did not involve any genetic change in the nature of the species. A strange new world was created, but its inhabitant was the same old species, *Homo sapiens*, late of hunter-gatherer fame.[6]

Much of the "return to nature" literature—from Rousseau to the "back on the farm" movements of the present century—has talked about "nature" as if it implied a pastoral or agricultural environment. An urbanized grandmother may look back with nostalgia to her childhood on the farm as a period of close communion with nature. A statesman or industrialist, sensitive to the pressures of the contemporary world, may retire to become a gentleman farmer.

We must remember, however, that although the agricultural world has a lot more in common with the original environment of our species than the present day techno-industrial world, agriculture is by no means "natural" for us. Quite the contrary. It was the technologies of agriculture that led to the creation of the first artificial, man-made environment. No longer was the ecological zone that was modified only a small envelope of personal or social activity. It stretched as far as the eye could see.

The new world of farms and farming was strictly a human artifact. Not only its tools but also its patterns of activity had never existed before, and would never have existed except for the hard work of human beings. The need for order and symmetry that forms a characteristic part of the inner world of our species was impressed upon an indifferent nature. Human goals were used to judge the outer world, and that world was redesigned to operate more efficiently to serve those ends. Some species of plants and animals were modified by selection and spread widely. Others were ruthlessly weeded out. A major feature of agricultural life is the fact that a relatively small number of plants and animals have ever been selected for domestication on any scale. Even today, most of the world's population is dependent on only a handful of species: four crops (wheat, rice, maize, and potato) and four types of meat (pork, beef, poultry, and lamb).[7]

By agriculture, a new kind of interrelationship was forged between the people and their environment. The old ecology was swept away. Instead of being used merely to react to the environment, the human effector system had been put to use to reorganize that environment along unprecedented lines. At the Zone four level, as far as the eye could see, stretched the man-made world. A new and more complex functional circle had been created for *Homo sapiens* by *Homo sapiens.* There was now a human element on both sides of the ecological equation. As the advantages of the new agricultural technologies became evident, hunting bands were encouraged to roam less widely and eventually to settle down in order to protect their increasingly valuable crop lands. Although hunting probably continued to be a major activity for many generations, it was conducted from a more firmly established base. This led to yet another very basic psychological change in the relation of man to environment. Man became landlord. He became more like the "territorial species" and less free-ranging in his movements within space. Soon the agriculturalists were almost as firmly rooted to the soil as the crops they grew. The political consequences of the new agricultural technology were as vast as they were unanticipated. Effective land management, especially that related to irrigation, demands the cooperation of large groups of human beings over a long period of time and under the discipline of central direction. Karl Wittfogel, in his discussions of the nature of "hydraulic society" has dramatized this point.[8] We do not have to agree with his specific political conclusions to accept his theses on the important relationship of agriculture to political forms.

Sexual patterns were most likely also affected by the new way of life. With the abandonment of the hunt, some of the *raison d'etre* for much of the sexual dimorphism that had arisen between adult male and female members of our species was lost. Sexual relationships may have been changed by the fact that the males were not away for protracted periods on hunting expeditions but worked in closer contact with the females and children, doing work more similar to theirs than had been the case in the earlier era.

The effect of agriculture on the bonds between the sexes has not yet been fully studied. I believe, however, that we can safely establish this as an area in which the second-order consequences of agriculture were very important and that the disruptions of human sexual life that followed from the agricultural way of life have affected the species ever since.

Since better methods made more of the solar energy pool

available, human populations grew with each technological innovation that improved the efficiencies of agriculture. The denser population of certain of the more fertile river valleys formed the early patterns for that type of village life which is still the prevalent way of life for the majority of the people in large areas of the earth, for example, in India, in China, and in Africa.

Once established, there could be no turning back on the process; abandonment of the more productive methods of agriculture and return to the hunt would have forced a large proportion of the population to starve. A trap had closed on mankind.

Crop-raising created a strikingly new environment for the peoples who practiced it. Even the shapes were new. Ditches were cut to divert water to irrigate dry lands. Fields of grain replaced marshland and withered scrub. The new world was one measured out in plots, often cut in a complex pattern of parallel furrows. Fields were leveled. Rocks were removed and used to mark out boundaries. Eventually even the hillsides were to be terraced, as we see today in intensive rice-growing areas like Southern China or Luzon. Throughout the new agricultural world, green and geometrical areas were carved out of what had been irregular zones of grassland, desert, forest, scrub, and swamp.

The shape of the new environment reflected, of course, tendencies inherent in man's inner world, tendencies to think in terms of geometrical pattern. For the first time, our ancestors were in a position to impose the contours of their *Innenwelt* upon the world in which they lived. They did not hesitate to do so, nor have the generations that followed.

The new agricultural life-style impacted intellectually in a variety of ways on the people that followed it. The new technologies went hand in hand with new sciences. Time became important in many new ways. The year needed to be properly measured, the planting seasons marked. In farm communities, complex patterns of holidays and festivals were developed to mark the changing agricultural tasks of the season. Measuring and counting became important, since contributions to granaries, trade, and property in land all required careful record keeping. Concepts expressed in geometrical or cyclical patterns undoubtedly became more widespread. Along with the new technologies, a variety of new sciences blossomed: botany, zoology, geometry, engineering, astronomy, meteorology, and many others. New symbols sprang up along with the new tools, not only to stand for the newly developed tools and processes but also to mirror discoveries in the related sciences.

People naturally talk about what is important to them. In vocabulary, the language of farming people is sharply different from that of a people that confines its activity to hunting and collecting. It must attune the agriculturalist's perceptors more accurately to the new types of sensory input needed, to the new distinctions. The Aymara, as a consequence of living in the Andes above the altitude at which maize will ripen, made the potato their staple, and distinguish in their native tongue over two hundred and fifty varieties of the potato genus alone; and all Aymara know the habits and the best way to prepare each one as food. Halfway round the world, the Cambodians reportedly have some two hundred ways to describe different types of rice or different stages in its growth and processing as food.

Beyond the names of the new crops and the new technologies needed to grow, protect, and use them, thousands of new ways of thought and new points of view about human society are required for adjustment to a fully agricultural way of life. New concepts were based on the analysis-systems that were already present in the *Innenwelt* of pre-agricultural man, but those systems were culturally extended to previously unknown levels of sophistication by the sharper demands of a more complex environment.

Although it involved very different behavioral patterns, the new agricultural way of life still had many characteristics in common with the old life of the hunter and collector. The scale and speed of life had not changed much, although the farming family might well be confined to a smaller territorial area of operation (except, of course, for the pastorialist who kept flocks that had to be moved between distant pasturages). The new way of life was, of course, usually more complicated and typically involved longer waiting. More was required in the way of preparatory actions keyed to distant events. Agriculture demanded bodily postures and activities, like sustained bending and digging, that had not been particularly typical for humans before. "If man had been intended to be an agriculturalist," goes the analysis, "he would have been born with arms that reach the ground."

One of the most important results of the agricultural revolution was, however, not simply the more efficient food-producing system that was created, but rather the new and more complex social system that it could support. This involved cities. We call the pattern "civilization."

THE CITY

Hippias of Elis, a contemporary of Socrates, was in his day a prototype of the modern individualist. Among other doctrines, he proclaimed self-sufficiency. An outspoken opponent of all occupational specialization, Hippias is said to have attended the Olympic games in ornate attire that was entirely of his own making, down to the ring on his finger. Although Hippias claimed proficiency in all the arts and announced that he was prepared to lecture on any subject, his ideas represent the negation of the basic premise upon which all civilization has been built. That premise is that it pays to specialize.

The first cities apparently arose in those regions where their development was favored by certain geographic relationships. Despite their inventive culture, the Eskimos were not on any road that would have led them to create a "civilization" in the sense usually given to the word. The city-centered way of life arose in all cases from an agricultural way of life, apparently as a direct result of the greatly increased productivity of the new farming techniques. As a large sedentary population developed in a fertile valley like that of the Nile, the Tigris, the Huang-Ho, or the Indus, the base was created for the development of civilization. Nonagricultural peoples like the Eskimos have never created large enough populations to sustain what we call civilization.

In the river valleys mentioned above, as residence became more established, personal and family status became more defined and groups were more sharply differentiated. As agricultural surpluses grew, more time became available for the pursuit of the various arts and crafts. The occupational specialization decried by Hippias of Elis became possible. As homes became more permanent, domestic architecture was defined. Large villages became possible. Since understanding of seasonal change was all-important to agriculture, the arts of astronomy and meteorology in particular, and prediction in general, became the stock-in-trade of a developing priestly class.

Organized warfare was another consequence of the development of agriculture. Growth of wealth in the new agricultural areas made defense of the area a prerequisite to group security. At a minimum, agriculturalists had to defend their crops and granaries from marauding pre-agricultural bands. Defense needs were met in the same way others were; by the creation of specialized groups trained for the role. The seed was thus planted for the professional military organization. Males, who no longer had the age-old chance to take part in the hunt, were the recruits. Conquests and defensive alliances, as well as economic necessities, led to the creation of larger political entities composed of several villages. The dominant or best-placed of the villages then began to take on urban characteristics that remain familiar today.

Clusters of satellite villages surrounding the newly dominant village-city could serve as the economic basic for a pattern of even greater occupational specialization. In the early village-cities, many new crafts were developed, with skills that were later to be passed on from father to son for scores of generations. The total *Zwischenwelt* of the urbanized culture became a vastly more complex structure, and different groups within society viewed the same world from increasingly variant perspectives.

Thus, the strangest of human environments was first created: the city. Crowded into a small area, often walled for defense and economic advantage, the members of various specialized artisan groups and social classes went their own way through life, perpetuating their own fragment of the total pattern. In contrast to villagers, most city dwellers no longer engaged in agricultural production, but instead carried on a variety of specialized activities—functions heretofore never performed by a single individual on a full-time basis. The urbanite had ceased to live the whole life. The family was no longer a self-reliant unit. The individual was dependent on a larger group, whose members were not all known to him and the interrelations of which were too complicated to understand fully. Urban dwellers dealt with each other in terms of highly segmented roles, rather than as whole persons.[9] With the new pattern of dependency, the individual—including his family and the larger social group—lost a kind of freedom that could never be restored. Civilization was closing in upon the individual.

Obviously, the anatomical foundations for human perceptions—the givens of our inner world—remained the same under civilization as they had been before, but the store of remembered data had become immeasurably larger. In fact, one of the major results of the growth of the cities was the manner in which the city was structured to accumulate information of value in taking future action. Within each craft, specialists passed on growingly complex techniques to their apprentices. Technologies that led to more efficient production also made possible the development of professional classes whose responsibilities centered in the field of memory, not only accountants, but also bards who sang of bygone days and a priestly class rich in liturgy.

"The City," Emerson perceptively observed, "lives by remembering." The need to record the activities of an increasingly complex urban economy led to the development of many types of record-keeping, including not only early forms of writing but also a variety of other systems like the knotted cords, or *quipu,* of the Incas. In most areas of sufficiently large population, these early systems of record-keeping seemed to lead quite naturally, though very gradually, to a full writing system and to the development of a broad literature. Writing, in turn, made many new things possible in the life of the city. Not only could complex economic records be kept but the results of additional types of experience could be recorded for future guidance. A new kind of human memory had been created—one that could deal in terms of centuries in much the same way as the individual had talked of years or decades.

The gradual accumulation of information and greater occupational specialization also opened the way for newer and more detailed sciences. Writing, moreover, facilitated those legal, military, and administrative activities that made larger and larger political entities possible. Larger states could in turn support more populous cities with more complex social structure. The significance of writing in urban development is sufficiently great that some students have considered literacy a virtual prerequisite to the development of the urban way of life.[10]

Adjustment to the new environment of civilization was not always easy for the people involved. The new urban life represented a major qualitative change from anything that they or their immediate precursors had ever experienced.[11] Old sensory systems had to distinguish new kinds of data. Old perceptual patterns had to deal with new needs. The attempt to perfect these adjustments continues in the modern world. "We are, in fact," remarked the anthropologist Ralph Linton, "anthropoid apes trying to live like termites, and, as any philosophical observer can attest, not doing too well at it."[12] The remarkable fact is, however, that we have been able to come as far as we have in making so unprecedented an adjustment. Now we face new adjustments that go far beyond any ever made by the social insects—or any other earthling species for that matter.

The most alarming aspect of our current situation is that the process of innovation and the culturally reinforced methods of preserving and passing on past innovations to the future shows all the classic features of a positive feedback system. Since the rise of civilizations a few millennia ago, the pace of innovation and change has continued to escalate. We will trace the outlines of that change in the next chapters and will then try to look soberly at the implications that it bears for human survival.

9
Man Meets Machine

"God makes all things good; man meddles with them and they become evil," declared Rousseau in the opening lines of *Emile*. "He forces one soil to yield the products of another, one tree to bear another's fruit. He confuses and confounds time, place, and natural conditions. He mutilates his dog, his horse, and his slave. He destroys and defaces all things; he loves all that is deformed and monstrous; he will have nothing as nature made it, not even man himself, who must learn his paces like a saddle horse. . . ."[1]

Much of the popularity of such iconoclastic ideas in the late eighteenth and early nineteenth century was the result of growing fear about the ultimate direction that industrial technology would take in changing the human environment. Today, the processes that alarmed Rousseau have been carried much further. The world of agriculture is now the old one. Although it continues to thrive in certain areas—those places we tend to call "underdeveloped" today—a growing proportion of the world each year moves toward the patterns of industrial life. At the same time, those areas that have long been industrialized have begun to move toward newer and even stranger ways of life.

How was it that "progress" could lead mankind so far from nature? What was it that impelled us toward the creation of an industrial society?

The agricultural revolution provided our species with unprecedented power. We could bend to our own purposes a larger share of the earth's energy pool than had ever before been expropriated by a single species. Nevertheless, people still had to supply the work that was crucial to keeping the new pattern going. The use of domesticated animals as beasts of burden had changed the pattern only slightly. Countless hours of back-breaking human work still had to go into hoeing and weeding, sowing and harvesting, threshing and winnowing. All the collateral arts and skills required similar effort. In some periods, this work force was composed of slaves; in other periods it was made up of serfs or indentured laborers. Women and children often contributed a major share of the heavy labor. Along with the other animals, the agriculturalists had domesticated themselves and their children into beasts of burden par excellence. Compared with the new work-centered life under agriculture, the ancient pattern of the hunt could be viewed almost as a recreation.

Agriculturalists could be freed from this heavy yoke of unnatural and inhuman toil only by further cultural innovation. Luckily, the process of innovation never ceased.[2] Better tools tended to be used to construct yet more complex tools and artifacts. Even during eras like the European Middle Ages, progress in tool-making and agricultural technology continued unabated. By the early modern period, the level of technological sophistication in Europe had advanced significantly above that of the Ancient World. Part of this technological advance took the form of better and wider use of non-animal sources of power: irrigation systems powered by windmills, flour mills run by water power, and the like. For example, the *Domesday Book* (*ca.* 1086) lists 5,624 water mills in England. But instead of lightening the load of the individual farmer, the new devices tended only to form the basis for a more complex social structure.

The development and improvement of clocks and similar devices had a great intellectual impact on the early modern period. Men like Leonardo da Vinci and Galileo obviously felt very much at home amid pulleys and levers. With the advent of printing by moveable type, mechanical methods were applied to human communication as well. By the seventeenth century, the elite of Europe were already accustomed to thinking about the world in terms of its mechanics. The symbolic side of the early modern European *Zwischenwelt* was already prepared for a new wave in tool-making. Then, in the the late eighteenth century, there began that rapid escalation in the everyday use of mechanical devices that has led to so many of the successes and so many of the problems of the contemporary world.[3]

THE DISCIPLINE OF INDUSTRIALISM

About two or three hundred years ago, the new economic revolution began, one that came to be as significant as the agricultural revolution itself. Our species began to develop a wide variety of new mechanical methods to channel energy directly toward human purposes, without using people as links in the energy chain. Development of purely mechanical links in the control and direction of the energy used in production formed the basis for what we usually call the "industrial revolution." In earlier epochs, solar energy had been trapped in the fields by the new agricultural methods and turned into the chemical energy of foods. Surplus foods were used in turn to feed the increasing numbers of urban workers who could then produce more and more specialized products by hand. With the advent of industrialism, however, sources of energy were directly tapped to run complex machines that made specialized products. With intermediate stages eliminated, productivity shot upward. At first, old sources of power like wind and running streams were simply used in more sophisticated ways. Gradually, however, new and previously untapped sources of chemical energy, like the fossil fuels, were put to direct use. The new potentials of chemical power were dramatized by the growing use of gunpowder.

Many of the first industrial inventions simply multiplied the effectiveness of human control over production. For example, the original spinning jenny, invented by James Hargreaves in 1764, was a hand-operated device that allowed the operator to spin eleven threads as easily as one. Soon devices were designed that could spin a hundred or more threads. With larger machines, new sources of power were needed to replace human energy. The first to be widely used was water, then steam. Water power, and the energy of the prehistoric sun trapped in fossil fuels like coal, could now be turned directly to meeting human purposes. But the new devices were large and costly machines and had no place in the home. As a consequence, factories came into being, usually located near sources of power such as rivers.

In 1769, James Watt patented the separate condenser, an innovation that made possible a much more efficient steam engine. Early steam engines had been effective largely as pumps, but now rotary movement became economical. When applied in industries like spinning, the steam engine allowed a factory to be set up more independently of geographic considerations. Factories no longer had to be confined to sites where water power was readily available. The new engines were big, but a single one might supply the energy for a very large factory containing a variety of individual devices. Power was generally transmitted by shafts, belts, pulleys, and other mechanical means to the various machines in the building. All this made the early factory a very noisy, dusty, and poorly lit environment, hot in summer and very cold in winter.

For the first time, there were created within shelters microenvironments that had less rather than more in common with the environment natural to humans than did the environment outside. They were fine environments, however, for machines. Within the factories the environment was good for machines but bad for people. Nevertheless, the machines produced what people wanted—a greater abundance of things.

We see here how desires basic to our inner world (our primate interest in things) could use abilities basic to our inner world (our sense of order and symmetry as exemplified in the repetitive industrial process) but at the same time create conditions that violated the psychological needs of the workers involved. This is a type of paradox of means and end that has only become more common with the passage of time.

Key to the accelerated development of true industrialism was the invention of a family of "machine tools," that is, generalized machines that operate to make parts of other machines. First of the modern machine tools was, perhaps, the boring mill, developed by Wilkinson in 1775 to make the accurate metal cylinders that were needed for Watt's new steam engine. Soon there were a variety of mechanical devices to work metal: to drill it, ream it, punch it, mill it, grind it, turn it, and polish it. Machines became cheaper and more productive in the process.

Coal quickly became central to the new way of industrial life. Not only did it power the steam engines of the new factories and replace charcoal in the making of iron, but it soon supplied the motive power for new forms of transportation. Run by coal, the first steamship crossed the Atlantic in 1819. Railways began to appear around 1830. But coal was not without its social cost. Coal mines of the early industrial period produced one of the most degrading environments to which humans have ever been subjected. Young and old alike worked long hours below the surface, in an environment more suitable to the mole than *Homo sapiens*.

Technology encompasses more than just tools and related devices but includes as well the techniques for manipulating tools, for organizing the productive process, and even for relating the culture to its system of production. The organizational techniques of mass production began to appear very early in the industrial period. By 1798, Whitney's "American System" was being used to manufacture muskets out of interchangeable parts. By 1818, the copying lathe had been developed by Blanchard to mass-produce gun stocks. Soon low-cost clothes were being machine made in standard sizes.

Instead of bringing increased leisure, however, the first impact of the new industrialism was to create a harder and more degraded life for the factory worker, the coal miner, and the average inhabitant of the increasingly congested urban areas. The new industrial way of life marked a traumatic change from an agricultural pattern that had been relatively stable for several thousand years. On the plus side of the ledger, many commodities became much cheaper. Even the urban worker, living in crowded and squalid conditions, tended to have more things than back on the farm. Communication and transportation systems were speeded. Even the workers were more mobile.

Cities grew rapidly, and with them problems of health, morals, and law and order. Workers, attracted to the cities, left family and other stabilizing ties behind. Even the nature of the world's armies began to change, from elite professional to mass conscript organizations. Repetition, an element that can bring natural pleasure in the arts, had become a frankenstein monster. Workmanship was replaced in the world of industrialism by repetitive labor; individuality became a wasteful luxury.

People were forced to act more machine-like during the

laboring part of the day, turning through a daily cycle like well-regulated cogs in the great machine of industrialism. "I am awakened almost every night by the panting of the locomotive," complained Thoreau, in an essay published posthumously in 1863. "It interrupts my dreams. There is no sabbath. It would be glorious to see mankind at leisure for once. It is nothing but work, work, work."[4]

Industrialism created a world of bigger and faster things, a world of more people and less space. System and symmetry were king of the productive processes, while social life became less orderly and stable. Relations between individuals became simultaneously more complex and more impersonal. As organisms, the industrial workers retained, however, the same anatomy that their ancestors had possessed during the hunting stage in which the species had been formed. Old sensory systems, old perceptual patterns, were adjusted to the strange new environment as best they could. There was no time to evolve new anatomical or neural systems. Adjustment had to be cultural. For this reason, accommodation to industrialism could only be partial. The gulf was too great.

The growing complexities of the modern era did not long escape the critical eye of observers. One of the most scathing of all attacks on the increased alienation of the species from its natural environment was that made by Rousseau on the eve of industrialization. Almost as a conscious antidote to the developing industrial way of life, the romantic literature of the late eighteenth and early nineteenth century conjured up an idyllic, pastoral way of life as a better norm for mankind. The utopian literature of the era had many of the same characteristics. Advocacy of an alternative life-style that would break sharply with the patterns usually associated with the industrial era has not yet come to its end, and is reflected in newer forms today, including science fiction.

The new industrial environment was quite unlike any that people had previously known. The scale and pace of all human activity was greatly increased. There was also physical crowding, strangely combined with a greater social distance between individuals and the total society on which they were dependent. Living in increased isolation from the kind of environment in

which *Homo sapiens* had originally developed, children grew
to adulthood in the new urban areas without having seen a tree,
much less having crossed an open plain or having heard the
whisper of a sea of grass in the wind.

To many it seemed that we had lost our birthright, had
been enslaved by a system of our own creation. In the words of
Toynbee, "The farmer and the nomadic herdsman are less free
than the food-gatherer and the hunter . . . The urban artisan and
trader are less free than the farmer and the herdsman; and this
gradual turning of the screw of regimentation has been speeded
up since the advent of mechanization."[5]

The impact of human activity on the natural environment
also began to be studied more seriously. "Man is everywhere a
disturbing agent," wrote George P. March in 1874 in his pio-
neering work on the needs for conservation: *The Earth as
Modified by Human Action.* "Wherever he plants his foot, the
harmonies of nature are turned to discords."[6] Much of the damage cited by March was, of course, the result of centuries of
agricultural activity. But the new industrial era had greatly
dramatized the problem.

The new world of the machine was not without its defenders. "A tool is but the extension of man's hand," Henry
Ward Beecher reminded his nineteenth-century contemporaries,
"and a machine is but a complex tool. And he that invents a
machine augments the power of a man and the well-being of
mankind." Most social critics of the nineteenth century could
not, however, ascribe to so simple and optimistic a view of
the significance of the machine. We had once again remade our
world, but the new industrial world had taken an unforseen and
threatening shape. Its processes served many of our purposes
and reflected the unique abilities of our species, but it surely
was not made in our image. Compared to the world of agriculture, the industrial city was even more alien. "Hell," said Shelley,
"is a city much like London—a populous and smoky city."

THE SECOND INDUSTRIAL WAVE

Around the beginning of this century—before the critics had
done much more than tentatively identify some of these major
problems of the new industrial society, and before more than

a quarter of mankind had begun to feel its full impact—a second wave of change began in the more advanced industrial nations. This new phase, sometimes called the "second industrial revolution," was marked by the development of a whole series of new and more sophisticated systems for the control of industrial activity.

Basic to the newer industrial system was the widespread use of electricity. The earliest electric motor seems to have been one that was designed by Gramme in 1873. In the first years, the use of electricity was important primarily because it allowed smaller, cleaner machines in the factory and cut down the noise level sharply; later it provided better lighting and cleaner systems of heating. The real significance of electricity was, however, the new systems of control over the the entire industrial process that it was to make possible. Electrical switching devices can provide an efficient substitute for much of human supervision. Moreover, a wiring system is much more flexible than any system of gears, belts, and pulleys. Inventions like the vacuum tube made it possible for a very small voltage to control very large currents. Electrical systems, such as those involving photoelectric cells, also took on some of the features of a sensory system, thus allowing nonhuman controls over the productive process. It is hard to imagine computers of present-day complexity without electricity. It is just as difficult to conceive a modern automated factory without electric power.

Electricity revolutionized not only the productive side of our world, but it also changed our communications systems into something quite new and different. With the development of the telegraph, it became possible for much of humanity to carry on almost instantaneous intercommunication; telephone, radio, and television only added new dimensions and greater efficiency to the new system. But electronic communication became possible not only among people, it also became possible among machines.

Charles Babbage, an English scientist and mathematician, had elaborated the basic principles of the computer in the 1830s, but the type of mechanism that he tried to construct—relying on cogs and wheels—could not be tooled to sufficient accuracy to do its job. Babbage's "analytical engine" thus joined the ranks of brilliantly conceived failures, and Babbage himself died in 1871 unaware of the impact that his ideas were to have once the era of electricity had dawned.

The first person to construct an electrical computing machine was apparently Herman Hollerith, a statistician tabulating the United States Census of 1890. The firm that Hollerith founded, after many mergers, eventually became part of International Business Machines (IBM). In 1915, the Ford Instrument Company was already producing an electrical analog computer of sorts, the Range Keeper Mark I. By the 1930s, both General Electric Company and Westinghouse were also producing electrical calculating machines. In 1936, a Chicago psychologist, Benjamin Burack, built the first "electrical logic machine" and the way was open for computers to go beyond the narrow field of handling numbers to areas closer to the basic processes of thought. The theoretical underpinnings for this new development were supplied by Claude Shannon in 1938. Development of "stored-program" logic by John Von Neumann in the 1940s further added to the possibilities of digital computers.

Computers, of course, can do much more than print out answers to mathematical and logical problems or recover stored data. They open unforeseen possibilities for information handling, with social as well as economic implications.[7] Computers can give instruction to other machines, to machines that print paychecks or type letters, to aircraft in the air or missiles in space, to factory lathes, to turbine generators. When such automatic control systems are applied to industrial processes, the need for human supervision over production decreases. As a result, the automated factory has become possible in industry after industry.

Despite the promises of the new systems, there has been widespread concern over the direction in which they will lead us. The industrial *Zwischenwelt* has surely alienated us from patterns of human life that were typical in the past. "The ordinary city dweller," says the philosopher Susanne Langer, "knows nothing of the earth's productivity; he does not know the sunrise and rarely notices when the sun sets; ask him in what phase the moon is, or when the tide in the harbor is high, or even how high the average tide runs, and likely as not he cannot answer you." Unless he has happened to live through a major earthquake, flood, or hurricane, he is not likely to consider nature as having any power over his life at all. As Langer put it, "His realities are the motors that run elevators, subway trains, the steady feed of water and gas through the mains and of electricity over the wires . . . the concrete and brick, bright steel and dingy woodwork that take the place of earth and waterside and sheltering roof for him . . . Nature, as man has always known it, he knows no more."[8]

The full impact of this new pattern has not yet hit us. Obviously, the higher levels of technological development made possible by automatic control systems will produce new dislocations, quite different ones in many cases from those created by the first industrial revolution. The new electronic systems for the control and direction of energy and information will give the species greater control over the environment than has ever before been possible. The term *post-industrial* has been coined to describe a new world in which the service industries play a larger role than production itself. But since that term seems to imply that we have left the industrial way of life behind, I more often use the term *techno-industrial* for the latest and most complex level of industrial life, one that had its origins about the time of the First World War and which has featured increasing sophistication in the field of electronics.[9] Brzezinski's term, the "technetronic era," apparently refers to the most recent decades of the techno-industrial period, as well as to what we can project ahead as the consequences of computers and evolving electronic communications systems.[10] Perhaps it will take the perspective of a bit more time to decide precisely when the new era began. That we are now in a new technological phase is, however, well established.

When the now emerging systems take full effect, a new generation of problems will arise. Some people predict, for example, so much human leisure in the future that there will be problems in finding satisfying and purposive activity to fill our time. This would have many implications. A mankind that turned all physical activity over to its machines could obviously not long survive, either physically or psychologically.

An important factor is that the rate of innovation has been

so rapid in recent years that the individual has for the first time come to think of change rather than tradition as the norm. The expectation of innovation has, in fact, become a strong tradition in our techno-industrial societies.

And the trend continues. We can today well understand the feeling of Benjamin Franklin when he wrote to Joseph Priestly in 1780: "The rapid progress true science now makes, occasions my regretting sometimes that I was born so soon. It is impossible to imagine the height to which may be carried, in a thousand years, the power of man over matter." But our thoughts today about this trend are no longer those of unalloyed enthusiasm. Hope has turned to dread. We have passed two hundred years beyond Franklin's era. The thought of another eight hundred years of the same accelerating pace of change is bound to make us somewhat uneasy about the final outcome.

10
Folded, Spindled, and Mutilated

When you fly the major air lanes of the world—whether from New York to Washington, from Paris to Amsterdam, or from Tokyo to Osaka—the land that you see below will almost all have been carved into aritificial forms: shining ribbons of highway, geometrical fields, lines of trees as windbreaks, the chaotic rooftops of the cities, walled-off tidal basins, black coal yards, the metallic gray of industrial complexes. Only the sea seems to keep its original shape or color. Although it is true that there remain well-traveled air lanes where the mark of human activity is not so apparent, like the approaches to the Grand Canyon area from the East Coast of the United States to Los Angeles, such areas are becoming more and more scarce on this earth. And even in the desert, the glint of an occasional metal roof and the winding brown lines of dirt roads below show that human encroachment has begun. Most of the surface of the globe has been altered in countless ways, great and small, by the activities of *Homo sapiens*.[1] In the areas of heaviest population, the contours of the new world have very little in common with the ancient home of our species.

Having made a new and much more complex environment, we find that one of the most old-fashioned and least adjusted features that is left is ourselves. Our species has turned most plains and river valleys into farmland, felled vast forests, reclaimed lands from the sea, carved paths and then roadways through the most rugged mountain terrain. We have built more and more cities with their new rectangular environments of streets and alleys, walls and windows. Our immediate precursors forged an even newer industrial environment of machine-laden factories, filled their world with tangles of wiring, poured vast seas of concrete, sped up the pace of travel and transport. But during all this, human anatomy remained the same. Even though we have modified the outermost zones of our interaction with the environment, the contours of our bodies, the network of our nerves, our natural ways of thinking about the world—our *Innenwelt*—have all remained those of the hunter on the ancient plains.

Although the agricultural revolution probably still remains the most basic of the changes brought about by human activity, it did not jolt the individual nearly as much as did the more recent industrial revolution. First, the development of agriculture took place over a very long period in most areas of the world. Only a few of the hunting tribes, like some of the dispossessed North American Indians, found themselves forced to make a rapid transition from one pattern to another. Secondly, the objects of the agricultural world were largely the same general kinds of things that had been important in the earlier way of life: animals, trees, grasses, flowing water. In most areas, the species of life on which people depended after the coming of agriculture were much the same as before. Goats and pigs that had been hunted were domesticated. Root crops, berries, and cereals that had been gathered were systematically planted and more efficiently harvested. New domesticated varieties of plants and animals were, of course, developed, but only over periods that encompassed many human generations.

We have no evidence, however, that a new, "domesticated" breed of *Homo* was developed at the same time. As a matter of fact, the evidence clearly indicates that this did not happen. If a child is taken from a modern hunting tribe and given an education identical to that of a child whose forebears have been agriculturalists or otherwise "civilized" for over a hundred generations, the two will grow up thinking and acting alike. City dwellers are separated from their primitive counterparts by cultural—not genetic—factors. An Australian aborigine child could be raised to live the life of a London cost accountant or a Buddhist monk.

This is not, however, all necessarily to the good. The very adaptability of the human race may carry with it a threat to our species. For the short run, people have seemed able to put up with what we are tempted to call subhuman conditions. In the ancient world, men and women toiled in slavery for generation after generation. In the modern world, industrial workers have endured the cramped quarters and foul air of sprawling cities. But the fact that such environmental change does not destroy the first generations that are subjected to it does not mean that our ability to adapt is unlimited or that future generations will not pay—perhaps with interest—the cost of having violated much of human nature. Let us then look at the relationship of our technological world to the natural environment in which our species originally evolved.

To begin, we must view the relationship realistically. We should not fool ourselves by talking as if our environment were now so completely man-made and man-controlled that we as a species need no longer worry about the natural world about us. We continue to depend on the sun's rays and would quickly die out if they should be blocked from falling on Earth for only a short while. We rely on other species of plants and animals for all of our daily food. And we remain part of a biosphere in countless other ways.

The very composition of our planet's air represents the result of its evolving biosphere, since it is the green plants that are responsible for the free oxygen that makes up some 20 percent of the present atmosphere of Earth. Abundant oxygen is, of course, crucial to terrestrial animal life; and it is the green plants that take back carbon dioxide from the air and in turn release free oxygen. Beginning with the appearance of land plants some half billion years or so ago, our planet's atmosphere gradually became richer in free oxygen and lower in carbon dioxide, with the excess carbon becoming the vast fossil deposits that we now mine and drill for oil, coal, and natural gas. The biosphere that existed by the time that our species was formed involved a complex cycle of interaction between oxygen-breathing animals which consumed carbon-dioxide-breathing plants—both of which faced the inevitable process of decay. It was a closed system, but one that maintained itself in delicate balance.

Today, however, we are burning fossil fuels at increasing rates, and the process is already changing the composition of the Earth's air. Recovery of sufficient fossil carbon and its reinsertion into the active biosphere could in theory return earth to an atmosphere more similar to that which preceded the evolution of terrestrial plant life. Although carbon dioxide is still a very minor constituent of the atmosphere, its proportion in the air we breathe has reportedly increased by 15 percent in the last hundred years or so. Unless countered in some way, such a trend would threaten all animal life with suffocation. Moreover, the so-called "greenhouse effect" of carbon dioxide in the atmosphere (since it traps solar radiation more effectively than oxygen) would lead to a rise in world temperatures. According to some analysts, only the concurrent increase in atmospheric dust has so far countered this effect.

But all this has only to do with the physical threat to our species, the creation of new physical conditions by upsetting our environment and making it more hostile to our bodily functions. I do not believe this to be the major threat, at least in the short term. Having recognized that even our techno-industrial society remains dependent on certain basic relationships with nature about us, let us move on to our psychosocial relationships with the new world of technology that we and our immediate forebears have fashioned. Here we will find the true threat. We will be particularly interested in assessing the degree to which our world has come to violate the intellectual, social, and aesthetic norms of the middle realm. Of especial interest will be those aspects which could threaten mankind in the very short term by increasing the intergroup tensions and fears that could make major wars more likely.

MODERN TECHNOLOGY AND THE MIDDLE REALM

Not only did we change our environment by industrializing, but we also changed our way of life—our view of the world about us and our relationship to it. Obviously, life in the modern industrial world has many characteristics that distinguish it sharply from that which was original to our species. The modern city represents a distortion of much that was characteristic of the middle realm. Differences can also be seen in terms of the variety, speed, complexity, closeness, and scale of the new environment.

What then are the strains and stresses that modern technology has put upon contemporary mankind? How does the new world violate the ancient norms of the middle realm? How is it that the new world that we have created could seem to run counter to our inner nature? Where did we go wrong?

I see several causes for the present disharmony between contemporary mankind and the techno-industrial environment. Most of these causes can, I believe, be attributed to three general factors, each of which is in turn the result of the very degree of the victory that human culture has won over the old environment. These basic problem-making factors are: 1) the fact that human populations have greatly increased as a result of humanity's victory over the environment; 2) the fact that people must now adjust to the new concepts, communication systems, and countless artifacts that were developed to gain that victory; and 3) the fact that rapid cultural change can have quite unexpected side effects, second-order consequences.

Perhaps it will be best to turn our attention first to the population problem as it has affected our relationship to the world about us, and our spacing as individuals on the surface of that world.

With their cultures of tools and weapons, humans long ago taught even the larger predators to avoid their presence. Modern science has extended the ancient victory over the larger beasts and has now conquered most of the dangerous insects and even many of the smallest organisms that cause disease. Death rates have fallen sharply and, at the same time, the birth process, long a particular source of danger for mankind, has been made much safer. Beginning with the development of agriculture, people learned to avoid many of the ancient dangers of drought and famine. With better and more secure food supplies, agricultural populations grew rapidly. More recently this growth has been accelerated by increased knowledge of our dietary needs. Improved transportation and communication have, in turn, had a major effect in decreasing the danger that local crop conditions might lead to famine. All this has tended to make ours an increasingly numerous species.

Already about twenty percent of all mankind live in cities with over 100,000 inhabitants. Not too long hence, a majority of the members of our species will live in such urban complexes, communities larger by far than those found among any of the social insects. It has even been projected that one day all the surface of the earth, at least the land surfaces, will form a single urban community, what Constantinos Doxiadis called "ecumenopolis."[2]

Although we do not know the exact environmental conditions under which *Homo sapiens* evolved, it seems quite safe to assume that pre-human and early human populations were thinly distributed in small groups, ranging over rather open territories. The human neural system was presumably developed to respond most effectively under these circumstances. But the ancient environment has been totally remodeled by now, and the old way of life has been abandoned for new and very different patterns. Eyes that once scanned an expansive horizon of grass and trees for signs of game now compile statistics. The five to ten thousand years that separate the later Neolithic period from the present are not enough to have played much of a role in adapting our species to the closer living conditions that have resulted from the higher population densities. And the challenges of the future are likely to be even greater.

If the present rate of population growth continues for another five hundred years, there will be trillions of human beings on this planet. The average population density for the entire land surface of the globe, counting in Siberia's wastes, the mid-Sahara, and the Antarctic, will rise to that of Manhattan Island today. Though most may agree that the prospects are alarming, individuals seldom plan their own families on the basis of worldwide, long-term considerations. They continue to think in terms of inner-zone priorities rather than the biosphere. Under these circumstances, world population is likely to continue to grow for some time at a rate that will present mankind with serious future problems of adjustment. Most animal populations evidence a breakdown in mental health if too densely crowded. Mankind is probably no exception.[3] If the actions of other species be any guide, overly dense populations will lead to the greater threat of intergroup and intragroup conflict. In a world armed with nuclear and other technologically sophisticated weapons, the danger is apparent.

Inhabitants of our techno-industrial world face the problem of adjusting to a complex technomass of cultural artifacts that often isolates the individual from the environment. This is part of an ancient problem. To some extent, we have not yet fully adjusted even to wearing clothes, for our skin seems still healthier when exposed to a degree of sun and circulating air; witness the sunbathing of the lighter peoples of northern Europe or the fact that Eskimos traditionally went nude once they entered the microenvironment of their warmed shelters. But clothing is only a small part of the inventory of artifacts that separate us from the raw environment. Modern technology continues to interpose additional man-made layers between our bodies and what remains of the old environment. In a sense, the *Zwischenwelt* has become a thicker and thicker intermediate zone. "Men," declared Thoreau, "have become the tools of their tools."

It is in the large city that the dehumanizing effect of modern life can most clearly be seen. The statistics on the social life of densely occupied urban areas are not comforting. In United States cities of more than 250,000 population, robberies occur ten times more often than in the suburbs and thirty-five times more often than in surrounding rural areas. When the statistics for the slum areas of larger cities are isolated, the contrast is even sharper. Statistics on not only crime but also other factors of social disorganization like unemployment and broken families tend to follow this pattern.

The concrete office buildings, canyon-like streets, and twisting of the modern metropolis are among the most characteristic shapes that surround us in the techno-industrial era. To these, also, we must try to accommodate. The new architectural shapes have in most cases been designed with a view to the needs of the builder, rather than their potential inhabitants. The economics of the techno-industrial system demands that skyscrapers be designed to minimize the cost per square foot of office space, that transportation routes be analyzed in terms of maximum capacities at peak hours. The limits of sheer human tolerance are consequently pushed to the brink by the nature of the system. What "human engineering" is done is too often centered on determining the limits of bare tolerance more accurately, so that any slack may be taken up.

But human limits are not so easily measured, and what

appears a safe limit may only be safe for the short run or under specific circumstances. An individual, or even an entire culture, can tolerate a great deal for a short period, but over a longer time the constant pursuit of the absolute limits of human tolerance may violate those very limits, with serious consequences for all concerned.

When we design a modern zoo in which to confine wild animals, we consciously and conscientiously do our best to re-create for each species something approaching its natural habitat. We realize there is no other way to keep animals alive and healthy. As we build additional units of our new industrial world for our own habitation, we often overlook these same basic considerations. We look at the "efficiency" of the unit to be added, not its impact on the life-patterns of those who will work or live in relation to it.

Kevin Lynch, a professor of city planning at Massachusetts Institute of Technology who helped direct a five-year research project on the perceptual form of the city, has characterized the contemporary city by: 1) the "perceptual stress" it creates, such as the city's noise and visual confusion; 2) its "lack of visible identity," which is to say urban tendencies toward monotony of form; 3) its "illegibility," that is, the sense of alienation that city life can create; and 4) its rigidity and lack of openness to individual action.[4] These are basic ways that the modern city can violate our middle realm.

The great concentration of people in the industrial cities of the world has led to an increased problem in coping with the side-effects of technology. Population density and the nature of industrial activity has led to the pollution of rivers and their shores, and even the nearby oceans and their beaches. With large-scale use of nuclear power, the disposal of even more dangerous by-products of human activity—radioactive wastes —will pose major problems over long periods of time.

We need some balance here, however. Despite the un-natural contours of its external shapes, city life does appeal to much that is basic to human nature. For the healthy person in a relatively stable society, the complexities of urban life are not necessarily destructive. The worldwide attraction of the big cities to rural populations reflects the human desire for variety over monotony. "Once they've seen the lights of the city," goes the comment, "how can you keep them down on the farm?"

Organisms—particularly mammals—are by their nature active seekers of varied and complex stimuli. We saw this in chapter 2. As we noted in chapter 4, sensory deprivation can even be injurious to the human being. The city is rich in variety of experience and meets our needs as curious mammals very effectively in that respect. Nevertheless, if environmental factors become so complex as to be unpredictable for the individual, stress leading to neuroses or even physical problems can result. Just as our bodies respond best within a certain range of temperature, we do our best when dealing within a certain range of complexity in the sensory information with which we are confronted. To go beyond this point would be to invite disorientation and even disaster.

The rapid pace of modern industrial life is stressful and can place a heavy strain on both the mind and body. Recent technology has created a variety of problems that touch on speed and its implication. The astronaut can only endure a certain multiplication of the normal gravitational pull during acceleration. Jet passengers who cross several time zones in a few hours upset their circadian rhythms, their built-in psychological clocks. For about four days, the effect of travel across the United States by air can be clearly seen in patterns of temperature, pulse, and respiration; and a continuing effect can be measured by testing the reaction time, attention span, or even the urine of the traveler. Personal mobility has increased sharply as the result of faster and more efficient means of transportation; and sociologists point out that, while mobility can be viewed as a human value, it may become so high that it creates either personal or social problems.[5]

To a great extent, the machine has become the pacemaker of techno-industrial society. Time is chopped into smaller and smaller significant segments, and the individual is often left subject to a tight schedule that is made up of disparate activities. We have come to be increasingly dependent on our machines; they have almost been integrated into our functional cycles. This has its obvious dangers. A machine may be just as difficult to control as those aspects of the environment it was designed to bring under control.[6]

Distortions of scale in modern life take many forms. To begin with, there is the very size of the architecture of the techno-industrial world. Its inhabitants are dwarfed by its cities, and their bodily strength is puny when compared to the size and power of the gigantic machines around them. To be objective, however, we must limit the length to which we carry conclusions drawn from size alone. We find modern skyscrapers awe-inspiring, but so were the snowy mountain peaks to our remote ancestors. It is probably not the proportions of our modern cities that are likely to intimidate you or me so much as it is the size of the human society with which we must deal.

If a skyscraper is more "intimidating" to us than the stony face of a mountain, it is precisely because the former is a human construction, one teeming with complex human activity, rather than just because it is large or strangely shaped. The increasingly large number of persons within our societies, that is to say, within our communication systems, is of inestimable benefit to the development of human knowledge, but the massive scale of the modern social system can also tend to make the individual feel insignificant. This is one reason why intermediate groups like families, extended families, and local communities cannot be dissolved without creating a flood of social ills. "Above all, one thought baffled my understanding." wrote Wordsworth:

> how men lived
> Even next-door neighbors, as we say, yet still
> Strangers, not knowing each other's name . . .
> Among the close and overcrowded haunts
> Of cities where the human heart is sick.[7]

CONTEMPORARY COMMUNICATIONS SYSTEMS

Very similar to the problem of the scale of technological society is that of the size and nature of its communication system. Modern systems of communication are not only incomparably larger and more complex than those of earlier communities, but their very nature has also been transformed by the techniques of the new industrialism.

One of the major characteristics of the contemporary communication pattern is the greater proportion of what we may call "non-cooperative links" (i.e., one-directional channels of communication) in the total system. In contrast, members of preliterate societies communicated almost totally by means of what we can call "cooperative links," channels that were two directional. The person spoken to or gestured to could almost always reply in some way. Written language began the change in this directional pattern. The readers of a book normally have no way to ask questions of, or to express their own views to, the author. Except perhaps for the occasional book reviewer, they can only accept or reject the information as presented; they cannot reciprocate in any systematic way by questioning or by supplying contradictory or supplementary facts. In the early modern era, the development of printing, by making books more plentiful, greatly increased the percentage of noncooperative links in the total communication system. Modern media like the newspaper, radio, motion picture, and television have all helped to increase the proportion.

A feeling of alienation from the community may result from too great a reliance on noncooperative communication links. This tendency, if carried to its extreme, could create a society in which we were no more than passive receptors, no longer active seekers, of information. There are, of course, some natural controls. As social beings, and true to our active mammalian heritage, we would probably be dissatisfied if too great a proportion of our communication links were of the noncooperative variety. We should be expected, for example, to get bored, turn off our television and to go out to enjoy the more substantial world of give and take. In fact, of course, our system may not be healthy enough to operate in so rational a manner.

Perhaps there remains, however, hope that a degree of natural balance in communication input/output can be maintained under industrial conditions. It was the children of the fifties who were so often described by their elders as glued to their television sets—and whom many had expected to become a passive generation—who became in the late sixties the generation of "youth in revolt." Most important, one of the basic tenets of that student revolt was revulsion against being "told what to think," against the lack of credibility in the mass media, against the trite and inane. Even more significant, it was that same generation which seemed to put a new value on simple human contact over more grossly material values. This reaction often took, of course, extreme, antisocial, and even absurd forms. But the important factor is that there does seem to have been a reaction. This very fact holds out some hope that natural feedback controls can continue to operate in even the strange world of industrialism. Our concern must remain, however, that any reaction be creative and not merely antisocial or negative.

SECOND-ORDER CONSEQUENCES
OF TECHNOLOGICAL INNOVATION

At the same time that technological changes were creating the new environment in which we now live, the so-called "pure sciences" were also developing in unforeseen dimensions, leading human understanding into intellectual fields far beyond the commonplace. This process has further strained our relationship to the ancient middle realm. Not only has our "outer environment" been changed, but the validity of our "inner world" has also been put in doubt. The human desire to understand the outside world goes far beyond the more descriptive aspects covered by the sciences; it includes as well those searching questions that we associate with philosophic discourse. The inability of modern science and philosophy to provide easy answers to the questions of the contemporary world has led some to conclude that both have failed us. Still others have challenged the very ability of those two disciplines to deal with the important issues of the techno-industrial world. Despite all of our new technology, faith in science has waned during the last generation.

The psychological implications of the new industrial way of life are far deeper than most suspect. Charles Reich referred to such problems as crime, antisocial behavior, mental illness, and psychopathic personalities as "the scurvy of today," caused not by the lack of a specific vitamin but more by a general lack of contact with the environment natural to mankind.[8] This is, I feel, likely to be a much more productive way to look at the problems facing us in a techno-industrial age than to ascribe modern ills simply to territoriality or aggression. All the facts seem to me to point toward a breakdown in our ecological (organism to environment) relationships as the basic psychological stress endangering our species. I will deal with this in more detail in the next chapter.

The degree of control that we have gained over our environment has led to many unexpected side effects. As stated in a study of the secondary impact of the space program, "any action, no matter how beneficent its purpose, has wide-ranging consequences beyond its primary intent."[9] There are the obvious mechanical side effects; but then there are many identifiable effects of a cultural nature.

The first, more physical, category might be characterized as noise pollution. There can be no doubt but that there is a physical hazard here, and one directly related to the fact that the contemporary world violates the acoustical boundaries of the middle realm. "Why should noise upset our health?" asked Dr. John Anthony Parr in testimony presented to the United States House of Representatives. "Well, it's all due to an inborn alarm system we have. A sudden loud noise spells danger and we react. In fact we automatically get ready to defend ourselves or flee." After describing the physiological effects caused by a sudden noise above a certain intensity, Dr. Parr added: "This internal upheaval if repeated again and again is exhausting physically and mentally, and ultimately can cause a nervous breakdown, and then it is but a step to contracting one of the stress diseases."[10] Here we have noises that are only incidental and normal by-products of the modern industrial world automatically eliciting startle and alarm reactions that were evolved by our precursors long ago on the ancient savanna. It is an excellent example of a breakdown in the proper relationship between our inner nature and the new environment.

The second-order consequences of specific technological changes on cultural factors such as the family, systems of authority, or ideological views of the world are much harder to isolate. Some may be anticipated, even though unintended. Some may be slow to surface. Second-order consequences of technological innovation need not, of course, be dangerous. Some turn out to be quite beneficial. But the problem of controlling the impact of change is increasingly difficult.

It is obvious that the increasing rate of recent technological change is in itself, a most important reason for some of the problems that we have today. Under such circumstances it is hard to sort out what is happening. It is no exaggeration to say that human cultures have normally changed very slowly. As an accrued body of more or less successful ways of coping with the environment, a culture is by nature conservative. Its members are usually most reluctant to admit that their world view is based on any misconception if that admission might seem to threaten the culture with institutional collapse. This tendency to conserve cultural values is in part a reflection of the fact that a cultural pattern can be destroyed much more quickly and easily than a new one can be established.

In most historical periods, the coming of each new generation allowed for a sufficient rate of gradual, almost unconscious, culture change. But today, major developments with cultural implications come with increasing rapidity. This can lead to alienation between generations and, consequently, to serious problems for the well-being of society as a whole. The generations need each other; a society can never be whole if the distinction between generations is too great.

The great number of technological changes that have taken place during a comparatively short period of time create confusion for both the individual and society. Without enough time in which to work out the effect of each change and its impact on other patterns of behavior in the culture, it is easy to make inadvisable—downright stupid—responses. With time, the mistakes may become apparent, but the rush of even newer techniques and devices leaves little time for putting the system back in order. The responses of one decade thus create the problems of the next. There is no time-out.

Technological change can often have its effect on quite unrelated sectors of the culture concerned. For example, the mass-produced automobile had a major impact on the courting customs of America in the two decades after the First World War. Recent agricultural techniques have greatly changed the structure of the rural family around the world. The side effect of an innovation may be even more oblique, and have only a long term or very subtle effect on attitudes. Take for example the following sequence: 1) new methods of transportation have made it easier for the average person to travel to other countries; 2) many people have thus come to realize for the first time that their own cultural patterns are not the only possible ones; 3) as a consequence, typical members of contemporary society tend to be somewhat more critical and open in their attitude toward their own culture's traditional ways of dealing with life. The particular phenomenon has had a great impact on the younger generation in today's Europe, where travel between cultural areas has become a more common occurrence than ever before in human history. The second-order consequences, particularly the social and political implications, of this change are beyond easy estimation.

Sexual roles and patterns have been greatly disturbed by the innovations of technology. We are a species that had developed some degree of sexual dimorphism in response to the needs of the hunt on the open plains. Yet in the modern techno-industrial world that dimorphism no longer serves the same purposes that it once served. Here again we see that human nature does not readily change to accommodate the second-order consequences of our innovations. Many men and women lead sexually unsatisfying lives as the result of the type of new technological world in which they find themselves.

It is precisely because we eventually see the results of previously unforeseen effects of technology that we can be so easily misled into viewing technology as if it were an "outside force," something impacting upon our species rather than something flowing from our own nature. The tendency to externalize technology is the major flaw in Ellul's analyses. For the individual, of course, the scale and complexity of modern technology— the size of the technomass—makes it seem an external factor, and its ramifications often seem to violate the personal goals it should serve. For the species, however, the situation is quite different.

Modern technology, in the sense that the term might be used to encompass the contemporary technomass, is nothing more than the accumulated effect of thousands of generations of technological activity in pursuit of human objectives. It has no force of its own that should compel us to do that which we do not want to do. We can even use social means to regulate the effects of inner-zone primacy in the decision-making process. The question then becomes one of coping with ignorance. Can we isolate the unforeseen and unwanted effects of modern technology early enough to take corrective action? Can we avoid crossing thresholds of catastrophe that would be destructive to human objectives? This will require knowledge of a high level of sophistication, and a very large input of information for each technological decision. Since in all our actions the *ignorance factor* that I discussed in chapter 4 will remain a consideration, there will remain limits on what we can safely do.

The study of the second-order consequences of the space program that I referred to above, concluded that "Our technology has reached the point where we can contemplate rejecting strictly technological advances if they promise to produce adverse social results."[11] If that is true—and if our powers of analysis will permit us to sort out the potential results of each possible line of action—then there is real reason for optimism. There is, however, in my opinion, no evidence yet that convinces me that we already have the vast information bank, or even the skills in hand to gather the type of information we would need to deal with the problem of second-order consequences.

DEFINING "TECHNOLOGY"

We need now to define the term technology. You may find it strange at first that, in a book about the problems of modern technology, I should hold off on introducing a definition of the word "technology" until chapter 10. To refine the concept of technology much beyond the simple dictionary level, however, it is first necessary to develop a series of other concepts. These have been introduced in earlier chapters, and are now available to help us understand the nature of technology and to clarify its relationships to science, to art, and to other aspects of human culture.

Definitions are arbitrary and cannot by themselves add much to human understanding. An interrelated series of definitions, can, however, provide a structure for our thought and help us sort out real-world relationships. As an example of this, the "Glossary of Terms" at the end of this book is designed to record the various definitions used in the book and to help explain the way in which I consider that they interface.

The literature dealing with technology in the major European languages shows certain readily identifiable translation problems. French, German, and Russian works often use a cognate of the word *technique* (*Technik* in German, *tekhnika* in Russian) in senses where *technology* would normally appear in English. For this reason, the translation of Ellul's work titled *La Technique* had to be called *The Technological Society* when it appeared in English. In the text, however, Ellul's translator uses "technique," "techniques," and "technical" in ways that would be very unlikely for anyone writing and thinking only in English.

To complicate matters further, the word *technology* in continental European literature is commonly associated with the *study* of *technique*—what might be termed the *scientific study of technology* or even *technicology* in English. Despite the fact that much of the most perceptive writing on the subject of technology has been in German and French, I will attempt to follow English pattern of use for terms like "technology" and "technique." To do otherwise would only lead to confusion in a book written in English.

As the word is commonly used in English, "technology" includes a rather wide variety of human actions and of artifacts that are the result of such action. When we wish to talk about the accumulated mass of technological products, excluding the processes, we can use the term *technomass,* much as *biomass* is used for the total living tissue in a system. In addition to covering the technomass, *technology* also includes the techniques of using tools, methodologies for organizing complex processes involving tools, and even the associated techniques for manipulating persons as if they were tools. It thus incorporates tool-making and design, all of the manufactured products of human industry and all of the works of engineering and construction—projects such as houses, roads, breakwaters, artificial reservoirs, and the like.

All of these usages of the term *technology* cover both the

processes of modifying our environment, and the artifacts that are the results of those processes. Technology thus covers, in the way I use the term, all of the physical and operational aspects of the output-facilitation side of our *Zwischenwelt*—all but the purely intellectual or symbolic side of that great zone of cultural activities that we use to mediate our relationships with our environment. I will try to use the word technology consistently in that sense.

In my usage, technology need not be "practical" or of value. It is a fact, a neutral concept. This differs from dictionaries that define technology as "a technical method of achieving a practical purpose" or "the totality of the means employed to provide objects necessary for human sustenance and comfort."[12] It also differs from John Kenneth Galbraith's definition of technology in *The New Industrial State* as "the systematic application of scientific or other organized knowledge to practical tasks."[13] If we prejudge technology as "practical," we are forced to artificial conclusions that are far from proven.

Some uses of the terms *science* and *art* overlap common usages of the term *technology*. We should try, however, to make a systematic distinction.[14]

Science—at least that which is called "pure science"—aims at systematizing our understandings of the environment. It relates to the intellectual and symbolic aspect of the *Zwischenwelt*. A "scientific discovery" creates a new "cultural set" in the minds of those who accept it. It conditions the inner world of the "knower" by the creation of concepts. Such a discovery involves finding new patterns of causal or other relationships. Science, although a form of cultural activity, relies upon our analysis-systems, and in turn sharpens or "tunes" them with new expectations so that they can be more effective for predicting events and manipulating the environment generally. It becomes then part of an input-facilitation system.

In its contemporary sense, the term *science* is usually used to refer to the results of a very specific, intellectualized methodology, the experimental or "scientific" method, rather than to information-gathering in general. The term is also commonly applied to the body of data in symbolic form that has been amassed by that methodology: research papers, formula, and the like.

Science attempts to create a matrix of symbols that reflect the reality of our environment as accurately as possible. A great deal of scientific activity involves the manipulation of features of the environment in such a way as to validate and to extend parts of that system of symbols; this is the experimental method. As dramatized in the works of Thomas Kuhn, however, the history of science is more than a record of accrued information being added to that already known.[15] It is marked by "scientific revolutions," where existing paradigms are rejected or modified by new paradigms. The rejection of a long-held concept is often one of the most productive events in scientific activity.

The term *applied science* is sometimes used as if identical with *technology,* especially when describing the design of improved and more economical production methods or the planning of new types of engineering and construction projects. To maintain a clearer distinction between the terms science and technology, however, I restrict the term *applied science* to the use of the experimental method in order to gather detailed information needed to make decisions in pursuit of clearly formulated and immediate objectives (e.g., a series of tests required to design a switch for a certain instrument to be put aboard a spacecraft). Hit-and-miss methods worked out during the process of production, particularly during repetitive production such as that on an assembly line, remain in the province of technology.

In practice, the distinction between *applied science* and *technology* is often reflected in terms of the professional background of the persons involved. *Applied science* is tagged onto the work of fully qualified scientists who are employed in industry or otherwise targeted in their research toward well-defined economic goals; *technology* is more often applied to the work of craftsmen, engineers, foremen, production teams, and the like. In reality, however, the distinction should not be made in terms of "who does it" but rather in terms of "what is done." Like pure science and even applied science, the technological process leads also to an increase of human knowledge, although that knowledge is more likely to be transmitted by word of mouth or by example rather than through a formal reporting system such as that of modern science.[16]

The term *art* is presently used in the English language in many confusing ways. Sometimes it is roughly employed to mean *technology*, e.g., "the art of motorcycle repair." Very occasionally the term *art* is extended to cover the sciences as well.

I believe, however, that the term *art* will be both a clearer and a more useful concept in our discussion here if we restrict it to a certain type of technology, that which can have a positive emotional effect of some type on those who experience the action or object created. This positive effect is what is sometimes called the "aesthetic effect." It assumes there is a "sense of beauty," a human tendency to react in a positive way toward certain shapes, motions, and the like. Art then can be defined as that part of culture which creates artifacts or actions (e.g., the dance) which are designed to produce this aesthetic effect.

The analysis-systems that we have seen to constitute a major aspect of human nature play a large role in the sense of beauty. Nothing mystic need be assumed. The physiological basis of the aesthetic response is shown by the fact that certain drugs can artificially activate the pleasure centers involved.

Analysis-systems evolved during the hominid period govern the way in which we respond toward the flow of incoming sensory data and how we reduce it to comprehensible patterns. Art requires the perception and exploitation of these patterns. Just as humans enjoy exercising their physical capabilities in sport, they enjoy exercising their perceptual and analytical abilities in art. By manipulating variables within the various analysis-systems, the artist creates feelings of emotion. The tempo of music represents pattern-making in time. The dance involves creating patterns by bodily motion. Painting (and artistic photography) requires the establishing of patterns between entities or the basic shapes that form those entities. Literature involves the abstraction of pattern from the chaos of individual experience and its controlled exploitation for emotional effect.

Art obviously has close ties to play. That kind of pride in one's personal creativity, often called "self-expression," is also a major factor in the appeal of art as an activity. Art thus differs from the other forms of technology in that, while all are designed to modify our *outer* world, art is designed to impact upon our *inner* world in a very specific and positive way.

The term *art,* like the larger term *technology,* can refer not only to processes and techniques, but also to the products of those processes and techniques, as when we talk of an "exhibition of Oceanic art." In the way I define the term, *art* should not, however, be used as a synonym for "skill" or "advanced technique." I also believe it would be misleading to treat art as if it were somehow contrasted with science or part of a dichotomy between emotion and intellect. Both art and science require the whole person. On one side, art demands a high level of intellect; on the other, many a scientist has described the strong aesthetic pleasure that he has felt from discovering a "beautifully simple" hypothesis to explain a variety of phenomena under study. Both art and science are deeply involved in the same processes of pattern finding.

A distinction can be made between *pure art* and *applied art,* following to a degree that between pure and applied science. Pure art would encompass artistic activity that seeks only aesthetic objectives. Music, oil painting, and the like would normally be examples of pure art. Applied art would include the design of utilitarian objects and much of what is considered architecture. The purpose of an artifact created by pure art would be its effect on the *Innenwelt.* The purpose of an artifact that was the result of applied art would be to modify the *Umwelt* as well. Oil paintings, novels, or even musical compositions that are designed to teach, exhort, or otherwise serve a political or social purpose could be considered in a narrow sense as not *pure* art. The line, like that between pure and applied science, is hard to draw sharply.

In the last several chapters we have seen that technology is not something new, a skill developed by industrialism during the modern period. It is as old as humanity, even older; there were tool-making hominids before *Homo.* It is not some kind of alien force, but one that arises from our inner nature, from the manner in which we manipulate objects in our minds, the way we interrelate them in terms of cause and effect and the like. It has deep roots in the mammalian tendencies to play and to be curious; many inventions are the result of a strong desire to "see if it will work." It reflects, also, the kind of creative planning that was required in hunting big game—the way of life that our precursors lived during the era when our species took its present form.

Like the first lungfish moving out onto the land, we face new opportunities as well as new dangers. Old understandings, old habits, will not be good enough in the centuries ahead. The fact that the contemporary industrial world is a human creation does not make any simpler the problem of adjustment and orientation faced by the individual or by our species as a whole.

For good or bad, we have emerged into a new and strange world. Can we survive the secondary effects of life in a man-made world long enough to adjust to it? Or are we, in frustration and despair, likely to destroy ourselves before we can do so? Are we already entrapped by our technologies?

11
How the Trap
Could Spring

It is easy to admit that the breakdown of the relationship between our species and the environment could, over the long term, create threats to our continued survival. But precisely how, in what time-frame, and in what manner would so dire a threat arise? What would trigger an ultimate crisis?

Most works being published today on human ecology tend to frame the threat to *Homo sapiens* in terms that are comparable to those which have been faced by other species. We are described as an "endangered species," one that could gradually become extinct because of disregard for maintaining the physical quality of our environment. We are seen as using too many pesticides or other poisons, upsetting our biological relationship with other species, "fouling the nest" with our own pollutants, changing the composition of the atmosphere with activities like the burning of fossil fuels or supersonic travel, and ignoring the balance between available resources and population.[1]

In the chapters above, however, we have seen that the point of the arrow that is aimed at our species is directed toward our most vital and most vulnerable point, the organ that makes us so different from other species. The arrow is aimed not at our lungs, not at our bloodstream. It is aimed at the head, at the brain, the one truly specialized organ of our species. In the structure of this brain reside the traces of a long evolutionary history—the structural result of ages of successful interaction of what-was-to-become-man with a variety of environments. Here resides our patterns of perception and of thought, analysis-systems that form the basis of what we call "human rationality." Here resides the organ that has created the complex patterns of indirect interaction with the environment that we call modern technology.

Technology is very much part of our nature, but that does not necessarily mean that its effects are completely benign. Nor does it even mean that we have full control of our technologies. There are those who believe that, as a result of something programmed into our systems, we are ruled by a sort of "technological imperative"—that once we develop the ability to create a certain technology or device, we are compelled by our nature to develop it and to use it, even if only to find out whether it will work. Exploration of the moon has even been justified on the grounds that we "had to do it" because we knew we "could do it."

A "technological imperative" of this type would represent the ultimate development of such drives as curiosity and diversive exploration. If uncontrolled, if unchecked in any way, almost any human drive is capable of becoming destructive. The biological value of curiosity, although particularly significant among the younger mammals as we have seen, has always required restraint. If we look at young mammals, we see both natural fears and the warnings of their mothers or other pack members pulling them back from the brink of dangerous activities or explorations. If it were not so, too many of the young would perish.

If we as a species have developed a drive toward the creation of technologies which is so strong that it cannot be restrained by other aspects of our goal-directed behavior, then we are in serious trouble. The existence of a "technological imperative," in the most absolute sense of the concept, would inevitably doom us as a species. It is obvious that many possible technologies are already available that could lead to human extinction.

To avoid such a fate we must be able to exercise the needed restraint. We must also be able to refrain from actions when we have insufficient information on consequences. If we cannot do so, we are a biological freak—a monstrosity—and will not long endure.

Whether our tendency to create technologies is the result of a dangerous overspecialization of certain aspects of our complex brain structure is not yet clear. By lateralization and other novelties of brain development we may have set in process a train of events that will prove our undoing. If that is to happen, war will probably play the major role during the final act.

The first nuclear explosion was the sum of generations of carefully conducted and carefully recorded human cultural activity. Countless physical tools and symbolic concepts had to be developed and integrated into the functional circle of our interaction with the world about us before such an explosion could be brought about. This does not, however, guarantee that the resultant abilities to exploit nuclear power will necessarily be used only rationally in the future. Far from it, one of the greatest immediate dangers to the species is that they may not.

Why, however, should there be danger that the fruits of human rationality will now be put to irrational use? I see two basic reasons for this danger. Both are of the nature of "second-order consequences." There are: 1) social frustrations created by our technologies that have undermined confidence in rational action, and 2) the fact that technological power can today be so easily concentrated in the hands of individuals and small groups.

Our highly technological, man-made environment puts several types of pressure on its subjects that could contribute to irrational decisions by nations or leadership elites. To begin with, there are the stresses of crowding, These are worse than global population statistics would indicate, since the move from the land to the cities is creating a rise in urban populations that is much steeper than that of the total population. Whether or not we accept that *Homo sapiens* is a "territorial animal," we do know that increased population densities can create tensions both within groups and between them. We know from our zoos that if we put too many animals into too little space they will not all survive. Deaths may be the result of intragroup conflict or other forms of social disorganization, not just of starvation or other shortages of needed resources.

Another basic tension in our world is the very rate of change. This tends to unsettle a variety of factors. Every year finds more people leading lives that are yet further from that which mankind lived in the ancient middle realm. Although the rate of change in our society is accelerating rapidly, the ability of individuals to accommodate to change cannot accelerate at the same pace. All peoples have a heavy streak of conservatism in their culture, and they will readily fight for what they believe to be their traditional rights and their traditional ways of life. Too much change tends to overwhelm human beings and leave them without the standards of conduct or the systems of expectation and prediction that they need for the daily conduct of life.[2]

Change also creates problems because it is not uniform in its impact. For many groups the "progress" of the world has seemingly passed them by. This is the concern of the less developed parts of the world; it is growingly the problem of traditional rural society as well. The populations of such areas increasingly feel that they are contributing their resources to the modern technological world and are reaping many of its disadvantages, but that they are not sharing fully its benefits. Thus there are many areas of the world that are key to the total functioning of the contemporary technological world but which do not feel any sense of loyalty toward or participation in that world. This is, of course, a dangerous situation. To borrow a phrase from Toynbee, the populations of such areas represent the "external proletariat" of our modern technological society. With sufficient levels of frustration, the aspiring leaders of such excluded groups will turn to increasingly desperate lines of action.

The mobility of the individual in our growingly impersonalized society makes today's citizen a homeless creature compared to our ancestors of only a hundred years ago. Old moral restraints on action are often removed before new ones are developed to replace them. The institutions on which traditional societies had depended are weighed in the balance of technological efficiency and relevance and often found lacking by our social commentators; but new institutions take a long time to develop. Institutional collapse is a danger that is surpassed in its immediacy only by global war.

Intragroup conflict becomes a threat wherever common institutions and basic values are not shared. Where change is sufficiently rapid, two generations of the same family may end up accepting totally different value systems. All of these factors of social instability weaken consensus, increase the possibilities for aggressive behavior, and make rational decision-making more difficult for the society in question.

During the last two centuries or so, rationality as a concept has come under heavy fire. There were two directions of attack upon the concept of rationality that had characterized the Enlightenment. First, there was the theoretical. The clarification by modern science of some of the limitations of human understanding brought a degree of intellectual disorientation. Einstein's Theory of Relativity was, for example, generalized into a new folk view that "all was relative." Heisenberg's Uncertainty Principle was popularized to imply that "all was uncertain." Space, time, causation—even matter—all seemed to become unreal under the critical scrutiny of science. The logic of our middle realm seemed discredited by new discoveries.

Secondly, but concurrently, there began a practical attack on the idea that people operate on the basis of rational patterns. This was expressed in the nineteenth century by that era's characteristic glorification of "heart over brain," a movement that in many ways represented a reaction to the new industrial environment. In the twentieth century, the mood darkened. Freud and his successors were widely interpreted as having shown for all time that mankind is driven by irrational forces. The phenomenon of two world wars, and particularly the fact that large populations could be rallied behind the policies by someone like Hitler, made this view of human nature seem quite credible.

Lack of confidence in the rationality of others carries heavy implications for one's own actions. Expectation of irrationality in the responses of other nations is bound to lead to increased fears in the international community and could even lead to a readiness to "think the unthinkable" about the need to take preemptive military actions. A high enough level of fear could also encourage those actions that might be interpreted by other nations as preparing the way for preemptive strikes.

Amidst the rapidly changing political and economic environments of the late nineteenth and early twentieth century, dogmatic ideological views of the world had already become popular. Cut adrift from the traditional authoritarianism of rural family life, many urbanized individuals sought new authoritarian groups in which to submerge their identities. Within the more dogmatic of such movements, intellectual debate was waged not with rational arguments of the type that characterized ancient Athens or the Enlightenment but in a spirit closer to the late Middle Ages, replete with bodies of doctrine that were beyond questioning and with cries of heresy followed by excommunication from the movement. In some cases, where the power was available, a new "Inquisition" was instigated.

The attraction of the dogmatic, ideological approach to solving problems continues to be one of the greatest threats to rational processes in the world today. It will continue to be attractive as long as we are as seriously out of harmony with the world about us as has been the case since the coming of industrialism. Some see in modern technology itself not only the power but also the propensity to submerge the individual in a system that is basically dehumanizing. Marcuse argues that individual freedoms are in the processes of being destroyed in all areas of human activity by the very demands of technological-industrial production, and that the mass media made possible by technology operate to mask this new tyranny by creating the illusion of continued freedom.[3]

Even our better systems of transportation can be seen as a potential threat to the well-being of the species. No community is really isolated anymore. But that also means that there is no place to hide anymore. Although our technologies allow for the rapid shipments of relief supplies to areas of disaster, they also make arms control more difficult. The most rapid means of transport, rocketry, is reserved almost solely for potential use in the delivery of weapons of destruction upon other nations. Today countries can attack each other across wide expanses which had in the past insulated them to a very real extent from each other.

The vastly more efficient communication systems of our technological world also carry new dangers along with the obvious advantages that they bring the species. While possibilities for intercommunication are increased, so are the possibilities for frictions between groups. The statement of a national leader intended for a primarily domestic audience, may reverberate in hours around the world with a variety of interpretations and misinterpretations supplied.

ARE WARS "INEVITABLE"?

The idea that we are driven to war by something in our nature is not a new one. Its most eloquent expression in this century was published in 1911 by a German general, Friedrich von Benhardi, and entitled *Germany and the Next War*. The book, which attained a wide audience throughout Europe, concluded that "war is a biological necessity" and that anyone who has studied biology should see that "war is a universal law of Nature." In the words of Benito Mussolini, written for the *Italian Encyclopedia*: "War alone brings up to its highest tension all human energy and puts the stamp of nobility upon the peoples who have the courage to face it." The social sciences have generally rejected such notions, but we must admit that we have little scientific information on the factors that lead to wars. And any historian can show us that warfare has been part and parcel of human activity throughout the entire period for which we have any record.

The historical record is also the record of agriculturalism. The thesis could be made that warfare as a human institution may be a second-order consequence of the agricultural revolution. *Homo sapiens* had developed as a hunter-gatherer species, with the two activities somewhat separated between the males and females in accord with biologically evolved patterns of sexual dimorphism. Agriculture destroyed the natural pattern, and denied the males the needed experiences of the hunting band. Young males in drudgery-ridden agricultural communities would thus become, the logic goes, natural recruits for the kind of activity in which the first armies engaged. Under such a thesis, war could be seen as a sort of substitute for the hunt, filling a needed social and psychological role for certain males that was otherwise lacking in the sedentary farming environment.

One factor not well explained by such a theory is that of "aggression." If war is simply a displacement of a need for hunting activity, it should be conducted with a sort of natural enthusiasm and not with anger or hate. The predator-prey relationship is not marked by the latter emotions. It is not a type of "aggression" at all. How then does "aggression" enter the picture? Despite the able work of the ethologists, we still know little of the biology of aggression.[4]

The hypothesis that "aggression is always a consequence of frustration," was advanced by the psychologist Dollard and his associates in 1939, but was rather quickly rejected by the scientific community.[5] More recent psychological studies are less dogmatic and stress the importance of a variety of "noxious stimuli" that often lead to aggressive action. In some cases, an aggressive attack may result when there has been neither frustration nor any "noxious stimulus." Attack may be a learned response and occur simply because it has led to rewards in the past.[6] Wars can be viewed as resulting not only from desperation but also from temptation and thus as resembling more closely the predator-prey relationship. The very riches of early agricultural regions and later cities were an invitation to nomadic marauders living at a much lower standard of living but able to engage in warfare effectively. They were also a temptation to better organized agricultural communities in the area. Simple words like "greed" and "envy" may still help us understand a good deal of the conflict in our world.

Scientists continue to argue about the nature of war and its relationship to human aggression. Some still consider both war and aggression to be negative responses to adverse environmental conditions, although not in the absolute terms that were asserted by Dollard. According to the zoologist John Crook, the literature of today's experimental ethology shows that aggressive behavior, instead of resulting from some innate or ineradicable force that demands repetitive expression, "occurs normally as a response to particular aversive stimuli and ceases upon their removal." Crook asserts that the history of aggression in modern man "may thus be attributed to aversive features in the complex overcrowded, overcompetitive, overstratified social world in which he lives rather than to some unsatisfied vital urge."[7]

We may be dealing in part with a problem of definitions. One of the advocates of "aggression" as a natural human trait, Anthony Storr, declares at one point that human aggression is much more than a simple response by the individual to frustration: "it is an attempt to assert himself as an individual, to separate himself from the herd, to find his own identity." Storr states that his own experience leads him to the view that "aggression only becomes really dangerous when it is suppressed or disowned. The man who is able to assert himself is seldom vicious; it is the weak who are most likely to stab one in the back."[8] I feel it is clear from such comments that many who talk about a natural human tendency called "aggression" are really thinking in terms of "self-assertiveness."

It might be argued that it makes no difference what terminology is chosen as long as it is consistently used. But here lies the problem. The word "aggression" has often been given more than one meaning by those writing on the subject. Sometimes it is used to mean a personal emotion, and at other times, marching armies. There is a real difference of connotation if we allow the term "aggression" instead of, say, "self-assertiveness" to stand for the more personal emotion or attitude. It sounds logical, for example, to assert that "Since man is by nature *aggressive*, wars will never cease." It is less convincing to assert: "Since man is by nature *self-assertive,* wars will never cease." The illogical jump from personal psychology to political phenomenon becomes apparent in the latter formulation.

Now, I believe that, if we are to talk of individual human drives, it would be safer to say that *Homo sapiens* is characterized by "self-assertiveness" than to make the same statement about "aggressiveness." But even here there remains a problem. Not all human beings evidence self-assertiveness to the same degree. In our culture at least, males have been conditioned to evidence more assertiveness than females. There may even be some physiological basis to this difference. Even among males, it could be said that only the more "dominant males" evidence the trait clearly. How the trait comes out in behavior also varies sharply from culture to culture. It becomes exceedingly difficult to sort the influences of human nature from those of social conditioning.

Nevertheless, I do believe a substratum of a common human heritage can be seen operative here. Several kinds of evidence can be cited. First, self-assertiveness is a basic drive to be found in all cultures, and especially among leaders. Moreover, certain types of brain damage seem to affect the level of an individual's self-assertiveness, suggesting that the drive has a physiological basis in our cerebral structure. Self-assertiveness also tends to be manifested in children (albeit at a diffused level) in accordance with a relatively predictable maturational schedule, a fact that strengthens the supposition that it has a physiological basis.

If it is true that there have always been wars and always will be wars since humankind is by nature highly aggressive, then our species is doomed. There can be no other conclusion. We are too clever in our tool-making (weapons especially) to be able to afford being so violent in our social relations. If, on the other hand, war represents a distorted replacement of certain hunting drives, there may yet be hope that by creating better social conditions we can in turn displace war as a human activity. Only history can prove or disprove the thesis of the inevitability of war.

I personally believe that wars have been characteristically fought as a means to some foreseen advantage, whether real or imaginary. If this is true, one cannot say that wars have been *ipso facto* irrational, based on deep emotional drives toward violence. It may be highly immoral for a bank official to attempt to embezzle a million dollars, but it is not inherently irrational if he has reason to believe that he can get away with it. A great deal of human warfare may have been the result of the pursuit of similarly perceived advantages by those who instigated the wars involved. Although not flattering to humanity, there is some ground for optimism in this fact.

Wars in the twentieth century do not, however, have much of a rational look to them. In the first place, the states initiating international conflict have as often as not come out the losers. This suggests that wars in the twentieth century have often been the result of fear rather than of simple hope for conquest. This atmosphere has been the result, I believe, of the stresses and insecurities of rapidly changing times. In a world free of the extremes of fear, there would be greatly increased hope for lasting peace.

The question of whether war can be avoided in the future is a broader one than whether war is the result of human aggressive drives, drives which make it inevitable. Even if we reject the idea of such drives, we may have to accept the likelihood of war for other reasons. Surely during much of human history warfare has played a role in social change, the mobility of populations, the expansion of trade, and even the spread of religions and other value systems. To avoid war, our society will have to find other ways to accomplish certain types of change. Given the level of our destructive technological skills, warfare has become too dangerous to be engaged in simply because it is an effective catalyst for change.

LOW-TECHNOLOGY WARS?

The question has been raised from time to time: Can we somehow limit future wars so that they will not pose a threat to human survival? Two basic approaches have been advanced. One would exclude specific types of known weapons from those to be used, but leave the rules otherwise open to innovation. The second approach would go much further and ritualize warfare into set patterns that would not allow for variation. A model of the first approach is the restraint in the use of poison gas during World War II. A model of the second is the patterned conduct of certain wars in certain eras like the European Middle Ages.

Unfortunately, both models have their limitations. During World War II, both sides were prepared to defend themselves from gas attack and to retaliate in kind. That neither side initiated the use of gas may well have been the concern of each that it might suffer the most from such an escalation. If there are to be countless future wars, it would be rash to assume that gas will never again be used—and used it probably will be as soon as one protagonist sees sufficient unilateral advantage to be gained from its use. There were some who had hoped after World War I that future wars would never again involve air attacks, at least on civilian populations. Yet Hitler did not hesitate to place great reliance on the dive bomber as an attack weapon in his earliest blitzkriegs. Nor was there much hesitance in using even so indiscriminate a weapon as the atom bomb when it was seen as an "efficient" way to end the war in the Pacific. There will always be a tendency to use readily available weapons when the advantage seems clear enough.

This does not mean that there may not be weapons that will go unused. The danger of bacteriological weapons to both sides may prevent their use. Neither side would see advantage in spreading forms of disease that might ultimately infect itself as well. But the principle in control remains that of perceived advantage—not restraint in the use of modern technology for the purposes of war.

Nor does this mean that nuclear weapons may not be used in some future war between powers so armed. Balanced deterrence may, of course, prevent their use. But if that balance were broken by means of other forms of warfare and one power felt it could use nuclear weapons with impunity, the risk of their use would rise sharply. The decision, once again, would more likely be made on the basis of immediate advantage rather than the long-term interests of humanity.

The idea of replacing all-out war with a safer and more ritual form of conflict is an ancient one. The Olympic games of ancient Greece represented an extreme form of the idea. Sport is obviously one of the activities that might be used to displace certain drives that find an outlet in war, whether based on ancient hunting drives or other human needs for adventure and physical contest.

The Geneva Convention did not go nearly as far in the process of displacing war, only attempting to humanize its practice to some degree. The claim is sometimes made that during certain eras, such as the feudal period in Europe, wars were fought within a code of conduct that restricted the bloodshed. The image is one of chivalrous knights jousting in accord with rigorous standards of conduct, of armies meeting in the field in set formation to fight at prearranged hours.

It would be pleasant to believe that such precedents might lead to patterns of restrained warfare in the future, but one does not have to go so far as to accept the concept of a "technological imperative" to believe that restraint would be most unlikely in any war that threatened the existence of any state. Anthropological studies of warfare are rare, but one recent study of three oceanic societies seems to indicate the existence of several distinct phases of warfare in that area.[9] The least violent forms had many ritual connotations and might well be conducted within set norms and without great loss of life. But if either side discerned significant weaknesses on the part of the enemy, there was a tendency for the war to escalate and the rules of conduct to become more violent. Genocide was a possible outcome of a clear victory in the third state. Not a very reassuring pattern.

There are some who believe that the very fact that awesome technologies are available for war will most likely be the factor forcing mankind to find other solutions for conflict of interest. In an era long before atom bombs and ICBM's, Thomas Edison prophesied: "There will one day spring from the brain of science a machine of force so fearsome in its potentialities, so absolutely terrifying, that even man . . . will be appalled and so abandon war forever." We can only hope that future leaders will live up to Edison's expectations.

Stress and the Roots of Conflict

Even if war is not something that is the inevitable result of human nature, there can be no question but that the consistent blocking of the natural self-assertiveness and self-realization of any social group will tend to prod it to desperate action. Given the dangerous technologies loose in our world, this is a situation that we should attempt to forestall whenever possible.

According to the philosopher Glenn Gray, "A happy person will never—or almost never—give way to the destructive passions of rage and resentment. On the other hand, the unhappiness that arises from the frustration of action and consequently thwarted self-realization and deprivation of freedom is nearly bound to be violent."[10] Similar theses have also been advanced by numerous psychologists, psychiatrists and historians.

Toynbee underlined the alienation of the "machine-tender" in our technological world. Noting the fascination of hunting and fishing and even the pleasure and mental stimulus involved in farming, he added, "Such pleasures are denied to the factory worker whose job is to repeat the same streamline motions, any number of times over, as any number of specimens of the same standardized part of some machine pass before him on a conveyor-belt." From this, Toynbee concluded that it is "not surprising that the bored factory-worker's 'recreation' in his leisure hours sometimes takes the form of anti-social violence and destructiveness." This is the machine-tender's "revenge on society for an injury. . . . In mechanizing his work, society has made the salt of his life lose its savour for him."[11] This type of alienated citizen can, of course, pose a major threat to the entire technological system, as interdependent as it all is.

The sources of social unrest are also the seedbeds of war. The stress of daily life, the frustrations of an unpredictable environment, fears caused by personal insecurity, the outrage of perceived injustices and inequalities—all these set the stage for the rise of leaders who would be willing to take the chances involved in war.

Economic and social collapse of the modern technological world has been predicted by some. Roberto Vacca, for example, has postulated that the present systems of human organization and association have been outgrowing ordered control and are nearing a critical degree of instability.[12] There are surely great instabilities in the present situation, but, in my opinion, a "breakdown" is not as likely to dissolve the very fiber of the industrial world as it is likely to pit parts of the world against each other in deadly conflict. Local breakdowns are more likely to appear in specific countries than there is likely to be a simultaneous collapse of the techno-industrial system throughout the world. These localized breakdowns could, of course, be most dangerous for all humanity by creating the kind of desperate circumstances that would make war seem a plausible option.

The nations with the greatest capacity for waging the kind of war that would threaten human survival are, of course, the major industrial nations. And these are precisely the nations that are most likely to be affected by social tensions resulting from the insecurities of an extremely rapidly changing environment. Only if rationality continues to rule within the leadership councils of each of those industrial nations, can the danger of eventual nuclear war be avoided. With the spread of industrialization and the proliferation of nuclear power, the danger of an irrational decision can only increase.

CRISIS LEADERSHIP AND DECISION-MAKING

John F. Kennedy, while president, gave his analysis of the threat of nuclear war in the following words: "Every man, woman, and child lives under a nuclear sword of Damocles hanging by the slenderest of threads, capable of being cut at any moment by accident or miscalculation or by madness." I have no reason to believe that Kennedy was attempting to exaggerate the gravity of the situation as he viewed it from a position of great responsibility as a leader.

As I stated earlier, two major dangers of the irrational use of weapons of mass destruction come from a breakdown of confidence in human rationality and the fact that modern technology allows increasing power over the destiny of the species to accumulate in the hands of a smaller number of individuals. Any individual human being is capable of going mad. It is most unlikely, however, that the majority of a group of twenty or a hundred decision-makers would suffer to the same degree and at once. Despite the phenomenon of mob psychology, there remains safety in numbers. Thus collective leadership can only be safer than one-man rule, even if it remains authoritarian in character.

Some will charge that there is no way of preventing some future madman or power-seeking nation from unleashing destructive forces of war and ultimately destroying the human race. There is surely no world government around the corner that will prevent it. Even if global controls were established, they could always break down into civil war between contending leadership groups. This is a depressing thought. If mankind is to survive, say, the next million years (not an unrealistic biological expectation in terms of the modest antiquity of *Homo sapiens*) there will be tens of thousands of future generations that must face the problems of government within the confines of planet Earth. It seems likely that vast technological power will be in human hands during most of that period. "Sooner or later," the pessimist will say, "someone will come along who will make a fatal decision for all mankind," and the cynic might add, "Probably sooner rather than later."

Dejection in the face of the long-term threat of irrational individual actions or miscalculations on the global scale overlooks one major factor: human societies are motivated by the will to survive. If people continue to evidence anything like the degree of ingenuity they have shown thus far, they may yet be able to devise social mechanisms that will prevent any one aberrant individual from destroying social groups or the entire species. The problem of preventing irrational action against the interests of the species by a larger group—whether a party, class, or nation—is a problem of another degree of magnitude.

The most difficult problem in terms of decision-making is not that of preventing irrational actions but that of knowing the implications of decisions that must be made. We have seen that the second-order consequences of technological changes are exceedingly difficult to predict. The fallacy which treats technology as if it were an extrahuman phenomenon with a force all of its own is probably the result of our perceptions of lack of control when past decisions continue to carry us in directions in which we did not plan to move. We begin to feel that we are victims of an abstract force we call "technology," and we forget that what we are being subjected to is no more than the unforeseen results of past human decisions which might have been modified or even not undertaken at all, if we had had sufficient information on second-order consequences. The ultimate danger is that a series of small but not easily reversible decisions will lead us into a situation from which there is no escape. We could discover, too late, that we are trapped in an unviable position, outside the boundaries of our ecological niche, as it were.

Under the impact of industrialism, the scale of human decision-making has greatly expanded, while at the same time there has been a great increase in the speed at which major decisions can be implemented. The complexity of our heavily technological society means that more and more decisions are taken by increasingly specialized technicians who are in no position to see all the implications that may be involved. The very pursuit of what appears the short-term efficiency of the system can lead to the results that are destructive to basic human goals.

Students of the decision-making process have recently gone so far as to talk about "the inefficiency of being efficient."[13] This is a somewhat poetic way of saying that true efficiency in decision-making may require that we not implement decisions too rapidly or too thoroughly when sufficient information is not readily available. Until it is, irreversible decisions can be exceedingly dangerous.

The most immediately identifiable danger to our species is, then, the continuing threat of large-scale war that might involve nuclear or other highly lethal weapons. This immediate danger is not going to be quickly lessened by any action to improve the total human environment. We can hope that present world leaders will have the needed restraint. But man will have to survive not only the next decade but the one following that, the next, and the next. We cannot project the international situation in the year 2000, much less 2050. We cannot even say which nations will be the major protagonists then or how many may be armed with weapons that could endanger the species. But a child born today has, medically speaking, a reasonable chance of living until 2050—and even beyond. It is not unrealistic for us to be directly concerned about the world of that year. Whether we can survive the challenges that will arise during the next full generation will depend on whether we can begin the process of recreating our world so that it will not be as deeply marred by stress, fear, and distrust as the world of the last generation. This can only be assured by reestablishing a better relationship between ourselves and our environment.

The necessity is even more stark if we are to consider the magnitude of dangers that may lurk for mankind in the year 2080 or 2180 if we do not begin the process of improving the human situation today. We must not view so distant a future as if it were someone else's problem. To the extent that we feel ourselves the better for people like Voltaire or Franklin who were active two hundred years ago, we must today feel ourselves responsible for preparing the way for those who will be here two hundred years from now.

The tendency of the last two hundred years has not only been toward increasing alienation in our relationships with our environment; personal insecurity has been increased by a lack of trust in the action of other human beings. This is not a context in which we can expect a high standard of rational decision-making, whether we are talking of the masses or of those in the positions of greatest power. Ills like panic, stress, insecurity, and fear can be communicated within a social group, creating the kind of mass hysteria that might be typified by mob action. They can also be evidenced in less extreme, but still dangerous, forms. It was from protracted group insecurity in Germany, particularly among certain social classes, that Hitler arose. This is the kind of cultural breakdown that we must seek to prevent.

STRAIGHT LINES AND CATASTROPHES

Discussion of the possibility of future trauma for the human race runs into criticism of several predictable types. There are those who will automatically characterize any concern for potential catastrophe as part of a "doomsday syndrome." They will often point to prior predictions of crises that did not materialize—as if they were proof that new predictions would not come to pass. There is no logic in such an approach. To begin with, human beings have only been predicting historical events for a few thousand years at the most. Even in that short time there have been many cases of institutional collapse—and there were some who saw the handwriting on the wall rather clearly in those cases. Civilizations, cities, whole cultures have been destroyed. Of course, there has been no crisis that has destroyed humanity—but if someone should be able to predict one successfully, the logic of the situation will allow for no postscripts on the accuracy of the prediction. So those who ask to be shown doomsday as a proof of the possibility of doomsday make no sense at all.

Some who are unwilling to address the possible dangers before mankind simply characterize them as unthinkable. There has always been a human race; there always will be. Somehow "man will prevail." The zoologist Kenneth E. F. Watt, in his book *The Titanic Effect,* has described what he considers a basic human tendency to ignore warnings about possible disasters that are enormous in scale.[14] If the good ship *Titanic* is unsinkable, what need for lifeboats or emergency drills?

Another common reaction to the discussion of possible

catastrophic events has to do with the time factor. There are those who assume that we will have adequate warning of any impending disaster well in advance of the danger and that we should be able to take appropriate corrective action in time. But what is "adequate warning?" Those who believe they detect the early warning signs of trouble may not have their analysis accepted. It may take the disaster itself to convince the most skeptical.

There is a strong tendency to view human events as if they move along an easily charted continuum. Terms like the "course of human events," the "flow of history," the "path of progress" tend to reinforce this perception. In reality, however, the world is full of sudden discontinuities. Some people incorrectly assume that a historical or social threshold can be treated as if it were, say, point 100 on a straight line marked off with a hundred-plus equally spaced points. According to this model, if point 100 involves danger, we should discover that fact at point 99, and pull back. Even if some momentum should carry us beyond the threshold to point 101, the degree of damage would only be 1 percent. Once a 1 percent correction were made, we would be back again to the zone of safety.

The world does not work that way, however. Many types of thresholds can be crossed in only one direction. Once over them, there is no return. Adding pressure to an eggshell will smash the egg; taking the pressure off will not put it back together again. Many other types of threshold can only be recrossed with great difficulty. A child can restack the house of blocks he has knocked down, but he will need longer to restack the blocks than it took him to knock them down.

In the last few years, mathematicians have addressed the phenomena of sudden change and developed a new discipline called "catastrophe theory." Using topological methods to conceptualize its principles, catastrophe theory has been used to analyze such disparate kinds of change as that of a dog from fear to attack, that of a crashing stock market, and that of a buckling construction beam.[15] Catastrophe theory can also provide a new way to conceptualize those discontinuous changes that are so common in social science, classifying them into examples of seven "elementary catastrophes," each with its own mathematical model. Whether or not one accepts all the mathematics involved, these models dramatize the fact that when we project change, we should think in terms of complex topographies replete with "falling-off places" rather than with straight roads on flat surfaces.

TRAPS AS MODELS OF OUR PREDICAMENT

By our dependence on technology, we have already entered into a cage-like trap, one from which we cannot easily emerge. We can, however, continue to thrive within its confines for the time being, and with some adjustments perhaps indefinitely. But within the trap there are also spring triggers which, if tripped, could destroy our species. These we must identify if we are to avoid the ultimate catastrophe.

The concept that we are threatened by the type of trap that could spring upon us is more than a convenient metaphor. It expresses reasonably well the idea that we are locked into lines of action that cannot be allowed to continue unchecked without peril to the species. It underlines the fact that we have within our technological capabilities a variety of means of destroying ourselves but over which we have not yet evolved adequate social control systems. High-technology war is only the neatest of such means. Whether the specific weapons are nuclear warheads, neutron bombs, or chemical agents makes little difference if the scale of use is large enough.

To lessen the threat of irrational action, we must try to establish a future ecological relationship between the various nations and peoples of the world and surroundings in which they live that will be healthier than the relationship that prevailed during the last century. A social group which finds its world interesting and pleasing, aesthetically as well as in terms of its material products, will identify with that world and is unlikely to take actions that would put it in jeopardy.

The 1978 mass murder and suicide at Jonestown, Guyana, provides a striking example of how irrational can be the actions of fearful and disoriented victims of the ills of our modern society.

Fear remains a major enemy of rational action, one that rivals ignorance of consequences in the dangers that it can create. I am not referring here to normal anxieties or concerns for day-to-day matters, but to that kind of overriding fear that can cause a herd of wild horses to plunge over a cliff. In the long term, the best way to assure that groups of men will not be subjected to destructive levels of fear would be by creation of a less stress-filled world, a world with which they have a more harmonious relationship.

As we use the image of a trap to illuminate our current relationship with technology, we must take care not to lead ourselves astray. Earlier chapters have amply demonstrated that technology is not something alien to our nature; it is not an outside force with the power to entrap us against our will. It is, instead, part of our very nature as human beings.

The trap in which we find ourselves as a species is one of our own making. Our precursors have willed it, step by step. The contours of our techno-industrial world were created by the countless actions of individual human beings, who were usually acting without conscious thought for the possible second-order consequences. They were acting in terms of what I have called "inner-zone primacy."

Thus, we have arrived quite naturally at where we are today. In this case "naturally" means "as would be expected, given the phylogenetic structures of our brains and sufficient time for our cultures to accumulate the data needed to support the current level of technological sophistication." The test ahead is whether our brains, and the social systems based upon them, will prove capable of coping with the technomass that we have created by eons of technological activity. The test, in a real sense, will be whether human nature is ultimately a viable thing, whether it reflects an approach to the environment that can long endure.

With our inner nature so key to our responses to the world about us, there are some who have asked whether we should not look into changing human nature rather than further modifying the outer world. We will look into that possibility in the chapter to follow.

Part Four

Can We Escape the Trap?

12
Can We Remake Man?

Are we, as a species, hopelessly out of step with our times? Having remade the world about us, must we now remake ourselves? Could we, for example, somehow redesign or reprogram ourselves to be less self-assertive and thereby increase the chances of avoiding the war and other turmoil that threaten the future of our species?

Organisms normally adapt themselves to their environment by a gradual series of evolutionary changes in their own makeup from generation to generation. As we discussed in chapter 3, when what-was-to-become-man left the forests for the plains, he set in motion a wide variety of adaptations to the new environment: bipedalism, nakedness, new eating habits, and a new way of looking at things, to mention only a few disparate aspects of the necessary change. These changes took, however, hundreds of thousands, if not millions, of years to accomplish.

It was only a comparatively few generations ago that our species made the next great leap and adopted a system that relied primarily on agriculture for food. As we discussed in chapter 8, this was a transformation of life-style that was as pregnant with implications for humanity as was the descent from the trees to the open ground or the change from a primarily vegetarian to a partially carnivorous way of life. In evolutionary terms, agriculture is a recent development. Perhaps ten thousand years have passed since the agricultural revolution began, and it was during the latter half of that period that the new system became widespread. The second major man-made change, the industrial revolution, has but two or three hundred years of history and is only now beginning to affect many areas of the world. In only the last two decades, the second industrial revolution has hit the technologically most advanced nations, adding a whole new dimension of change.

Present rates of human population growth will require that we adjust relatively rapidly to these new and increasingly complex ways of life. We must do so before the forces of disorganization and conflict overtake the new system, and threaten it—and perhaps the species that created it—with catastrophe. As we discussed in chapter 11, war is probably the most immediate danger, and general institutional collapse the second, but these are by no means the only forms the threat could take. Obviously, we must explore all options that would make humanity more secure.

Rapid adjustment of our species to new environmental factors and challenges will require, some specialists think, nothing less than the remaking of our physical structure. The logic is that our species, having remade its environment, must now use its ingenuity to "remake" its own nature and thus to adjust more properly to its chosen surroundings. In this chapter, we will explore the possibilities of "remaking" *Homo sapiens* by several means: by surgery, through chemical changes in the body induced by drugs, or by artificial stimulation of the rate or direction of genetic change. The result in each case would be the same: creation of a new or modified human nature. We will want to examine the implications of each for the onward survival of our species.

RESTRUCTURING OUR ANATOMIES

The most direct method that has been proposed by which we could consciously speed our bodily adaptation to new or changed environments would involve artificially altering human anatomy. Several possibilities have been suggested by which we might make a new form of human out of the old. These include inserting various types of mechanical devices into the human body or otherwise altering the anatomy by surgery. (An even more basic approach, the surgical restructuring of the genetic makeup of the fertilized human egg cell so that it would develop a revised human organism will be discussed later in this chapter.) Any of these methods would make possible a much faster rate of change than would be likely to result from the traditional drift of evolution. They would also be much more open to conscious control, i.e., to systematic planning to meet identified needs.

Dr. Manfred Clynes has coined the term cyborg—an abbreviation for *cybernetic organism*—to describe a being made up of a living organism and one or more mechanical devices. In the widest sense, a man with an artificial hand, or even a person wearing glasses, could be called a sort of cyborg. But such tame examples are not what I am talking about here. The same methods that now allow us to equip a person with an artificial hand could be used to create people with physical abilities quite different from those that anyone now has, while operations on the human neural and/or glandular system could be used to alter behavior, to make a person who is less "aggressive" and more placid, for example.

Relying on already developed methods of plastic surgery, a human being could be surgically reorganized for space travel over great distances. With further development of techniques, an astronaut's digestive system could be removed (or bypassed) and replaced with a much more efficient system based on intravenous feeding. Various special-purpose limbs could be designed for space voyagers, replaceable in universal sockets much as artificial limbs can be attached today.

Though the very idea may seem to most of us today to require unnecessary "mutilations" of the human body, certain problems encountered in the new environment of space may encourage us to create cyborgs of some type if we intend to probe far. The ultimate in bodily change would be to discard the entire outer form of earthling *Homo sapiens* and to transplant a human brain into an entirely redesigned body.[1] There could even be specialized interchangeable bodies—of a mechanical nature—for extreme conditions of heat or radiation, greater gravitational pull, weightlessness, and the like. A human brain could thus select a body appropriate to the un-Earthly environment to be entered, much as we choose our clothes to meet the expected weather conditions of the day.

The sensory apparatus of a cyborg could also be made much more sensitive than that of the average person today, and replaceable parts could be designed to provide the cyborg with, say, telescopic or microscopic vision. Whether the human brain could be artificially altered in order to think better, or to operate in a way more in keeping with modern needs, is another question, and one on which we have little data. The idea of artificial limbs seems to me, however, a quite unnecessary refinement. The human hand is already a sort of "universal socket" that can manipulate a wide variety of specialized tools without having to suffer surgical modification.

Surgical possibilities for altering human nature are not limited to changing the mechanics of limbs or extending the range of sensory capacities. The same means can obviously be used to alter at least certain aspects of behavior, by modifying either our neural or glandular systems. Of the possibilities of the first, little is presently known, although we do have ample evidence that radical changes of personality can be effected by frontal lobotomy.[2] Presumably, as our knowledge of the workings of the brain increases, we may find more subtle ways of altering the human personality by brain surgery. Thus far, such methods appear to hold promise only as a drastic means with which to deal with the effects of organic disease or insanity. With universal frontal lobotomy the danger of war would surely diminish, for the effect is to make the subject more placid. Ironically, the same operation would remove the drive necessary to sustain a techno-industrial civilization. A culture demanding such surgery could not even be self-sustained, for a complex medical technology of the nature required to perform so many operations of such sophistication could not be maintained in a world inhabited only by persons with as little drive as those who have had a frontal lobotomy.

Electrical manipulation of the brain can accomplish some of the same effects of brain surgery. "Pleasure centers" have been turned on in humans by such means. Bulls have even been "tamed" by the push of a button. One author has coined the term *electro-sociology* to describe the potential science of the electronic control of patterns of social interaction.[3]

Given the present state of our skills, operations on the human neural system are likely to remain very expensive for a long time and to be insufficiently predictable to hold out much hope for helping the species as a whole to readjust itself to the world about it. The same is probably true of electronic manipulation of our brains by means not involving surgery. Even more important, this type of approach is most likely to be limited by its very nature to removing or blocking some aspect of human mentality. It is unlikely to open the way for any substantial improvement in human capabilities. What we would prefer is a better race, not a subhuman or semihuman one, but a superhuman one!

Alteration of human nature by the change of the glandular system poses much the same possibilities. It also faces somewhat similar limitations. Here there is some precedent. Several cultures traditionally created one form of "modified man" by castration. The eunuchs of the Chinese and Ottoman Empires were notable examples.

Is there not some hope here? In many ways it is the human males who seem to show the worst record for adjusting to civilized life. Could not some reduction in "masculinity" be at least a partial answer? Although castration is a relatively simple operation to perform—at least when compared to other possible methods of glandular modification—the eunuch system was never extended to more than an extremely small portion of any human population in any era. To extend it to most males would create significant second-order social consequences. More important, castration does not seem to affect many of the sex-linked characteristics. The strife-ridden history of the eunuch systems of China and the Middle East hardly recommends the idea to us today.

The restructuring of other glandular systems would involve much greater medical sophistication. Though a more placid race might be produced by, let us say, the systematic reduction of all thyroid glands, the attempt would in itself threaten our continued existence. The danger of inhibiting necessary human drives would probably be as great as any hope that such surgery might hold for creating people better designed to cope with the conditions of modern technology.

The real problem that stands in the way of using surgical means to modify people so that they would be better able to adjust to the demands of our technological world is not inadequate technique or even our ignorance of the likely effects of specific lines of action. It is a more philosophical one. Can a species, limited as each is to reflecting only its own evolutionary past, possibly design by its conscious acts a successor species (or subspecies) that would be superior to itself? In evolution it is long-term, successful interaction *with the environment* that shows the profitable direction for change. The input of information involved during such millennia-long processes is vast beyond comparison with all our accumulations of historical and scientific fact. Use of surgical means in the attempt to alter human nature quickly and radically would have to rely on what would be, in evolutionary terms, very scanty information. The decision/information ratio would be most alarming. We would simply be reduced to having to guess—and a wrong guess on so vital a matter could well further disturb the functional circle of our species and create a threat to our survival far greater than that which it was intended to meet. People would also find it much more difficult to accept the decisions of a planning authority in such matters as their bodily structure than they have in present areas of conscious planning for future adjustments like urban redevelopment and family planning.

CHEMICAL MODIFICATION OF HUMAN BEHAVIOR:
DRUGS AND MEDICINES

Surgical means are not the only ones that we could use to alter radically our relationship to the world about us by changing our nature. People can, for example, greatly modify the workings of their minds by introducing certain chemicals into their systems. Drugs are much quicker and easier to use than surgery. They also tend to be less frightening and their effect more easily reversed if necessary.

The chemical approach is not new. It has been used to varying degrees by many cultures in the past, particularly during eras of rapid cultural change. Narcotic drug addiction in China during the period when that nation came into traumatic contact with the Western world comes readily to mind. Another example would be the Ghost Dance Cult that arose among the Indians of the Western United States during the late nineteenth century—a cult based on eating the hallucinogenic peyote cactus.

The hope that is seemingly expressed in the use of LSD or the other hallucinogens today is much the same as that which prevailed in the Ghost Dance Cult, that drugs can bring us into a more sharply perceptive relationship with the inner realities of the world about us. This view appears to be based on the mystic idea that the human mind contains deep within it some type of secret power that only needs to be "unlocked" to be liberated. The chemical changes induced by the drug would then bring about this liberation and create a better or more perceptive mental state, perhaps allowing us to understand more of the total-environment or to relate to it more effectively. Such hopes have been shared by those in the medical profession, and are by no means to be found only among mystics. One expert on psychopharamacology has described such experimentation as "part of the most ancient and almost instinctive efforts by man to search for a new dimension of the human mind."[4]

Once again there is a serious flaw in our logic if we think we can "unlock" new powers of the mind by chemical means. I can see nothing in the manner that evolution operates that would give us any reason to expect that we or any other species has ever evolved, even temporarily, anything that could be called a "hidden power." There is every reason to assume that we evolved what powers we have on a day-by-day basis, under conditions of use that increased the chances of survival of our forebears over their less successful contemporaries. All logic indicates that without active and open use within a gradually altering functional circle, no new power would be developed; and that there could be no "hidden power" in any species awaiting release. Obviously, there may be powers or abilities that were developed and used by our forebears but that are blocked or inhibited at times by certain aspects of the modern world. That is, however, another question and would lead us in other directions in our search for solutions.

The effect of a drug of the nature of LSD is to make the human brain operate in a way that is markedly different from the way in which it was evolved to operate through countless generations of successful contact with the environment. On this basis alone, the overwhelming odds are that the widespread use of "consciousness-changing drugs" could only serve to alienate their users further from the realities of that world with which we are prepared to deal by our biological heritage. Use of the hallucinogens under scientifically controlled conditions may teach us much about the nature of our brains and thereby add to our surprisingly meager knowledge of this vital subject—but this is quite another consideration.

Recent interest in the hallucinogens is only one example of the long history of experimentation with the effect of chemical substances on the mind and body. In addition, there are the stimulants like coffee, tea, and tobacco that have long been used to sharpen human perceptions and awareness. With the opposite effect, there are the depressants, chemicals which lower the rate of muscular or nervous activity. The most common of these is, of course, alcohol. In recent years, a wide variety of additional drugs have been developed by medical science with more precise stimulant or depressant effects.

In terms of implications for contemporary man's adjustment to the modern industrial world, the tranquilizers are one of the more interesting types of substances recently developed to modify the workings of the mind. These substances, whose numbers and variety increase with every passing year, have been conclusively shown to be valuable in helping certain individuals to maintain their feelings of well-being and even their sanity under the strains imposed by the increased pace and complexity of the modern techno-industrial environment. Tranquilizers act as selective depressants, affecting primarily the subcortical structures of the brain such as the midbrain recticular formation, the thalamus, and the hypothalamus, the areas seemingly most involved in what we would call the emotions.

At the same time, those tranquilizers most commonly prescribed by the medical profession exert much less influence than the other depressants on the cerebral cortex and its functions: thought, memory, perception, coordination, and the like. To varying degrees, these preparations can affect the endocrines, block conditioned-avoidance behavior and certain motor-reflex activity, relax muscles, and even inhibit seizures. For the individual, they can reduce anxiety tensions and lower the level of aggressiveness. Some lessen tendencies toward hallucination and delusion.

As useful as the tranquilizing drugs have been and will continue to be for the treatment of certain of the ills occasioned or aggravated by the conditions of industrial life, it seems quite apparent that man's proper adjustment to modern technology cannot be brought about wholly or even in significant measure by their use. First, even the safest of these preparations must be used under medical supervision, and many can have serious side effects; that is to say, their effects are not sufficiently selective. Second, as depressants, they naturally tend to slow down reflex activities and to relax the general level of human responsiveness. The pace and complexity of the modern world tends to demand the contrary. We need quicker and more efficient responses rather than slower and less efficient ones. Many necessary processes of the industrial world could not be safely performed by persons taking heavy doses of tranquilizers. The labels on bottles of such pills often spell out the dangers of driving or operating machinery while taking the medication. Third—and for reasons similar to those discussed above during consideration of other means for modifying human behavior— the area of usefulness of the tranquilizers seems limited primarily to a negative role, and a narrow one at that, in alleviating certain tensions. The proper adjustment of contemporary man will involve much more than blocking out certain pathological distortions of human nature.

All in all, the tranquilizers appear of some value only as stop-gaps for those unable to participate fully in industrial life: the ill, the afflicted, the aged. For the person who is to be a full participant in that world, a better solution must be found. Much the same may be said of the chemical approach in general.

BREEDING A NEW RACE

A quick look at a chart of all the varieties and bloodlines of dogs will dramatize for anyone the great change that can be brought about by selective breeding. A Saint Bernard, a dachshund, and a Chihuahua hardly look like representatives of the same species; dog fanciers will also know that the various breeds of dog exhibit very different behavioral patterns as well. Manipulation of human genes could presumably produce just as dramatic lines of change within our species, leading perhaps toward human populations better able to adjust to the stress of our techno-industrial age.

The genetic approach would have some advantages over the use of surgery or medicines, since it would bring about a more permanent change in human nature. Two general methodologies have been proposed to speed genetic change. The more radical method would be to use modern knowledge of biology to operate, as it were, on the structure of individual genes within the fertilized egg and thus to change them in some predetermined and predictable manner into completely new conformations.[5] The other possible approach would be the more traditional eugenic one: selecting among those genes now in the human gene pool and thereby changing the future proportions of variants within the breeding population. The latter method is a tried and true one. It is how we have created countless varieties of domestic plants and animals.

We would have to define our goals, of course. A very basic decision would be between a unidirectional and a multidirectional approach. Under the former, we would seek to move all of mankind toward a single ideal. Under the latter, we would seek to create a series of new subspecies of differing types to meet different problems or needs—much as we have created special-purpose breeds of dog.

The unidirectional approach has obvious difficulties. There would be great danger that we might pick erroneous directions in which to move, since the area of possible development is by its nature unchartable. Mankind could, in a sense, drag itself out on a limb. We could as readily make ourselves less viable as a species rather than more so. Caution would then seem to dictate that we leave a portion of mankind unchanged as a control group or that we change parts of mankind in different ways on an experimental basis so that through the real-life process of interaction with the environment we could choose the most successful variant. But there are also severe dangers in any multidirectional approach. Most important, it could render mankind asunder to a degree that would make present-day racial conflict seem superficial. It is hair-raising to think of a half-dozen "test races," each hoping to prove itself superior to the others.

The use of artificial methods to create new genes and new

gene combinations represents the more challenging method for remaking our species. There have been a variety of suggestions for radical revision of our organic structure. It has even been proposed that genetic engineering could develop the primitive gills that are present in the human embryo into usable organs. This would open the way for human beings to reenter the sea. Thus, goes this proposal, human beings could recapture the genetic vestiges of a long-abandoned world and use them to regain effective use of that world. Re-entry into the seas would, of course, require much more than usable gills. Many other modifications would be required, and many features long typical of man would no doubt cease to be functional. What value would bipedalism be in the sea? What value hair on the head? What value shoulders or a pelvis? Moreover, unless lungs were also present, the new form of breathing apparatus would cut off the new creatures from the long-accustomed life on the land—and presumably from that part of humanity remaining there.

Here the problems of this type of proposal really begin. It would seem likely that new genetic forms, like one designed for the sea, would not long remain similar to what we call mankind. If it were not to remain *Homo sapiens,* what value would it be for our species to have launched it into the seas? Unlike present-day human beings, who have only their own kind to blame for their frustrations and maladjustments, these mutant creatures might justifiably hold those of us who remain on the land guilty for much. The same could also be said of all variants that might be the result of a multidirectional strategy in genetic engineering.

To be dangerous, the multidirectional approach would not require that we create strongly divergent forms like human beings capable of living in the seas. Dangers are inherent in almost any genetic planning that would not retain a single gene pool for all humankind. If we discovered how to create a somewhat modified form of human being that was better adapted to urban life, we would have to decide whether the new genetic form should be restricted to the larger cities, or whether all humanity should be replaced by the new form. It would be difficult to keep such variants from interbreeding with the remainder of the population—if that should remain genetically possible. Think of the possibilities for future *Romeo and Juliet* tragedies! If

differing variants were allowed to marry and have children, pro-
vision would have to be made for fitting the intermediate off-
spring into some type of environment in which they could be
reasonably happy.

All in all, a continued commitment to the essential unity
of humanity seems the safer course. This in turn sharply limits
the immediate value of the genetic approach, for it would be a
slow process indeed to leaven the entire loaf of mankind with
new and improved genetic characteristics.

As has already been discussed, the problem that now faces
us is not so much one of finding ways to occupy new environments, like the seas or outer space, but to find our proper place
in the new world that we have created during the last several
millennia. The adjustment that we must make to this new
environment is not one that is likely to require new arms or
legs or even new and improved sensory capacities. It is one that
has to do with our inner nature, including both our thought
processes and our social propensities.

I must register my most serious doubts about the hope of
using genetic engineering to find answers to the problems of our
technological world. There is the matter of timing. If the ability
to re-engineer genetically the outer man seems distant from our
scientific abilities today, how long will it be before we can learn
the techniques that would be needed to engineer our inner nature, to redesign and reorder our very perceptual and intellectual patterns? But more basically, even if the techniques could
be found in time, the same logical problems that we discussed
earlier would arise in a new form. How could we, using our
minds as presently constituted, be expected to model a new
mind that would surpass our own present capabilities? How
could we ever gain enough information about consequences,
particularly second-order consequences, to make informed
decisions?

Consequently, I cannot agree with the molecular biologist
Robert L. Sinsheimer, that our cultural development and our
knowledge of the genetic component of human nature has "pro-
ceeded so far that we can soberly envision the means to remould
these innate patterns" and thereby "make supple our heredity."[6]
I do not see how we can transcend our own nature in such a

manner. I also believe we could not achieve a safe decision/ information ratio for so significant an action.

Although genetic solutions do not seem to be what we need to solve the problems of our techno-industrial age, we cannot afford to ignore the genetic factor. By conscious selection we could gradually eliminate certain defective genes and increase the percentage of the more successful traits, thus speeding human evolution along the tracks that it is already following. In this way, we might be able to improve the memory, to increase the perceptual abilities, and to sharpen the general intelligence of the average man. Since more intelligent persons are probably better able to adjust to a wide variety of environmental factors, there is a little relevance here to the issue before us. But intelligence as such cannot guarantee adjustment. There are, moreover, different kinds of intelligent behavior and some may even turn out to be mutually exclusive. The problem would be to define which are the effective and which are the defective traits. Although I do believe a certain degree of consensus could be reached on many factors, the philosophical problem remains, especially if the process of change is to be extended very far.

THE REAL AND THE ARTIFICIAL IN EVOLUTION

We have come, again and again, to the basic epistemological problem facing all forms of artificially promoted change in our species. The only assurance we have that our genetically transmitted patterns of perception and thought have something in common with the nature of the real world about us is the fact that they have evolved over countless generations of contact with that world and have served to bring us—like our ancestors —safely through the challenges of daily life in our middle realm. Those patterns bring to all our decisions a vast amount of built-in information. Once we started altering the genetic endowment of our children in any way, they and their descendents would have a lessened assurance of the adequacy of their relationship to the real world. We would have disturbed the functional circle of perception and response that has related us to the world as we understand it, and programmed us to deal with it with some certainty.

For these reasons, the more basic and permanent nature

of genetic change, instead of being an advantage over surgical or medicinal methods, would represent a major disadvantage. Certain changes may be easier to make than to unmake, and a past genetic error would have to be detected and corrected by a future generation that was itself the spawn of that error. Whether we are talking about the surgical, chemical, or genetic approaches, the only corrective for such problems would be to leave an unmodified but elite "control group" in command of supervising the process of change—an idea that we have shown to be pregnant with possibilities for trouble.

All in all, the manipulation of human nature seems a very risky business. Multidirectional strategies for changing our nature run the danger of pulling apart the basic unity of mankind, while unidirectional strategies would leave no control and could lead to disorientation and disaster for the *whole* race. Not at all encouraging alternatives.

After surveying all the above mentioned possibilities for remaking our species, I can only conclude that adjustments on the scale that we will have to make to our new techno-industrial environment cannot be safely made by changing the physiology or psychology of our species by surgical, genetic, or chemical means.

If we cannot remake ourselves to fit the pattern of the techno-industrial world, perhaps we should seek some way to renounce those patterns as our chosen way of life. Couldn't we turn our back on technology and return to nature? That will be the topic of the next chapter.

13
Down with Technology!

A second proposed answer to the problems of human nature vs. human technology emphasizes the importance of protecting our original nature and consequently advocates that we abandon all technology or at least those phases of technology that do violence to our nature as human beings. "Back to nature" philosophies and movements are almost as old as civilization itself.

The literary tradition of almost every nation shows evidence of the idea that mankind should return to the simpler ways of the past. Some writers who immediately come to mind are Lao-tze, Tolstoy, Rousseau, and Thoreau. It was a common theme in ancient Greece and Rome. In the Judeo-Christian tradition, there can be no doubt but that the idea of a return to nature is often closely linked to a concept of a lost Eden. But traditions of a long-past Golden Age, more primitive and more happy, are to be found in widely disparate cultures. Perhaps they all trace to dim memories of the trauma of the agricultural revolution, when, as we saw in chapter 8, mankind left the hunting and fishing stage in which the species had developed and took up the back-breaking work of farming and the social regimentation that went with it. Rather than idealizing the hunting and gathering stage, however, it was often a pastoral pattern that was used to symbolize the simpler and more natural way of life.

Portrayals of life in the pastoral setting were a major feature of the literary traditions of most of the European countries during the early modern period. The idyll or pastoral poem portrays mankind in harmony with nature. In the pastoral, the shepherds and their maidens have great leisure to indulge in the arts, such as music and poetry, and to dally in the pursuit of love. Economic reality, like the need to care for the demands of the sheep and other domestic animals, seems almost to disappear in the idyllic mist. Several of Shakespeare's plays were of this genre, and those were commonly based on a long series of earlier plays with similar themes. The landscape painting of that era, and well into the so-called Romantic period of the nineteenth century, often portrayed specific scenes from pastoral plays or other views of an idyllic life in such a dreamland. It is not hard to see, of course, that these visions were evidence of a natural reaction to what was really going on in European culture at the time: an increasing alienation of Western man from the kind of environment that was natural to the species. Literary escapism is nothing new.

Jean Jacques Rousseau and his works formed a kind of watershed in the development of back-to-nature ideas. Writing in the late eighteenth century, he picked up the early modern and neoclassical concepts of a Golden Age of pastoral life and recast them in a more serious and systematic form in which they remained highly influential throughout the nineteenth century and to some extent until the present. Rousseau's vision contrasts the "noble savage" unfettered by civilization with "modern man" contaminated by the advance of the arts and sciences.

Despite the many philosophic, educational, and political concepts that emerged from the ideas of Rousseau and his followers, there were few programs actually worked out by which mankind might in fact "return" to anything similar to the pastoral way of life. There were, of course, those who were inspired to leave their cities for the occasional trip through the countryside, and a new wave of interest in nature and the outdoor life was set in action. But this was no substitute for finding a solution to the problem perceived by Rousseau.

As we have seen, a literal "return to nature" by our species would not involve establishing a pastoral-based economy, but would instead require reestablishing a way of life that is even more primitive: one based on hunting and gathering. Abandonment of agriculture, both farming and pastoralism, would be required. One recent book, Paul Shepard's *The Tender Carnivore and the Sacred Game,* has actually proposed the abandonment of agriculture for a technological/hunter-gatherer society.[1] Otherwise, there have been few serious proposals that would involve turning away from agriculture. To the contrary, there have been a variety of "back-to-the-land" movements, like that proposed by the social reformer Bolton Hall around the turn of the century and which sought to get the urban poor onto garden patches in the suburbs. Such programs stressed the valuable role of agricultural activity as a means of improving the human condition.[2]

One writer on the technological problems of the present era, Gordon Rattray Taylor, has proposed what he calls a *paraprimitive solution,* i.e., the creation of a society that, while not actually primitive in all ways, would be parallel to or somewhat similar to a primitive society.[3] For Taylor, this means picking the patterns of some earlier era as a compromise between the truly primitive way of life and that of today. Interestingly, Taylor picks as his compromise era "the eighteenth century, in advanced countries"—precisely the period in which Rousseau lived and to whose "unnatural" conditions Rousseau had reacted so strongly.[4]

AWAY WITH THE MACHINE!

Reactions against "the machine" have played an interesting role in the history of attacks on modern technology and its ways. For many, it has become the symbol of a hated regimentation, of the dehumanization of modern culture.

Machines can be sharp taskmasters, of course, since they demand a high level of discipline on the part of their would-be masters. The first machines had to be watched carefully and served continuously, otherwise minor misfunctions could lead them to self-destruction. More recent machines have internal controls (negative feedback systems) designed to preclude this danger. The discipline of the modern machine is largely a function of its great cost; it must be operated at high levels of efficiency to be economical. Its very expense demands a high level of human support.

The question has been raised, in fiction as well as in serious studies, whether we are today still served by our machines or have embarked upon the road of serving them. "May not man himself become a sort of parasite upon the machines?" asked Butler in a tongue-in-cheek "Erewhonian" manuscript called *The Book of the Machines,* "an affectionate machine-tickling aphid?"[5]

As early as 1675, there were attacks on those kinds of machines that threatened to put large numbers of laborers out of work. In that year, the weavers of Spitalfields rioted for three days against the introduction of machines that did the work of twenty men. In early nineteenth-century Britain, especially between 1811 and 1816, there was a rash of attacks on machines by workers in the hosiery and lace industries. Called the Luddite movement, from the pseudonym "General Ludd" taken by several of its leaders, the attacks were part of a general movement for better working conditions and pay. The machines were only convenient targets in the workers' effort to put pressure on their employers. There was no evidence of philsophical opposition to the use of machines *per se.* Nevertheless, the terms "luddite" and "luddism" have remained in the language to describe "machine-breaking" or any form of violent opposition to the use of machines in the manufacturing process.

The twentieth century has been marked by a variety of literary and philosophical attacks on "the machine." Jünger, in his book *The Failure of Technology,* epitomizes the tradition that looks upon the mechanical as diametrically opposed to the organic.[6] He sees technology as representative of some sort of "death principle" that is subtly and gradually invading and destroying the organic world. The growth of modern technology in Jünger's eyes represents a kind of "will to power," recalling the psychological theories of Alfred Adler.

Machines were not without their defenders. Proponents of the rapid introduction of automation into industry in the 1960s were, for example, quick to term their opponents "intellectual luddites," and to ascribe to them an irrational hatred for the machine. This usage was designed, of course, to condemn as reactionary those labor leaders and others who were concerned about the economic effects of automation.

All things considered, human history shows very little evidence of hatred for machines. Most people are either intrigued by them or take them for granted and ignore them. There is, however, some fear of too high a level of dependence upon them. Science fiction has often used the theme that we might somehow be rendered obsolete by our own machines. The term *robot,* for example, was introduced into the international vocabulary in *R.U.R.,* Karel Capek's dramatic satire upon mechanized society, which appeared in 1921.

Most twentieth-century analysts have considered it possible for mankind to prevent the creation of machines that would "make the human race obsolete." The relationship of man and the machine must be symbiotic, not parasitic, declared Lewis Mumford; and man must be ready "to dissolve that partnership, even forego temporarily its practical advantages, as soon as they threaten his autonomy or his future development."[7] Thus far, it has only been specific groups of workers threatened with unemployment who have opposed certain specific machines, and there have been few practical proposals, such as legislation, that would oppose or limit the use of machines as such.

POLITICAL IDEOLOGY AND OPPOSITION TO TECHNOLOGY

The ideologies of both Soviet communism and German national socialism glorified the industrial process and the technology of mass production—to the point that virtue was even seen in the discipline of the machine. But many other twentieth-century political movements have reflected an antitechnological streak. In India, Mohandas Gandhi took quite the opposite position to that of the Communists and Nazis and actively opposed large-scale industry, while making efforts to protect the traditional handcrafts of the village artisan. The choice of the spinning wheel as the symbol of the Congress Party dramatized this Indian viewpoint. Much of what was involved was opposition to foreign imports, for example, machine-made British textiles, but with Gandhi, the purpose went deeper. It did not, however, take long for modernizers like Jawaharlal Nehru to reverse this aspect of Gandhi's ideology and to launch out on a path desired to bring modern technology to India as rapidly as possible.

The interplay between the advocates of technology and those with doubts is not as easy to trace in the Peoples Republic of China as in India. Both Marxist doctrine and the experience of Soviet communism strongly inclined China toward the path of rapid industrialization. The economic plans of the PRC show the same efforts to maximize "industrial progress" as those of the USSR. But, one perceives, not at any cost. In China, even in the post-Mao period, there appears to be a lingering concern about the side effects of modern technology that is not apparent in the Soviet Union. Specifically, there are those who still fear that the degree of specialization required by a high level of technology will create a new elite class of technicians who will work for their own personal and in-group interests rather than in the interests of all the Chinese people. There also appear to be some who fear that modern technology will bring with it greater reliance on a world economy that is "capitalist" in nature and that this could jeopardize the purity of the ideology of the Chinese communist party. Most of the Chinese leadership seems prepared, however, to accept large-scale modification of natural features within rural environments along the lines made famous at Tachai.

In the industrial democracies, a variety of political movements have picked up the theme of opposition to technology. Environmentalism as a movement has been strongly influenced by some of the earlier Utopianisms.[8] Opposition to technology has taken the form of experimentation with new life-styles, whether neoprimitive or anarcho-socialist in concept, and to efforts to legislate controls over technology—such as Proposition 15 in California, which if it had not been defeated in June 1976, would have virtually put an end to the expansion of nuclear power in that state.

The issue of technology in much of the so-called Third World can, however, still be summed up by the question: How can we get as much as possible, as soon as possible? The urge is primarily "to catch up" with the technologically advanced nations. Although some lip-service is given to the concept of avoiding the errors made by the already developed nations, the level of concern for such matters as pollution is relatively low. "First, let us get the factories; then we will worry about the side effects" is a common attitude.

More significant, Third World leaders often react with ill-disguised suspicion to expressions of environmental concern on the part of specialists from the technologically developed nations. Their concern is that the developed countries, having attained power in the world by means of technology, will use exaggerated environmental concerns to keep the rest of the world from ever catching up. They do not want to see their nations treated as good only to be set aside as wildlife sanctuaries, soil banks, tourist attractions, and "native preserves," while the industrialized nations increase their technological sophistication and consequent power in the world.

This problem of differing perceptions of technology between "developed" and "developing" nations has thus become another basic obstacle to efforts to find solutions to the environmental problems on the global scale. A Russian, a Frenchman, and an American can discuss their perceptions and philosophies of technology with some degree of shared experience and common concern. But can they enter into the same type of dialogue with friends from Burma, Rwanda, or Surinam? And by the time those countries are fully industrialized, what will conditions be in Moscow, Paris, or New York?

THE DIFFICULTIES OF PROGRESSING BACKWARD

The tactic of disassembling modern technology, or stopping its progress, as a solution to the current problems of our relationship to the world around us is fraught with difficulty. To begin with, we would have to decide how far back in history to go in our search for a "natural" world. Anything less than reversion to the original hunting and gathering stage that was natural to *Homo sapiens* would be only a partial step; and if it were artificially forced on unwilling persons and nations, it could well lead to a situation that was much more arbitrary—and therefore dangerous for our own survival—than that in which we are now living.

The most obvious flaw in any plan to "return to nature" is that no form of primitive technology would be able to support human populations of the size that we have today. According to estimates, hunting and gathering as a way of life would under the best of circumstances provide only for millions, not billions, of persons on the globe. With pastoralism and a bit of undemanding agricultural technology, we could perhaps sustain a hundred million persons in small villages and nomadic settlements. What would happen to the rest of mankind?

There are those who believe that a collapse in our techno-

industrial culture could well force the issue, and lead to a
dramatic drop in human numbers that would provide one of the
requisites for the needed step backward. Roberto Vacca, for
example, predicts a new "Dark Age" as the result of a breakdown of modern technology; and he expects the period to be
marked by a sharp decrease in world population, beginning with
the more advanced countries.[9] But failing such an automatic cut
as the result of trauma, how could we ever reduce numbers?
Fifty years of a Draconian birth-control program would help,
but even that would probably leave too many old people in the
remaining population. We thus appear trapped by our very
numbers, at least within the time-frame of the next several
generations.

Planning any move back toward primitivism would present
almost insurmountable problems. Beyond the question of who
should be allowed to live, someone would have to decide exactly
how far back to move and then to design ways of establishing
culture at that point around the world. What would we do with
anyone who did not want to regress? What would we do with
any country, religious sect, or ethnic group that refused to
comply? If, say, Madagascar alone were to remain as is, it could
easily establish dominion over much if not all of the remaining,
primitive world—and thereby set the stage for the whole cycle
to repeat itself. If all nations were forced to comply, who would
be the policemen? Would you have to create a new class of Luddites, playing such a role as the "guardians" in Plato's *Republic*,
who would smash any new machine that might be developed?

We must remember too, our discussion of the human drive
for a complex and varied environment. In chapter 4, we reviewed the more specifically human need for diversity of sensory
input. These understandings make it hard to imagine the human
race opting for a return to the tedium of village life as it has
been lived in the past. As we have seen time and again, technology is neither something new nor something that stands outside our nature. The fact is that people enjoy technological
activities. Children of all cultures are intrigued by mechanical
toys, by "things that work." To turn our back on our nature as
manipulators of things about us would be to deny our primate

origins. It would not be a "return to nature" but a violation of nature.

There also seems no point in efforts to eliminate only the specifically modern aspects of technology. We are trapped by our large populations and by our psychological natures, and also by the lack of natural mechanisms or processes that could be used to motivate or compel retrogression. This does not mean that nations, or city governments for that matter, cannot make conscious decisions against developing certain technologies or technological programs like the SST or expanded highway building. It does not make impossible international agreements to destroy certain specific lines of technological development like ABM systems, or even all nuclear weapons. But it is probably safe to conclude that we cannot turn our backs on technology as a whole.

The only remaining approach, then, is to use certain of the methods of technology to regulate the other aspects of technology. This is to say that we are forced once again to rely on the same means to adapt to our uncertain future that the Eskimo used in the past to accommodate to the Arctic wastes, that the Polynesian used to adapt to life on the sea, and that the Bedouin used to adjust to life in the blazing desert: cultural ingenuity. Nothing more. Nothing less.

14
Environment as
Art-Form

If we cannot remake ourselves so that we will fit the Procrustian mold of our new techno-industrial world, if we cannot throw off the vast technological structure that keeps so large a population of us alive, what can we do? Is there any pattern of adjustment that could bring together the inner needs of human beings and the immense potentialities of modern technology?

We have looked at the vast new artificial world that our species has built for itself; and much of it, while imposing, does not seem very attractive. Much even appears alien to our deeper needs. But we have seen that one area of human artifice is closely linked to the psychological nature and needs of the individual: the arts. In the arts, an artificial world is created, but not one that is alien to our inner feelings, needs, and desires. By its very nature, art cannot violate our *Innenwelt* and still be art.

TECHNOLOGY VS. ART?

Those, like Jacques Ellul, who tend to view technology as if it were an extraneous force, as if it were something extrinsic to human nature, often conclude that in the modern world art is doomed to be subordinated by technique.[1] Technology is viewed by Ellul as absorbing art and as corrupting it in the process. This tendency to treat technology as an "outside force" has almost theological overtones at times. Natural man has been corrupted by the fruit of the tree of mass production. In the process, he has lost his innocence and his birthright, and the wages of his sin against nature is seen to be his inevitable extinction as a species. Technology is virtually treated as if an

218

independent, sinister force, a modern devil that has led man astray. Against such a force, the more artistic side of human nature is considered doomed to have no influence on the course of human events.

If one accepts, however, the evidence that I believe demonstrates that technology is the result of tendencies intrinsic to our species—that it too is a reflection of the ecology of the human mind—then the pragmatic side of technology must be recognized as nothing inherently unnatural and also as a phenomenon closely related to the arts. Operating from such a premise, there remains some hope that the artistic side of our nature may yet be able to coexist harmoniously with the more narrowly pragmatic. There is some hope that we may be able to design a world system that creates the aesthetic values important to the fulfillment of our psychological nature as efficiently as it can produce the things essential to our bodily nature.

The view of technology as an "outside force" is not, however, the only concept that we will have to come to grips with here. Other philosophers of technology tend to describe technology as if it were a dangerous, potentially fatal, "inner force" over which we do not have the essential means of control, often treating it with the same theological overtones mentioned above. This "demon within" concept is in many ways more difficult to come to grips with than that of the "devil without." It is in fact much more compatible with the scientific and evolutionary world view—if we equate the "demon" in question with nothing more mystical than an internal phylogenetic trait that would tend *Homo sapiens* toward certain patterns of action that would not be conducive to long-term survivability as a species.

In accord with the definitions reached in chapter 10, I will not look upon art and technology as competing forces. Art will be treated as a form of technology designed less for its impact on our *Umwelt* than for its positive impact on our *Innenwelt*.

Can art so conceived be expected to help us in our efforts to control the other aspects of technology? Can we use it to control unwanted second-order implication of technological progress? Or is it itself subject to those negative forces many associate with modern technology? I for one have not lost hope in the power of the arts.

THE ROLE OF CONSCIOUS DESIGN

As the general level of industrial sophistication rises, the possibilities of conscious control increase. Our hope must be that the highly industrial world of the future can, through art, be increasingly given the external features of the more ancient human habitat, and that it can be designed so that most social interaction can be conducted in accord with patterns true to our natural temperaments. We must apply our artistic sensitivities to the techno-industrial world and bend it to our ways, not allow its features to control and perhaps destroy human values. The contours of our future technology should not be permitted to violate the more basic norms of our middle realm, the scale, pace, or degree of complexity that are comfortable to our bodies and minds.

Conscious effort will be essential, especially in our efforts to deal with the wider zones of our interaction with the environment. To forge a more humane future world in the time available will require that we use our full repertoire of artistic skills to harmonize the technomass with our needs.[2] In the long run, and especially at the inner zones of the individual's interaction with the environment, the solution of many problems posed by our new man-made world will result from countless small personal decisions by individuals. But considerations of timing and scale require that there also be planned, conscious effort.

Certain problems can only be addressed at the global scale, since they affect the entire biomass and our relation to it. Especially here, consciousness must play for mankind the role of the indicator in a healthy negative feedback system, and thus assure that the relationship between our inner nature and the outer environment is held within endurable limits. Without conscious design, some adjustments would not come rapidly enough to prevent the large-scale dislocations and frustrations that would threaten the peace and security of our species. Others might not come at all, given the force of inner-zone primacy.

Change has been almost unbelievably swift in the last few decades, and it has not been a respecter of the aesthetic side of human life. Robert Frost's old farm, depicted in the poem "Westrunning Brook," was, for example, turned into an automobile junk yard. Unbridled aesthetic pollution is as much a threat to human well-being and ultimate survival as are other forms of environmental pollution.

The intellectual as well as the physical environment of young people today is astonishingly different from that of their grandparents. As we have seen, we do not have time to evolve new organs or new intellectual powers in order to make the needed adjustments. In many areas of interaction, we will not have time to wait for gradual, unconscious, historical processes to rescue us from our present problems. Thus, for the first time, certain processes of environment-creation by our species will have to be carried out on the conscious level. At various levels, especially at the larger zones of interaction, we will have to *design* many aspects of our future world, not just hope that they will fall together helter-skelter. Objectives that fit into our aesthetic needs will have to be clearly identified and research done into the alternative ways in which these objectives can be obtained. Finally, on the basis of that research, lines of action will have to be consciously chosen that lead us toward the kind of world in which our kind can be comfortable and secure.

Basic to our efforts to find the necessary patterns of accommodation, there must be a wide recognition that there is such a thing as human nature, and that people are not infinitely adaptable. Human nature, not the short-term needs of industry, will have to be taken as the long term "given." In the final analysis, it must be industry that is humanized, rather than people who are industrialized. Art will have to be recognized as the highest form of technology, taking precedence over all others, because it serves the needs of our inner, not just our outer, nature. The arts and aesthetic considerations will have to be recognized as of central value to mankind, not as mere frosting on the cake of daily life. As Theodore Roosevelt declared, "There is nothing more practical in the end than the preservation of beauty."

THE ROLE OF IDEAS IN DESIGN

In addition to the artistic talents required to design future habitats, a wide variety of scientific and social activities will have to be undertaken to show us the way out of our present problems.

These will include deeper research into human nature (including both its anatomical and behavioral aspects), the control of population and a survey of means for its better distribution over the available surfaces of earth, more systematic city planning, accelerated programs for the conservation of natural resources, and the expansion and better utilization of recreational areas. Cities of the future must be better designed to preserve the identity of the family and other small social groups. The pace of urban life, the scale and complexity of cities, must be held in check so that they will not grossly violate the norms of the middle realm.

We will, of course, need to understand ourselves much better than we do now in order to know what kind of surroundings would be most harmonious with our own well-being and thus create the type of environment in which our kind has the maximum long-term chance to endure. All this will require much learning. We will also have to design more effective methods to share what data we have developed. Success will require, however, the arts as much as the sciences.

It is unfortunate that resources on the same scale that have recently been put into space programs are not being earmarked for further research into ways to protect our more ancient earthly environment, or being devoted to the creation of the new arts that will be needed to adapt our cities to a healthier and more humane way of life. Before we spend the vast sums required to build space stations, we should be willing to spend the sums needed to build experimental villages on Earth.

The drive to find new planets that might be habitable by our species is a very long-term project. If it is ever to succeed at all, we will in the interim need to accommodate to very many bizarre new things here on planet Earth. Without forgetting the outward reach that leads us to wish to explore space, we must also remember the significance of this planet to the preservation of our species. Most specifically, we must not allow pressures and frustrations to build up within or among the industrial nations that could lead to strife on a global scale.

We cannot, of course, ignore the housekeeping side of our relationship with our environment while we are increasingly focusing on the psychological aspect. We must find ways to control the unwanted by-products and unexpected side effects of our industrial surroundings, or at least to isolate those effects so that they will produce the least possible impact on the everyday life of the average man. We must improve our understanding of the second-order consequences of our decisions, particularly those that relate to the outer zones of our interaction with the world about us. Levels of atmospheric pollution must be carefully watched, for example. Mankind has, it is to be hoped, a long time left to inhabit this planet and we cannot ignore the long-term effects of various forms of contamination.

"In wildness is the preservation of the world," said Thoreau. It would be a very dangerous experiment to attempt to replace all the features of the old *Umwelt* with a totally artificial creation, to allow our *Zwischenwelt* to expand to a point where we are no longer part of any naturally based ecological system. We will have to work harder to protect and preserve the natural resources of our planet, since to the extent that we neglect or destroy what remains of the ancient ecology we are destroying not only part of the heritage of our species but probably also reducing the odds for future survival.

For several decades, increasing attention has been given to city planning, urban redevelopment, and the like. More recently, the term "environmental engineering" has been coined to describe the overall effort to provide a more suitable environment for people to live in—an effort that goes beyond city lines to encompass the countryside, the seas, and the atmosphere as well. Many problems of environmental design have already been assayed.[3] Nevertheless, most efforts so far have been very modest, given the scale of the problem. More important, many studies have failed to appreciate the intellectual dimension of our relationship to the new worlds of things and symbols that we have created. Scholars have only just begun to see the value of looking at the ecological dimensions of human activity in order to better integrate the many disciplines into which their knowledge has been categorized.[4]

THE ROLE OF SCALE AND VARIETY

The vastness of the problems before us in planning for a more humane world should not lead us to think that our plans must be aimed at the creation of bigger and and bigger social, political, and economic structures. Obviously, there must be effective global institutions if we are to continue to endure in a world shrunken by the impact of technology. But individuals do not normally perceive the world in global terms, or even in national terms for that matter. The British economist, Schumacher, has eloquently made the point that smaller-scale institutions are generally better adapted to the needs of the individual.[5] We have seen in previous chapters that the human realm has in most areas of activity its characteristic limitations of scale and that we cannot violate those limitations with impunity. Economic activity is no exception.

We must also avoid concluding that the pattern of conscious design involves the discovery of "the proper environmental pattern" and its uniform imposition on all of humanity by means of the "planning process." The unidirectional approach would be a very dangerous one to follow in the design of human environments. Since there are limitations to the number of persons that one person can know, and since there are limits as well to the number of places that one can visit and the number of roles that one can play in a lifetime, we must recognize that even in our shrinking world, different individuals will continue to live in different social worlds of interaction.

Our carrying capacity for information will simply not allow enough two-way or "cooperative" communication links to create any type of "global village" that would impact upon the individual in the way in which smaller social groups impact. Marshall McLuhan's concept that new communications media such as television are bringing together all of the peoples of the world, previously isolated by the variety of written and printed languages, becomes misleading, in my opinion, when he talks of the creation of the "global village"—a universal culture that will somehow once again be basically tribal in character. Terms like "tribe" and "village" conjure up limitations of scale that can hardly be reconciled with McLuhan's metaphorical usages.

In a practical sense, we must continue to think of the global environment as plural in nature, as a cluster of thousands of more specific cultural, religious, economic, and even personal worlds. Rather than striving to find or create the single "best" culture for all of mankind—that is, a world "monoculture" of some type—we must work to preserve the diversities of the human cultural heritage. We must prevent the reduction of all existing cultures to any sort of common denominator.

To accept a universal monoculture of the "lowest common denominator" type would be to destroy the rich variety that interests people as curious mammals and stimulates much of our creativity as a species. Like sensory deprivation, cultural uniformity would, in my opinion, stifle human creativity and ultimately destroy us all. Even within a particular culture, environmental planning should make room for a multiplicity of lifestyles, providing varied patterns among which the individual can choose. Mass culture is one of the dangers of the techno-industrial age, and should be consciously treated as such. Diversity is always a good insurance policy.

Looking at history, we can see examples in which uniformity of outlook contributed to cultural decline. The very success of Han Chinese culture in the East Asian geographical zone was a factor that eventually led to the ossification of many aspects of that culture. Chinese culture was recognized to have no equals among the "barbarian peoples" who lived on the fringes of its known world. Its stereotypes, life-styles, and clichés were considered a natural part of the life of all civilized men. Only cycles of invasion during periods of institutional collapse brought new ideas to the fore. Similarly, the narrow orthodoxy and fear of heretical ideas that marked medieval Europe was a factor in holding back intellectual progress.

Our approach to cultural planning must be multidirectional. I can see no safe alternative. Thousands of diverse human communities must be allowed to live side by side. The idea of a common world ethos or metaculture should be limited primarily to a universal respect for all mankind, an interest in all the many cultures and subcultures it encompasses, tolerance for differences of approach, and a sense of common destiny.

This final aspect is of importance, for I would not advocate an atomized world, with communities out of contact with each other. We all have much to learn from each other, and people and goods should be able to move from culture to culture and from community to community. I do not agree with the Taoist ideal, whereby you may see the smoke of your neighboring village's fireplaces and even hear the crowing of their roosters, but never feel any desire to visit them.

In this context, the development of an international language would be of great value as an auxiliary for intercommunication, and for the more effective transfer of information. It should not, however, be designed to replace the variety of existing language systems. As a matter of fact, the existence of an international auxiliary language could well play a role in protecting some of the smaller ethnic groups from absorption by larger nationalities, since members of the smaller groups could use the international auxiliary when they had the need to communicate with those outside their own culture rather than having to assimilate to a major national language such as French, English, Hindi, or the like.

THE ARTS AND TECHNO-INDUSTRIAL MAN

There is a distinction that we must make here between "metaculture" and "monoculture." The first concept, as I will use it, describes 'a cultural umbrella of sorts, above and protecting other cultures. Under the metaculture concept certain very basic values may be generally accepted by all cultures—primarily those values designed to insure the perpetuation of the species. A world metaculture might include universal acceptance of standards for the prevention (or at least limitation) of war, for the maximization of world economic gain through trade, for protection of the common environment, and for intercommunication, including both the sharing of general ideas and specific scientific knowledge. A metaculture would not prescribe such things as life-styles, art-forms, and the like. In sharp distinction, I will use the term "monoculture" for the idea of worldwide uniformity in all areas of cultural activity.

A multidirectional strategy for the design of human environments does not suffer from the same dangers as a multidirectional genetic strategy; it can allow for the maintenance of economic contact, the interflow of individuals, and the exchange of ideas. It would at the same time help inhibit the development of a single, homogenized, mass culture which would restrict human creativity and accelerate the dangerous practice of making too many decisions on a global scale.

Over time, of course, the patterns of our relationships to the environment and to each other are going to continue to change. Some cultures will disappear; new ways of life may be tried on an experimental basis. Features of the more successful communities will tend to spread to other communities. The evolution of social forms is not a greatly different process than the evolution of species. If the more fit human societies are those that tend to thrive during the short and middle term, the only consequence can be to increase the long-term chance of the survival of mankind itself.

Now this may lead some to worry that what we call a global *metaculture* would, in fact, represent little more than a first step toward the creation of a *monoculture*. Gradually, they might assert, any global metaculture would tend to expand its areas of concern, eventually absorbing the other cultures into it, much as certain ethnic groups have absorbed others throughout history. Some people might even see this as a historical necessity, as part of the inevitable march of progress. Surely there are tendencies toward universalism in all the major religions. Pressure toward uniformity has also been charged as an inevitable result of our technological explosion; many writers have declared that the inexorable discipline of the machine will make all cultures alike simply by forcing them all to be efficient in the same mechanistic ways.

This latter thesis is closely related to the concept of "Industrial-man." Alex Inkeles and others have argued that irrespective of preexisting national traditions, the introduction of industrial modes of production with the characteristic large-scale and bureaucratic approach to management will lead to the creation of structural environments, institutional features, and attitudinal patterns that will be relatively consistent around the world. In Inkeles's study, his conclusions were primarily based on a comparison of Western and Soviet industrial societies.[6] Somewhat similarly, one of the major theses advanced by John Kenneth Galbraith in *The New Industrial State* is that all states, whether capitalist or communist in economic doctrine, tend to converge in character under the imperatives of technology.[7]

Jacques Ellul and others of the more pessimistic philosophers of technology have also accepted the concept that industrialism will force all cultures into a single mold, one that Ellul sees as necessarily unresponsive to the aesthetic side of human life. Science fiction is full of future worlds in which human culture is brutalized by a uniformity imposed by technology. *Brave New World* and *1984* are examples.

Some scholars of world affairs, including Galbraith, have come to reasonably optimistic conclusions, even though accepting the thesis that we are on the road toward creating a single, prototype "Industrial-man." In contrast to the pessimists; they see value in uniformity. They feel the world would be a safer place if the ideological and other differences that currently separate the cultures of the major industrial powers were to be lessened by the convergent forces of technological society. Those who believe that they discern patterns in techno-industrial society that favor totalitarian methods do not agree. In fact, many anti-Utopian novels project a future world in which mirror-image technological states are locked in eternal conflict, while the cultural level of the average man is degraded by mass culture to the very lowest common denominator.

I believe that we do not yet have enough evidence to determine whether the expansion of technology is itself leading to the creation of such a standardized "Industrial-man." The issue has not yet been properly addressed. To begin with, we must separate technology from other historical influences when we interpret the evidence thus far. When the Soviets pushed rapid industrialization during their early Five-Year Plans, they did not start *de novo* and reinvent the patterns of industrialism; instead, they borrowed entire cultural and organizational systems that had been proven useful in the earlier industrial states. The same is true of the developing countries of the Third World today. It is hard to separate the trends of modern Western European culture from those of modern techno-industrial culture *per se*. But there is surely a difference. The Japanese example shows that a distinct, and in many ways still non-Western, culture can have a technology as advanced as Western Europe. Recent research in Europe also tends to remind us that even in countries as close as Britain and Sweden there have been major differences in the direction that social institutions have evolved under the impact of industrialization.[8]

A second factor that is often overlooked is that, although technology may have the effect of reducing certain cultural differences, it also provides the economic wherewithal that can allow for creation of new types of cultural diversity. As long as there is creativity in the system, new complexities and new diversities can arise under the rubric of the techno-industrial world at a rate that might well surpass the pressures toward leveling. Just as city life is more diverse than village life, sophisticated technology could as easily provide the basis for a richer and more diverse pattern of culture, rather than necessarily push us toward a dehumanized mass society.

All too often, those concerned in the modern world with the design of human communities have tried to operate on the basis of narrow ideology or insufficient scientific fact. First they have attempted to formulate the general laws of social development and, having done so to their satisfaction, have then sought to apply those laws mechanistically to as large a proportion of humankind as possible. I believe that there is no individual human being, no matter how scholarly or well-informed, who can pretend to tell humanity as a whole precisely how it should interact with the world about it. The best that can be done is to work toward a system that will continue to allow the selective processes of culture to operate as openly and freely as possible. In this way, the countless small but creative acts of individual human beings each seeking the fuller life for himself or herself will show the proper direction of change. Here, close to the inner zone of personal interactions, we find the limits of global design.

The artist does not expect to paint a "perfect painting," only to have all future artists do nothing more than to copy it endlessly as the standard of all time. Too often, the political theorist has tried to conjure up a Utopia that would so well express human needs that it would never change. We are, however, a species that has had a very complex evolutionary history.

Our functional circle is not very close to perfectly round. It is more what I have called a "dynamic circle." A heavy dose of change is surely built into our future for some time to come. Nor is the human future something that can be prescribed. It is something that must be lived. If we are to survive the immediate future, however, I do believe that we must balance off the recent successes of our technologies with greater attention to the aesthetic side of our creative nature. The building of human homes in socially and aesthetically satisfying communities must be treated as among the most important of our art-forms.

AESTHETICS AND SURVIVAL

The aesthetic side of the entire environmental problem is, in my view, most important. It is often overlooked. Our technological traditions often treat the arts as if they were merely peripheral to human ends, incidental to productive life. It is my thesis that the arts lie nearer to the core of human life and that the productive processes remain primarily the means that we use to attain what are primarily aesthetic values. And I charge that even those businessmen, farmers, construction workers, military men, and others who pride themselves on being "realistic" or "hard-headed," follow the same priority of values. You need only look at the houses, estates, yachts, and other purchases of those who are financially successful to see the principle in action.

Artistic traditions vary sharply from culture to culture, but underlying all these are certain basic considerations which have deep roots in human nature. The arts are not in conflict with the rational element in man. To the contrary, both find their roots in the same natural perceptual patterns: the analysis-systems by which we categorize and rationalize the phenomena of our outer environment. The graphic arts play with space, music plays with time and tempo, the dance and cinema play with motion, sculpture plays with the outer form of entities, and dramatic tragedy plays with the laws of cause and effect. All art-forms, like the sciences, impose order on a chaotic world. The artistic approach differs primarily in that it uses more complex, asymmetrical patterns rather than the starker, more easily demonstrable, symmetries preferred by the sciences. The same inner-world of human psychology is reflected in both.

If we are to be capable of transforming our world so that it will respond more adequately to the deep-felt, ancient needs of our species, we will surely require creation of new directions and priorities in the arts. The medium for human artistic expression must become the entire environment, including the activities of the people who live within it.

We must plan not only the pictures we hang on our museum walls, but more importantly what the average person sees out of the average window. Our artists must design not only the choreographies of future ballets, but also the pattern of movement through space of people on their way to work—the visual and kinetic impressions upon each individual as he or she moves through the appointed rounds of the day. We must think not only of musical compositions, but also about how we can assure that each individual is exposed only to pleasant sounds, full of variety and well modulated by silence. We need literature and drama on the stage and television, but also social institutions that put meaning and interest into all hours of every human life, not excluding those of the very old. In sum, our arts, our skills in design, must be applied to the totality of human sensory input.

I will concede that many of the underlying features of the industrial world are here to stay. They may continue as long as our species survives. But the very complexity of that world and the great power that technology has harnessed open a vast number of possibilities. I see no reason why many of the uglier aspects of the industrial world cannot be modified so that they no longer touch our daily life. Others can probably be altered so they will have less impact. Certain glaring examples of "aesthetic pollution," such as the odor of a chemical plant or the accumulation of litter along the highways, can be controlled by the same methods that are used to control the pollution of the air we breathe or the water we drink. In other cases, bits of the more natural environment can be used to screen off the less beautiful aspects of industrial life from the eyes and other sense organs of most people most of the time. In still other cases, redesign and reprogramming of certain features of our technology may be the best approach.

Modern industrial methods have already shown themselves capable of producing abundance for the average citizen beyond the dreams of the Pharaohs or the Caesars. Those methods also raise the possibility that, if we can survive the threat of war and the other immediate problems of the next fifty years, while at the same time continuing present trends of material progress, excess leisure may begin to pose as great a future problem for our species as excess work has posed in the past. Out of such abundance, there should come also new possibilities for creating a more humane industrial environment than has thus far been thought possible. Although the use of complex machines, systems of mass production, and continued high inputs of energy under man-made control systems seem necessary to any possible industrial world, the way in which that world affects the individual can be transformed by our conscious efforts. We need not live amidst the oily gears of our technology to reap its benefits.

If there is really some factor in the present world situation or in human nature that will force the more narrowly technological side of our nature to ride roughshod over all our aesthetic sensitivities, I would have to conclude that the extinction of *Homo sapiens* is only a matter of time. In that case, we are already well into a dance of doom and need only wait out the last act and the final curtain.

The "devil without" theory, I believe, can be pretty well rejected by anyone who accepts the evidence of science in general and human evolution in particular. The "demon within" concept cannot be easily proved or disproved, when the "demon" involved is conceptualized as an internal genetic defect of some sort that would tend our kind toward patterns of action that increase the danger of our extinction. We could be so flawed. Many species carry such defects for a long time. We have discussed the dangers of overspecialization; we as a species have developed the brain to an unprecedented level of complexity. The hopeful thought, however, is that our brains are the source not only of our tool-making powers but also of our aesthetic sensitivities and that they are designed to function as feedback mechanisms that should provide us the ability to see future alternatives and choose by a rational method the way we wish to go. While there is no proof we will make the proper decisions in time, I believe that there is also no proof that we cannot.

Part Five

Conclusion

15

How to Survive
though Civilized

"In this world there are only two tragedies," wrote Oscar Wilde
in *Lady Windemere's Fan*. "One is not getting what one wants
and the other is getting it. The last is the real tragedy." As a
species, we have perhaps been too successful for our own good,
our victory over our natural environment too complete. The
very successes of recent technology are now putting our species
in real danger. Pogo, the philosophical possum of the comic
strips, summed it up: "We have met the enemy, and they are us."

There is no turning back. We have abandoned the type of
hunting and gathering environment in which our species was
evolved. This act of abandonment represented, to be sure, a
dangerous step for the human future. Species usually become
extinct as a result of some alteration in the organism's relationship to its environment. "The general, true cause of extinction,"
wrote the anthropologist George Gaylord Simpson, "seems to
be change in the life situation, the organism-environment integration, requiring in the organisms concerned an adaptive
change which they are unable to make."[1]

Here we stand, in the midst of a man-made world that,
while it reflects the accrued residue of generations of our own
technological activity, is a very strange environment indeed.
Whether we endure as a species will depend on our ability to
adapt to that new environment. The fact that our contemporary
world is so largely man-made does not diminish the danger,
since many of its most important features are the unexpected
side effects of technological activity rather than reflections of
the human needs or desires that motivated that activity.

Let us begin to look forward by reviewing some of the
major points developed in the chapter above. The modern in-

CONCLUSION

dustrial world is the product of our mental nature, a nature evolved during a long evolutionary history marked by numerous changes of environment and way of life. Technological activity reflects a type of ecological relationship with the world about us that is characteristic of our species. It is not a superhuman force that imposes its will upon us. A civilization created by any other species would differ sharply from that which we have built.

We should not underestimate the continuing influence on contemporary man of patterns originally set by the ancient environment in which the species evolved. As we saw in chapters 2 and 3, some of these influences were physical. They combined to shape the outward form of our bodies and to set the patterns of our sensory organs. Others were programmed into our neural systems and provide us with our natural analysis-systems, the patterns by which we manipulate the world about us as well as the most basic ways in which we think about that world. The conservation of our own species in the centuries ahead will require that we gain fuller understanding of these influences, especially the latter. We must learn more about how our minds figure in the ecological equation, about the "ecology of the human mind."[2]

The most characteristic features of human interaction with the environment are not, as some recent works have suggested, specific behavioral instincts such as territoriality or aggression. Though *Homo sapiens* does appear to have a strong drive toward self-expression and self-assertiveness which can be distorted into antisocial forms, I see nothing that forces it to take such forms, given proper environmental conditions. The environment is not just a place to be, it is a place to act. Proper environmental conditions for our species do require outlets for ancient needs, such as the chance for a certain degree of exploratory and adventurous physical activity among the younger males, who had once formed the core of the hunting band. But it would be simplistic to think of that fact as making war either natural or inevitable. To the contrary, war may be viewed as a pathology flowing from the unnatural social environment of the agricultural world.

The factor that most clearly characterizes all men and

women of all cultures in their contact with the environment is that series of patterns that we all use to analyze and then to re-synthesize the chaotic sense data that we receive into systems that can be used to make decisions about future actions. These universal analysis-systems, by which we contrast, compare, or otherwise relate environmental data, include: space, time, entities, number, causation, symmetry, and the like. They form the basis of what we call rational action.

Like all forms of life, our species must maintain a functional circle of sensation and response within its environment. We are a complex and highly adaptable kind of organism, but our senses remain selective and their range limited. So are our abilities, both physical and intellectual, to respond effectively to all aspects of our environment. The natural scale of size and complexity at which human beings can best respond, what I have called the "middle realm," has its limitations. The boundaries of our middle realm were originally set by the controlling factors of the way of life that was lived by our precursors as they evolved into what we now call *Homo sapiens*.

That middle realm still lives on in us, having been programmed into the very genetic makeup of our species. It is part of that which defines what it is to be human. It sets both the limitations on our intellectual ability to understand the world about us and the limitations on our physical ability to adapt to changes in that world.

All of the analysis-systems we use for understanding our world—time, space, entities, motion, number, and causation, for example—are still perceived in ways that were evolved by our species for dealing with the problems of the middle realm. They are part and parcel of the ecology of the human mind. Together, these understandings create for all of us the natural boundaries of the "outside world"—the world we see and measure against our own internal copy of the ancient middle realm. The industrial revolution has not changed this fact. *In this sense, we all remain prisoners within the middle realm.*

Through the intermediacy of culture—evidenced externally by tool-making and more inwardly by symbol-making activities—human beings first learned to expand their world to occupy areas previously uninhabitable. Paleolithic hunters

moved into the sub-Arctic, the Quechua and Tibetans conquered the higher altitudes of the Andes and Himalayas, the
Polynesians sailed out into the vastness of the Pacific. Our progenitors were also learning, however, to fashion new worlds of
their own creation. They abandoned the ancient world of the
hunt, first for the settled world of agriculture, and their descendents more recently abandoned that for the crowded, anonymous
world of modern industry. Each successive stage was in turn
more alien to the original nature of our species. The contemporary world has little in common with that in which humankind evolved. *In this sense, we have exiled ourselves from
the middle realm.*

Herein lies the paradox that underlies so many of the
problems of our species today. Although we remain bound by
our inner natures as subjects of the middle realm—virtual
prisoners within its boundaries—we have by cultural means
exiled ourselves forever from the way of life normal to that
realm. Thus we have created a conflict, a state of tension, between our internal and external environments, our inner and
outer worlds.

A species, particularly one as adaptable as *Homo sapiens,*
can tolerate a considerable degree of tension and live. Five
thousand years of civilization show that severe tensions can be
maintained for rather long periods without more than partial
breakdowns of morale, occasional institutional collapses, and
a chronic tendency toward a major war every generation or so.
During our contemporary technological era, however, the degree
of divergence between our unchanged inner nature and the
rapidly changing external environment has increased greatly and
continues increasing at an accelerating pace. It is an open question whether this alienation can continue for more than another
generation without dire consequences. Most immediately dangerous would be the creation of a world of tensions and frustrations that could lead to a general war using all of our most recently developed weaponry. Global institutions that are essential
to maintaining our current population levels might even collapse
under circumstances short of all-out war. We see revealed a
psychosocial ecological problem that is much more complex

than the more strictly physical issues of human ecology, like conservation of resources or industrial pollution.[3]

As bad as the air is in some of our big cities, we are not likely to be threatened with extinction through our respiratory system. We are not lungfish testing out an unstable evolutionary innovation. Rather than the lungs, the organ most likely to be our equivalent of Achilles' heel remains the brain. Events set in train by psychological ills could lead to complete extinction. It is quite possible to imagine a scenario in which the frustrations of crowded living, social disorganization, increased intergroup conflict, intellectual rejection of the rational processes, increased control of dogmatic ideologies over human decision-making, and political instability on a global scale could set the proper stage of a series of irrational decisions that would bring on a war that would spell the doom of every last member of humankind.

Human rationality is the only hope that this or similar future threats will never come to such a denouement. The greatest assurance that people will act in accord with the rational processes that have made *Homo sapiens* so dominant a species would be to recreate, insofar as possible, the type of surroundings in which people can be expected to react most rationally. This is the most urgent motive I see in reexamining and reordering the ecological balance of our techno-industrial world.

How then can we readjust? As we have seen, we cannot readily change our inner nature, but even if it were possible, it would be exceedingly dangerous to try to change it much very quickly. Our only immediate hope is to adjust our outer environment to reflect better our inner nature. We can damn technology all we wish, but we are going to have to use more of our technological skills, not less. We will have to use them differently in a more subtle way, and much more consciously in the pursuit of human values. We have trapped ourselves into a way of life that we cannot reject, since our populations are far too large to support without a high level of technology.

Recasting our technological world will require the arts as well as the sciences. It will not come about "naturally" or unconsciously. Inner-zone primacy and the ignorance factor loom too large in our decision-making process to allow that. Conscious effort alone holds any hope for effecting many of the necessary changes within the available time. This will not be easy, since we are not in the habit of giving conscious attention to such matters. It will also be an expensive process, for we will no longer be able to deal with the world about us as if it were open to unlimited exploitation. The relationship of man to environment can no longer be that of spoiler and spoils. It will have to be more like that of the patient gardener and his garden.

Time is short. There are many exponential trends in our global system that tick on like ever speeding clocks, racing toward a less and less stable state. We must give the highest priority to supplying the needed controls and humanizing this new world of our own creation so that it will be a better home for those who live in it. If we do not, it will become the graveyard of yet another extinct species.

The proper strategy cannot be one designed to find the "final answer" to human adjustment to the environment in order to put it into universal effect. To begin with, the problem is far too complex for such an approach. But more important, we must expect that human accommodations to the environment will vary over time in the future, just as they have varied in the past. The strategy we need is an open one, one that will permit variety within the global system and an ongoing selective process that will allow the more fit approaches to prosper over time on the basis of their recognized merit. The world society must remain a cellular structure, as it were, with the primary function of the whole being the maintenance of communication between communities, the maximization of economic benefits, the enforcement of toleration, and the husbanding of common resources.

The community at the local level will remain very important to the whole. It must be made more vital than it has been under the impact of recent industrialism, for it is here that people operate on a social scale that is by nature the most intelligible and meaningful. Here too, not just at the national level, must variety be allowed to exist. Traditional subcultures, such as the Amish in rural Pennsylvania, must be permitted to flourish. Experimental approaches designed to find alternative life-styles should be allowed wide latitude to develop. A good case could even be made for maintaining a few hunting and gathering tribes completely outside of modern culture—much as we provide sanctuary for other life-forms. Maintenance of a rich panoply of varied human communities would do a great deal to increase the lasting power of *Homo sapiens*.

Uniformity remains a prime danger, since a uniformly applied error of sufficient magnitude could bring global castastrophe. If the thesis of "Industrial-man" is correct—that is, if technology is forcing all human cultures toward a single norm of cultural activity—then *Homo sapiens* is doomed. The chance that a monoculture so imposed would represent a way of life that would be viable is almost infinitesimal. It would represent a brittle crystallization of chance elements in our inner nature, elements that had never come out before in the same form. It would not have the flexibility and pliability that would allow for the proper accommodation to the real world about us. It is to be hoped, however, that the industrial revolution, like the agricultural revolution before it, will lead to more rather than less variety in the cultural adaptations it makes possible.

The global dimension is also important. Successful efforts to safeguard what remains of wild environments and to humanize the industrial areas that have replaced the rest of those environmentss will require the cooperation of all nations. International action is needed to protect migratory wildlife, our common atmosphere, and the high seas and their shorelines. Formalized bilateral and multilateral measures directed at particular problems will have a role to play. Specialized international organizations may also have to assume a degree of regulatory responsibility, much as such organizations have assumed responsibilities for matters of common interest like the international mails and weather prediction. During the last decade there has been evidence of a growing realization of the need for international cooperation of this type.[4]

To be successful, international cooperation in environmental affairs cannot end with programs to control activities that foul the environment or endanger species of wildlife; it must extend as well to broader and more positive programs—to joint efforts in the basic research needed to understand better our inner nature so that the nations can plan more effectively to meet human needs, to the exchange of information on experimental projects that hold hope as possible new patterns for future adjustment, to the pooling of resources for projects that can only be conducted on a scale larger than is possible for individual nations, to efforts to slow the current rate of population growth and distribute existing population more rationally over the land, and finally to patronage of all the arts that will be required in conscious environment building.

Knowing the problem does not mean that we will succeed in coming to grips with it. As I see it, the basic question can be framed in terms of a system badly in need of feedback controls. Can those persons who (like the thermostat in a well-regulated oven) have become aware of the problem turn themselves into an effective control mechanism (like the switch in the overheated oven that responds by turning down the gas) and thereby redirect the course of technological progress along a more humane path?[5]

This must remain an open question. No species on planet Earth has ever before had to face the need for conscious action at such a level. We have no past evidence on which to estimate whether it is possible for a species to establish control over its own destiny. We are the first case; we may be the last.

We must, however, not be intimidated by the scale of the project before us or by its unprecedented nature. All we can do is attack today's problems with the degree of determination that has marked countless other human communities in their adjustments to their environments. Our precursors went through many strange and unprecedented adjustments on the road to becoming human. Individual human cultures, like that of the Eskimo, have adjusted to the most inhospitable surroundings. We may well be able to adjust to the need for conscious design in the regulation of our relationship with the world about us. The verdict is not in.

I am reminded of the final lines of Voltaire's *Candide,* where, after a series of crises and misfortunes on several continents, Pangloss (the professor of Metaphysicotheologicocosmonigology) and his pupil Candide have settled down on a farm in Turkey, and Pangloss says:

"There is a concatenation of events in this best of all possible worlds: For if you had not been kicked out of a magnificent castle . . . if you had not been subjected to the Inquisition . . . if you had not lost all your gold . . . you would not be here eating preserved citrons and pistachio nuts."

"All that is very well," answered Candide, "But let us cultivate our garden."

Notes

1. Conqueror in Peril

1. George Gaylord Simpson, *The Meaning of Evolution* (New Haven, Conn.: Yale University Press, 1964) p. 204.

2. Many theses along these lines have been advanced, although most have not been systematically developed. Two recent works are Eugene S. Schwartz, *Overskill: The Decline of Technology in Modern Civilization* (Chicago: Quadrangle Books, 1971); and Roberto Vacca, *The Coming Dark Age* (Garden City, New York: Anchor Books, 1974).

3. José Ortega y Gasset, *History as a System* (New York: Norton, 1941).

4. Much of the change in attitude toward the concept of "instinctive behavior" was the result of the works of the "ethologists" who studied animal behavior in the natural environment, men like Nicholas Tinbergen and Konrad Lorenz. See Claire H. Schiller, ed., *Instinctive Behavior: The Development of a Modern Concept* (New York: International University Press, 1957); and Vernon Reynolds, *The Biology of Human Action* (San Francisco: W. H. Freeman, 1976).

5. Benjamin Franklin, *A Dissertation on Liberty and Necessity, Pleasure and Pain* (London, 1725).

2. The Legacy of Past Environments

1. The fossil record of brain evolution and its implications for the nature of intelligence is traced in Harry J. Jerison, "Paleoneurology and the Evolution of Mind," *Scientific American* 234 (January 1976): 90-101.

2. Alfred Sherwood Romer, "Major Steps in Vertebrate Evolution," *Science* 158 (Dec. 29, 1967): 1629-37, p. 1635.

3. Romer, "Major Steps." Mammalian evolution is also discussed by Romer in: *The Vertebrate Story* (Chicago: University of Chicago Press, 1959); and the *Vertebrate Body* (Philadelphia: Saunders, 1962).

4. W. C. Alee, "Distribution of Animals in a Tropical Rain-Forest with Relation to Environmental Factors," *Ecology* 7 (1926): 445-468.

5. Marston Bates, *The Forest and the Sea* (New York: Random House, 1960), pp. 20–25.

6. For a general discussion of primate patterns of action, see A. Jolly, *The Evolution of Primate Behavior* (New York: Macmillan Co., 1972).

7. Geoffrey H. Bourne, *The Ape People* (New York: G. P. Putman's Sons, 1971), pp. 243–45.

8. Joe T. Marshall and Elsie R. Marshall, "Gibbons and Their Territorial Songs," *Science* 193 (July 16, 1976): 235–237.

9. J. H. Crook and J. S. Gartlan, "Evolution of Primate Societies," *Nature* 210 (1966): 1200–1203; T. E. Rowell, "Variability in the Social Organization of Primates," in *Primate Ethology,* ed. Desmond Morris (London, 1967).

10. George Schaller, *The Mountain Gorilla, Ecology and Behavior* (Chicago, University of Chicago Press, 1963).

11. V. Reynolds, "Some Behavioral Comparisons Between the Chimpanzee and Mountain Gorilla in the Wild," *American Anthropologist* 67 (1965): 691–706.

12. Robert Ardrey, *African Genesis: A Personal Investigation into the Animal Origins and Nature of Man* (New York: Atheneum, 1961), p. 57.

13. Ibid., pp. 112–16.

14. Robert Ardrey, *The Territorial Imperative* (New York: Atheneum, 1966), p. 222.

15. David Premack, "Language in Chimpanzee," *Science* 172 (May 1971): 808–822; similar research is detailed in Duane M. Rumbaugh, ed., *Language Learning by a Chimpanzee* (New York: Academic Press, 1977).

3. The Unique Nature of Our Species

1. Bernard Campbell, *Human Evolution* (Chicago: Aldine Publishing Co., 1974), p. 372.

2. Elwyn L. Simons, "Ramapithecus," *Scientific American* 236 (May 1977): 28–35.

3. David R. Pilbeam, *The Ascent of Man* (New York: Macmillan Co., 1972), p. 99.

4. W. E. LeGros Clark, *Man-Apes or Ape-Man?: The Story of Discoveries in Africa* (New York: Holt, 1967); M. A. Edey, *The Missing Link* (New York: Time-Life Books, 1972).

5. Jane B. Lancaster, "Carrying and Sharing in Human Evolution," *Human Nature* 1 (Feb. 1978): 82–89.

6. John E. Pfeiffer, *The Emergence of Man* (New York: Harper and Row, 1969), pp. 109–111.

7. Raymond A. Dart, "The Predatory Transition from Ape to Man," *International Anthropological and Linguistic Review* 1 (1953): 201–208. Also see the same author's *Adventures with the*

Missing Link (New York: Viking Press, 1959); Robert Ardrey, *African Genesis: A Personal Investigation into the Animal Origins and Nature of Man* (New York: Atheneum, 1961).

8. G. Teleki, *The Predatory Behavior of Wild Chimpanzees* (Lewisburg, Pa.: Buchnell University Press, 1973); Jane van Lawick-Goodall, *My Friends the Wild Chimpanzees* (Washington, D. C.: National Geographic Society, 1967), pp. 65–71.

9. R. B. Lee and I. DeVore, eds. *Man the Hunter* (Chicago: Aldine Publishing, 1968), pp. 30–48.

10. Konrad Lorenz, *On Aggression* (New York: Harcourt, Brace and World, 1966).

11. J. T. Robinson, *Early Hominid Posture and Locomotion* (Chicago: University of Chicago Press, 1972).

12. One discussion is R. W. Newman, "Why Man is Such a Sweaty and Thirsty Naked Animal: A Speculative Review," *Human Biology* 42 (1970): 12–27; a popularized discussion is in Desmond Morris, *The Naked Ape,* (New York: McGraw-Hill, 1967).

13. Kenneth P. Oakley, "Possible Origin of the Use of Fire," *Man* 61 (1961): 207.

14. Lewis Mumford, "Man the Finder," *Technology and Culture* 6 (Summer 1965): 375–381.

15. Jane van Lawick-Goodall, *In the Shadow of Man* (Boston: Houghton Mifflin, 1971), p. 114.

16. Pfeiffer, p. 10–11.

17. Phillip L. Stein and Bruce M. Rowe, *Physical Anthropology* (New York: McGraw-Hill, Inc., 1974), pp. 271–72.

18. Campbell, pp. 196–201.

19. Mary D. Leakey, "Early Artifacts from the Koobi Fora Area," *Nature* (London) 226 (1970): 228–230.

20. Mary D. Leakey, *Olduvai Gorge,* Vol. 3 (Cambridge: University Press, 1971).

21. D. L. Wolberg, "The Hypothesized Osteodontokeratic Culture of the Australopithecinae," *Current Anthropology* 11 (1970): 23–37.

22. Philip V. Tobias, *The Brain in Hominid Evolution* (New York: Columbia University Press, 1972), pp. 134–37.

23. Jacques Ellul, *The Technological Society* (New York: Knopf, 1973), p. 79.

24. Martin Heidegger, *Being and Time* (New York: Harper and Row, 1962).

25. Raymond A. Dart, "On Evolution of Language and Articulate Speech," *Homo* 10 (1959): 154–165.

26. Pfeiffer, pp. 410–12.

27. A useful survey of much that is known about *Homo erectus* is: Edmund White and Dale Brown, *The First Men* (New York: Time-Life Books, 1973).

28. Pfeiffer, has addressed the subject of the rise of big game hunting and the psychology of the hunt, pp. 112–132.

29. Pfeiffer, p. 133ff.

30. A. Kortlandt, "Comment on the Essential Morphological Basis for Human Culture," *Current Anthropology* 6 (1965): 320–25.

31. Anthony Storr, *Human Aggression* (London: Allen Lane, 1968), p. 94.

32. D. S. Brose and M. J. Wolpoff, "Early Upper Paleolithic Man and Late Middle Paleolithic Tools," *American Anthropologist* 73 (1971): 1156–94.

33. We should not ignore those cultural differences in space relationships so well dramatized by Edward T. Hall in his books *The Silent Language* (Garden City, New York: Doubleday, 1959) and *The Hidden Dimension* (Garden City, New York: Doubleday, 1966).

4. The Intimacy of Mind and Environment

1. Woodburn Heron, B. K. Doane, and Thomas H. Scott, "Visual Disturbances after Prolonged Perceptual Isolation," *Canadian Journal of Psychology* 10 (1956): 1355.

2. These tendencies are the subject of: H. Fowler, *Curiosity and Exploratory Behavior* (New York: Macmillan Co., 1965).

3. John Cohen, "Subjective Time" in *The Voices of Time*, ed. J. T. Fraser (New York: George Braziller, Inc. 1967), p. 262.

4. Jacob von Uexküll, *Umwelt and Innenwelt der Tiere* (Berlin, 1909).

5. Marston Bates, *The Forest and the Sea* (New York: Random House, 1960), p. 175.

6. G. D. Scott and Paul Gendreau, "Psychiatric Implications of Sensory Deprivation in a Maximum Prison," *Canadian Psychiatric Association Journal* 14 (1969): 337–41.

7. Benjamin Franklin, *A Dissertation on Liberty and Necessity, Pleasure and Pain* (London, 1725), Sec. II, spelling modernized.

8. Charles S. Sherrington, *The Integrative Action of the Nervous System* (New Haven: Yale University Press, 1947), pp. 388–89.

9. Garrett Hardin, *Nature and Man's Fate* (New York: New American Library, 1961), p. 247 ff. The subject of the perfection of biological adaptations is also addressed in: François Jacob, "Evolution and Tinkering," *Science* 196 (June 10, 1977): 1161–66.

5. Limits of the Human Scale

1. Jacob von Uexküll, *Die Lebenslehre* (Potsdam: Muller and Kiepenheuer, 1930), p. 131.

2. Wolfgang von Buddenbrock, *The Senses* (Ann Arbor: University of Michigan Press, 1958), p. 131.

3. Julian Huxley, "The Size of Living Things," *Man in the Modern World* (New York: Mentor Books, 1948), pp. 75–90.

4. Claude Lévi-Strauss, *The Savage Mind* (London: Weidenfeld and Nicholson, 1966), p. 154.

5. Peter H. Ravin, Brent Berlin, Dennis E. Breedlove, "The Origins of Taxonomy," *Science* 174 (December 17, 1971): 1210–1213.

6. George A. Miller, "The Magical Number Seven, Plus or Minus Two: Some Limits on our Capacity for Processing Information," *Psychological Review* 63 (1956): 81–97; reprinted in Miller's *The Psychology of Communication* (London: Allen Lane, 1967).

7. *The Psychology of Communication,* p. 25.

8. Herbert A. Simon, "How Big is a Chunk," *Science* 183 (1974): 482–88.

9. An early, but very perceptive discussion of the size of vocabularies is to be found in Otto Jespersen's *Growth and Structure of the English Language* (New York: Appleton, 1927)—Chapter IX, especially pages 214–18.

10. J. S. B. Lindsay, "On the Number in a Group," *Human Relations* 25 (1972): 47–64; pp. 58–59.

11. Anthony F. C. Wallace, "On Being Just Complicated Enough," *Proceedings of the National Academy of Sciences* 47 (1961): 458–64.

12. Wallace, p. 464.

13. C. Kegan Paul, trans., *The Thoughts of Blaise Pascal* (London: Kegan Paul, Trench and Co., 1888), Number 72.

6. The Fig Leaf of Culture

1. Theodora Bynon, "Leo Weisgerber's Four States in Linguistic Analysis," *Man: Journal of the Royal Anthropological Institute* I (1966): 486–83.

2. Kenneth P. Oakley, *Man the Tool-Maker* (Chicago: University of Chicago Press, 1959), p. 4.

3. George A. Miller, "Communication and the Structure of Behavior," *Proceedings of the Association for Research on Nervous and Mental Disease,* 42 (1964): 29–40.

4. Lewis Mumford, *The Myth of the Machine: Technics and Human Development* (New York: Harcourt Brace and World, 1966), p. 24ff.

5. Ashley Montagu, *The Human Revolution* (Cleveland: World, 1965), p. 17.

6. Barbara Harrison, *Orang-Utan* (London: Collins, 1962).

7. Belle J. Benchley, *My Friends, The Apes* (Boston: Little Brown and Co., 1942).

8. A. M. Hoyt, *Toto and I: A Gorilla in the Family* (Philadelphia: J. B. Lippincott Co., 1941).

9. Jane Goodall, "My Life Among Wild Chimpanzees," *National Geographic* 124 (August 1963): 272–308.

10. Jane B. Lancaster, "On the Evolution of Tool-Using Behavior," *American Anthropologist* 70 (February 1968): 56–66.

11. Lewis Carroll, *Through the Looking Glass,* Chapter XII. First published 1872.

12. Harry J. Jerison, "Paleoneurology and the Evolution of the Human Mind," *Scientific American* 234 (January 1976): 90–101.

13. See, for example, Victor W. Turner, "Symbols in African Ritual," *Science* 179 (March 16, 1973): 1100–1105.

14. E. L. Thorndike, "The Orgins of Language," *Science* 98 (1943): 1–6.

15. Eric H. Lennenberg, ed., *New Directions in the Study of Language* (Cambridge, Mass.: MIT Press, 1964), pp. 65–88.

16. This issue is covered in Eric H. Lennenberg, *Biological Foundations of Language* (New York: Wiley, 1967).

17. Konrad Lorenz, *On Aggression* (New York: Harcourt, Brace and World, 1966), p. 238.

18. *Chuang-tzu,* Chapter 17. My translation.

19. Melville J. Herskovits, *Cultural Anthropology* (New York: Alfred A. Knopf, 1965), p. 305.

20. Samuel L. Clemens, *Letters From the Earth* ed. by Bernard De Voto (New York: Harper, 1938), p. 129.

7. Primitive Technologies and New Environments

1. Marston Bates, *Gluttons and Libertines: Human Problems of Being Natural* (New York: Random House, 1967), p. 226.

2. The role of learned behavior in a monkey species is addressed in: G. Gray Eaton, "The Social Order of Japanese Macaques," *Scientific American* 235 (October 1976): 97–106.

3. C. Loring Brace, "The Fate of the 'Classic' Neanderthals: A Consideration of Hominid Catastrophism," *Current Anthropology* 5 (1964): 3–43; also, the same author's *The Stages of Human Evolution* (Englewood Cliffs, N.J.: Prentice-Hall, Inc., 1967), p. 104.

4. One of the best presentations on the earliest discovered traces of human shelters is in: J. Jelinek, *The Pictorial Encyclopedia of the Evolution of Man* (London: Hamlyn, 1975), part III, "Dwellings and Settlements of Stone Age Man," pp. 211–274.

5. Feodor Dostoevsky, *The House of the Dead,* (1862) Part I, Chapter 2. Everyman edition. (London: Dent and Sons, 1962) p. 8.

6. Gabriel W. Lasker, "Human Biological Adaptability," *Science* 166 (Dec. 19, 1969): 1480–86.

7. Most of the groups considered will be ones primarily engaged in hunting and gathering as an economic system. The way of

life of such groups is covered in: Carlton S. Coon, *The Hunting Peoples* (Boston: Little, Brown and Co., 1971) and Elman R. Service, *The Hunters* (Englewood Cliffs, N.J.: Prentice-Hall, 1966).

8. Surviving hunter-gatherer peoples are described in: Lewis Cotlow, *The Twilight of the Primitive* (New York: Macmillan Co., 1971); Frederick G. Vosburgh, ed., *Vanishing Peoples of the Earth* (Washington, D.C.: National Geographic Society, 1968); and M. G. Bicchieri, *Hunters and Gatherers Today* (New York: Holt, Rinehart, and Winston, 1972).

9. Richard B. Lee and Irven DeVore, editors, *Kalahari Hunter-Gatherers* (Cambridge, Mass.: Harvard University Press, 1976).

10. Elizabeth Marshall Thomas, *The Harmless People* (New York: Vintage Books, 1965), p. 105. Scooped-out pits in the ground are also recorded in use as "shelters" among the aborigines in: Richard A. Gould, *Yiwara, Foragers of the Australian Desert* (New York: Scribners, 1969).

11. Daryll Forde, ed., *African Worlds: Studies in the Cosmological Ideas and Social Values of African Peoples* (London: Oxford University Press, 1954), pp. 4–6.

12. Colin M. Turnbull, "The Lesson of the Pygmies," *Scientific American* 208 (Jan. 1963): pp. 28–37.

13. Colin M. Turnbull, *The Forest People: A Study of the Pygmies of the Congo* (New York: Simon and Schuster, 1962), p. 74.

14. John Nance, *The Gentle Tasaday: A Stone Age People in the Philippine Rain Forest* (New York: Harcourt Brace Jovanovich, 1975), p. 22.

15. Ibid., p. 115.

16. M. H. Segall, D. T. Campbell, and M. J. Herskovits, *The Influence of Culture on Visual Perception* (Indianapolis: Bobbs-Merrill Co., 1966), p. 213.

17. Aime Vincent Perpillou, *Human Georgraphy* (London: Longmans, 1966), pp. 201–202.

18. A survey of the artifacts of one Polynesian island is: Hiroa, Te Rangi, *Material Culture of Kapingamarangi* (Honolulu: Bishop Museum, 1950).

19. Edwin G. Burrows, "Culture-areas in Polynesia," *Journal of the Polynesia Society* 49 (1940): 349–63.

20. J. M. Lubart, *Psychodynamic Problems of Adaptation—Mackenzie Delta Eskimos* (Ottawa: Department of Indian Affairs and Northern Development, 1970), pp. 27 ff.

21. Paul T. Baker, "Human Adaptation of High Altitude," *Science* 163 (March 14, 1969): 1149–56; Raymond J. Hock, "The Physiology of High Altitude," *Scientific American* 222 (Feb. 1970): 53–62.

22. Paul Shepard, *The Tender Carnivore and the Sacred Game* (New York: Scribner's, 1973), p. 157.

8. Ecology by Artifice

1. Alexander Bryan Johnson, *A Treatise on Language* (Berkeley: University of California Press, 1959), p. 29.

2. Kent V. Flannery, "The Ecology of Early Food Production in Mesopotamia," *Science* 147 (March 12, 1965).

3. Eugene Ayers and Charles Scarlott, *Energy Sources* (New York: McGraw-Hill, 1952).

4. On agriculture and energy generally, see: G. H. Heichel, "Agricultural Production and Energy Resources," *American Scientists* 64 (January-February 1976): 64–72.

5. According to Harrison Brown, *The Challenge of Man's Future* (New York: Viking Press, 1954), p. 14, a hunting-gathering economy could not support more than ten million persons worldwide.

6. The various effects of civilization on the individual and social human being are addressed in: S. V. Boyden, ed., *The Impact of Civilization on the Biology of Man* (Toronto: University of Toronto Press, 1970).

7. Jack R. Harlan, "The Plants and Animals that Nourish Man," *Scientific American* 235 (September 1976): 88–97.

8. Karl A. Wittfogel, *Oriental Despotism* (New Haven, Conn.: Yale University Press, 1957).

9. Louis Wirth, *On Cities and Social Life* (Chicago: University of Chicago Press, 1964), pp. 70–71.

10. Gideon Sjoberg, "The Origin and Evolution of Cities," *Scientific American* 213 (September 1965): pp. 54–63. On the development of city life generally, see R. J. Braidwood and G. R. Willey, eds., *Courses Toward Urban Life* (Chicago: Aldine, 1962).

11. Richard G. Fox, *Urban Anthropology: Cities in Their Cultural Settings* (Englewood Cliffs, N.J.: Prentice-Hall, 1977).

12. Ralph Linton, *The Tree of Culture* (New York: Alfred A. Knopf, 1964), p. 11.

9. Man Meets Machine

1. J. J. Rousseau, *Emile*, trans. Barbara Foxley (New York: Everyman's Library), p. 5. First published 1762.

2. Early technology is surveyed in: Henry Hodges, *Technology in the Ancient World* (New York: Alfred A. Knopf, 1970).

3. A major, two-volume review of the technological history of the Western world is: Melvin Kranzberg and Carroll W. Pursell, Jr., *Technology in Western Civilization* (New York: Oxford University Press, 1967).

4. Henry David Thoreau, "Life Without Principle," in *The Portable Thoreau*, ed. Carl Bode (New York: The Viking Press, 1947), pp. 631–655. Originally published in *The Atlantic Monthly* of Oct. 1863.

5. Arnold J. Toynbee, *Change and Habit: The Challenge of our Time* (London: Oxford University Press, 1966).
6. George P. March, *The Earth as Modified by Human Action* (New York: Charles Scribner's Sons, 1974), p. 34.
7. Herbert A. Simon, "What Computers Mean for Man and Society," *Science* 195 (March 18,1977): 1186–99; Zenon W. Pylyshyn, ed., *Perspectives on the Computer Revolution* (Englewood Cliffs, N.J.: Prentice-Hall, 1970).
8. Susanne K. Langer, *Philosophy in a New Key* (New York: Mentor Books, 1948), p. 226.
9. Philip H. Abelson and Allen L. Hammond, "The Electronic Revolution," *Science* 195 (March 18, 1977): 1087–91; the history of the computer is covered in the same issue of *Science* in Ruth M. Davis, "Evolution of Computers and Computing," pp. 1096–1102.
10. Zbigniew Brzezinski, *Between Two Ages: America's Role in the Technetronic Era* (New York: The Viking Press, 1970), pp. 9–23. "The Onset of the Technetronic Era."

10. Folded, Spindled, and Mutilated

1. W. L. Thomas, Jr., ed., *Man's Role in Changing the Face of the Earth* (Chicago: University of Chicago Press, 1956).
2. C. A. Doxiadis, *Ekistics, An Introduction to the Science of Human Settlements* (New York: Oxford University Press, 1968).
3. Edward T. Hall, "Proxemics," *Current Anthropology* 9 (April-June, 1968): 83–95.
4. Kevin Lynch, "The City as Environment," *Scientific American* 203 (Sept. 1965): 209–219.
5. Nils Petter Gleditsch, "Slow is Beautiful: The Stratification of Personal Mobility with Special Reference to International Aviation," *Acta Sociologica* 18 (1975): 76–94.
6. On this point see: Siegfried Giedion, *Mechanization Takes Command* (New York: Oxford University Press, 1955).
7. William Wordsworth, *The Prelude*. Book VII (1805).
8. Charles A. Reich, *The Greening of America* (New York: Random House, 1970), p. 168.
9. Raymond A. Bauer, *Second Order Consequences, A Methodological Essay on the Impact of Technology* (Cambridge, Mass.: M.I.T. Press, 1969), p. 18.
10. *Congressional Record*, U.S. House of Representatives, April 21, 1966.
11. Bauer, p. 20.
12. *Webster's Seventh New Collegiate Dictionary* (Springfield, Mass.: G. and C. Merriam Company, 1965).
13. John Kenneth Galbraith, *The New Industrial State* (Boston: Houghton Mifflin, 1967) p. 12.
14. See also: Cyril Stanley Smith, "Art, Technology, and Sci-

ence: Notes on their Historical Interaction," *Technology and Culture* 11 (October 1970): 493–549.

15. Thomas S. Kuhn, *The Structure of Scientific Revolutions* (Chicago: University of Chicago Press, 1962).

16. Edwin T. Layton Jr., "Technology as Knowledge," *Technology and Culture* 15 (January 1974): 31–41.

11. How the Trap Could Spring

1. A survey of ecological threats of this type is contained in Gorden Rattray Taylor's *The Doomsday Book,* (Greenwich, Conn.: 1970).

2. This issue is the subject of Alvin Toffler in *Future Shock* (New York: Random House, 1970).

3. Herbert Marcuse, *One Dimensional Man* (Boston: Beacon Press, 1964).

4. Nicholas Tinbergen, "On War and Peace in Animals and Man," *Science* 160 (June 28, 1968): 1411–18.

5. J. Dollard, L. Doob, N. Miller, O. Mowrer, and R. Sears, *Frustration and Aggression* (New Haven: Yale University Press, 1939), p. 1.

6. Arnold H. Buss, *The Psychology of Aggression* (New York: John Wiley and Sons, 1961), p. 198ff.

7. John Hurrell Crook, "The Nature and Function of Territorial Aggression," pp. 141–178 of *Man and Aggression,* ed. by M. F. Ashley Montagu (London: Oxford University Press, 1968); quote is on pages 172–173.

8. Anthony Storr, "Possible Substitutes for War," pp. 137–144 of *The Natural History of Aggression* (London: Academic Press, 1964), J. D. Carthy and F. J. Ebling, editors, p. 140.

9. Andrew P. Vayda, *War in Ecological Perspective: Persistence, Change and Adaptive Processes in Three Oceanian Societies* (New York: Plenum, 1976).

10. J. Glenn Gray, *On Understanding Violence Philosophically* (New York: Harper and Row, 1970), p. 29. See also Erich Fromm, *The Anatomy of Human Destructiveness* (New York: Holt, Rinehart and Winston, 1973).

11. Arnold J. Toynbee, *Change and Habit: The Challenge of our Time* (London: Oxford University Press, 1966), p. 217.

12. Roberto Vacca, *The Coming Dark Age* (Garden City, New York: Doubleday, 1974). A somewhat more optimistic view is that in: L. S. Stavrianos, *The Promise of the Coming Dark Age* (San Francisco: W. H. Freeman and Co., 1976).

13. M. A. Goldberg, "On the Inefficiency of Being Efficient," *Environment and Planning A* 7 (1975): 921–939.

14. Kenneth E. F. Watt, *The Titanic Effect: Planning for the Unthinkable* (Stamford, Conn.: Sinauer Associates, 1974), p. 7.

15. E. C. Zeeman, "Castastrophe Theory," *Scientific American*

234 (April 1976): 65–83; a critique of its mathematical basis is: Gina Bari Kolata, "Catastrophe Theory: The Emperor Has No Clothes," *Science* 196 (April 15, 1977): 287, 350–51.

12. Can We Remake Man?

1. D. S. Halacy, Jr., *Cyborg: Evolution of the Superman* (New York: Harper and Row, 1965).
2. P. M. Tow, *Personality Changes Following Frontal Leucotomy* (Fair Lawn, N.J.: Oxford University Press, 1955).
3. David M. Borvik, *As Man Becomes Machine: The Evolution of the Cyborg* (Garden City, N.Y.: Doubleday, 1971), p. 162.
4. Luigi Valzelli, *Psychopharmacology: An Introduction to Experimental and Clinical Principles* (New York: Spectrum Publications, 1973), p. 1.
5. Robert L. Sinsheimer, "Genetic Engineering: The Modification of Man," *Impact of Science on Society,* 20 (October-December, 1970), pp. 279–291.
6. Ibid., p. 288. The larger issue of genetic experimentation is reviewed by Robert M. May, "The Recombinant DNA Debate," *Science* 198 (December 16, 1977): 1144–1145.

13. Down with Technology!

1. Paul Shepard, *The Tender Carnivore and the Sacred Game* (New York: Scribner's 1973).
2. Bolton Hall, *A Little Land and a Living* (New York: Arcadia Press, 1908).
3. Gordon Rattray Taylor, *Rethink: A Paraprimitive Solution* (London: Secker and Warburg, 1972).
4. Ibid., p. 155.
5. Samuel Butler, *Erewhon* (New York: Modern Library, 1955), p. 23.
6. Friedrich Georg Jünger, *The Failure of Technology* (Hinsdale, Illinois: Regnery, 1949).
7. Lewis Mumford, *Art and Technics* (New York: Columbia University Press, 1952), pp. 72–73.
8. A useful article on this issue is: Steven Cotgrove, "Environmentalism and Utopia," *The Sociological Review* 24 (February 1976): 23–42. See also: Langdon Winner, *Autonomous Technology: Technics-out-of-Control as a Theme in Political Thought* (Cambridge, Mass.: MIT Press, 1977).
9. Roberto Vacca, *The Coming Dark Age* (New York: Anchor, 1973).

14. Environment as Art-Form

1. Jacques Ellul, *The Technological Society* (New York: Alfred A. Knopf, 1973), pp. 128ff. and 404ff.

2. The hope of creating a more humane technological society is addressed by Erich Fromm in *The Revolution of Hope: Toward a More Humanized Technology* (New York: Harper and Row, 1968).

3. For example, see Ian L. McHarg, *Design with Nature* (Garden City, New York: Doubleday, 1971); Jon Berger, "Toward an Applied Human Ecology for Landscape Architecture and Regional Planning," *Human Ecology* 6 (June 1978): 179–200.

4. Eugene P. Odum, "The Emergence of Ecology as a New Integrative Discipline," *Science* 195 (March 25, 1977): 1289–1293.

5. E. F. Schumacher, *Small is Beautiful: Economics as if People Mattered* (London: Blond and Briggs, 1973).

6. A. Inkeles and R. Bauer, *The Soviet Citizen* (Cambridge: Harvard University Press, 1959); and A. Inkeles, "Industrial Man: The Relation of Status to Experience, Perception, and Values," *American Journal of Sociology* 66 (1960) 1–31.

7. John Kenneth Galbraith, *The New Industrial State* (New York: New American Library, 1968), especially pp. 396ff.

8. Richard Scase, "Industrial Man: A reassessment with English and Swedish Data," *British Journal of Sociology* 2 (1972): 204–220.

15. How to Survive though Civilized

1. George Gaylord Simpson, *The Meaning of Evolution* (New Haven, Conn.: Yale University Press, 1964): p. 204.

2. The idea of an "ecology of the human mind" has been suggested in other works, for example, Gregory Bateson, *Steps Toward an Ecology of Mind* (New York: Chandler Publishing Co., 1972), but in a sense somewhat more restricted than discussed here.

3. Some aspects of this dimension of the ecological problem are addressed in Konrad Lorenz, *Behind the Mirror: A Search for the Natural History of Human Knowledge* (New York: Harcourt Brace Jovanovich, 1977).

4. René Jules Dubos, "The Human Landscape," *The Department of State Bulletin* 60, No. 1546 (February 10, 1969): 127–136.

5. Problems of mobilizing public opinion are addressed in: Russell E. Train, "The Environment Today," *Science* 201 (July 28, 1978): 320–24.

Glossary

Note: Since these terms form an interrelated matrix, they are cross referenced. Any word in italics in a definition appears on its own in the glossary.

Adaptation—In biology, any structure, physiological process, or behavioral pattern that makes one *organism* better able to survive and reproduce in a particular *environment* than others of its kind. Secondarily, a process of *evolution* that leads to the development of such traits. In *culture,* any learned pattern of behavior that performs the same function as biological adaptation; and includes both *input-facilitation* and *output-facilitation* processes.

Aesthetic effect—The elicitation of a positive emotional response to aspects of the *environment;* the sensation of beauty.

Aesthetic pollution—Introduction into the *Umwelt* of factors that, when sensed, decrease the species' total enjoyment of its surroundings. May include noise, offensive odors, "unsightly" litter, or the destruction or distortion of aesthetically appreciated natural features of the *environment.*

Aggression—A physical act or threat of action by one *organism* that is designed to injure or reduce the freedom of another organism of the same species or a species that cohabits the same ecological *niche.* Does not include the predator-prey relationship. Characteristically involves the creation of *stress* or other hyperactive emotional states.

Agriculture—The artificial manipulation of plants and animals in order to increase their yield, a stage in human *culture* that has generally replaced that of the hunter-gatherers. A form of *technology*.

Analysis-systems—*Phylogenetic* mechanisms (determined by genetic inheritance) used by an *organism* to analyze and synthesize the perceptual *data* that it receives from the *environment*. Analysis-systems in *man* include what we think of subjectively as: time, space, motion, categories, cause and effect, and the like.

Anxiety—A feeling of *uneasiness* or threat, often due to the recognition of an unacceptable level of *ignorance* and the consequent expectation of danger or some other uncontrollable or unpredictable event.

Applied science—Scientific activity conducted in pursuit of a specific goal, which is often of an economic nature.

Art—A form of *technology* designed to create *artifacts* or actions that produce a positive emotional effect (an *aesthetic effect*).

Artifact—Any man-made object or by-product. Includes *works-of-art* and *tools*. Many well-designed artifacts combine features of both the tool and work-of-art.

Australopithecus—Genus of *hominids* thriving in various forms in Africa during the Pleistocene period. Apparently had *cultures* of a sort, practiced *tool-making* on a large scale, and were probably similar in many ways to the forms ancestral to *man*—although they may represent an offshoot from the line that led to the genus *Homo*.

Biomass—The total weight of any arbitrarily chosen group of plants or animals. With *man,* can be contrasted with the *technomass*.

Biosphere—The totality of the biological part of all the Earth's *ecosystems*.

Catastrophe—Change of sudden and not easily reversible nature.

Civilization—Postagricultural stage of *culture* in which food surpluses are large enough to permit the development of specialized proefssions and *urbanization.*

Communication—Action by one *organism* (the transmitter) that modifies the probable behavior of another organism (the receiver), especially by providing *information.*

Communication link—A channel of *communication* that connects a transmitter with a receiver over time or space. May be *cooperative* or *noncooperative.*

Concept—An idea, existing as part of a *language* system, which is designed to play a role in *communication* or to extend or sharpen the human abilities to understand the *environment.* By *perceptor-mediation,* concepts play a major role in human *input-facilitation* systems.

Concept-creation—A *symbol-making* process, using the biologically based human *analysis-systems* and the input of experience within *cultures* in order to identify higher generalizations that can be used to interpret and manipulate the *environment* more efficiently. Performs a similar function in respect to the *receptor system* that *tool-making* performs in the *effector system.*

Cooperative-links—Two-way (or multidirectional) channels of *communication.*

Culture—Patterns of learned behavior, transmitted within a group from generation to generation by *language* or other *communication* systems.

Culture-building—The creation of complex patterns of learned behavior or *culture,* usually in response to changes in the *environment,* the opportunity to enter new environments, or to exploit old environments more effectively.

Curiosity—Drive of an *organism* to gather *information* about its *environment,* especially significant in *Homo,* where it involves not only *diversive exploration* but also intellectual activity.

Cyborg—A cybernetic *organism;* that is, one that has incorporated into its body and its *functional circle* one or more mechanical devices.

Data—Physical events within a *sensory system* or *communication* channel, measured in terms of the alternative number of states possible within the system involved. See *information*.

Decision/information ratio—The ratio between the magnitude of a decision (based on such factors as: numbers affected, area covered, time elements, and difficulty of reversing) and the available, pertinent *information*.

Diversive exploration—Pattern of activity whereby an animal seeks out the needed amount and variety of sensory *data* by moving about within its *environment*. Characteristic of the mammals. Part of the animal's *input-facilitation* system.

Ecological niche—See *niche*.

Ecology—Scientific study of the interaction between *organisms* and their *environment*.

Ecology of the human mind—A study of the way in which the processes that we call *mind* reflect the interaction of *what-was-to-become-man* with various past *environments*. Includes the way that human *analysis-systems* are used in *concept-creation*.

Ecosystem—All of the *organisms* in a specific habitat along with the other features of that *environment* with which they interact.

Effector-mediation—The process by which *culture* increases or extends the ability of an *organism* such as *man* to deal with its *environment*. That part of the *Zwischenwelt* which includes *tools,* technological processes and the like. See *perceptor-mediation*.

Effector system—All those mechanisms of an *organism* that allow it to respond to needs and perceived changes in the *environment*. Includes certain parts of the brain, part of the nerve system, the muscles, etc. Forms one direction of the flow of change within the *functional circle* of the organism.

The *Innenwelt* of a species greatly influences the actions of its effector system.

Environment—The surroundings of an *organism,* especially those with which the organism interacts. See *Umwelt.*

Ethology—The scientific study of the total pattern of behavior of a species in its natural *environment.*

Evolution—In biology, the gradual change of life-forms from generation to generation; basically, the changing frequency of genes within the *gene pool* as a result of interaction with the *environment.*

Feedback—A method of control within an *organism,* mechanism, or other system whereby perceived changes in the *environment* are picked up (sensed or registered on a mechanical indicator like a thermostat) and used to regulate the future action of the system.

Frustration—A condition in an *organism* when its normal pattern of *telic activity* is blocked or retarded.

Functional circle—A pattern by which an *organism* is fitted into its *environment* by an equilibrium between its *receptor system* and its *effector system.* Perception and response form an integrated whole within this pattern.

Gene pool—All the genes present in a population of *organisms.*

Goal-seeking—The pursuit of certain environmental conditions by an *organism. Telic activity.*

Homeostasis—Maintenance of stability within an *organism,* population, or other system by means of internal *feedback* systems which provide for self-regulation.

Hominid—Present day *Homo sapiens* and a variety of related *man*-like forms known only from the fossil record. Refers to any member of the family Hominidae, which includes *Australopithecus* and other genera as well as the genus *Homo.*

Homo—See *Man.*

Ignorance—An *organism's* lack of all the available or certain necessary *information* on its *environment*. A degree of ignorance is present in all biological activity, but no organism could be absolutely ignorant and survive.

Imperfection of adaption—*Concept* that nothing in *evolution* requires that a species be perfectly adapted to its *environment*, or that a *functional circle* provide complete equilibrium.

Input-facilitation—Those systems, *phylogenetic* and learned, that increase the effectiveness of an *organism's* outreach for useful data on its *environment*. Includes *perceptor-mediation* processes. Contrasts with *output-facilitation*.

Industrial convergence—The *concept* that all industrial societies are impelled by the disciplines of the technological system toward an identical cultural pattern, i.e., a type of *monoculture*.

Industrial-man—The *concept* that the forces of industrial *technology* create a similar type of person out of individuals originally belonging to quite distinct *cultures*. Related to the concepts of *industrial convergence* and *monoculture*.

Industrialism—A stage in technological development, beginning in Europe in the modern period, which features the use of heavy machinery to achieve large-scale production; the social and political structure created by such development.

Information—A collected body of *data* or flow of data within a *communication* system which is of at least possible value to an *organism* or similarly constructed mechanism in making decisions because it is not random and is thus capable of describing conditions external to the organism/mechanism. Organisms must seek information in order to deal effectively with their *environment*. Information is quantified by the number of possible alternatives that could occur.

Innenwelt—The inner world of a species. In *Homo*, strongly conditioned by the use of a series of complex but innate *analysis-systems*.

Inner-world—See *Innenwelt*.

Inner zone primacy—The concept that the individual will normally give priority in the decision-making process to factors impinging on zones of personal and social activity that are closer over those that are more remote.

Innovation—Process of creating new *artifacts* or technological methods.

Intellect—Total capacity of an *organism* for collecting *information*, organizing it in accord with *analysis-systems* that provide for its effective use in dealing with the *environment*, and remembering that information. Properly includes systems for both *input-facilitation* and *output-facilitation*.

Irrationality—The abandonment, usually under conditions of *stress*, of *rationality;* breakdown in making decisions by properly applying the biologically determined *analysis-systems* to all available and pertinent *information.*

Language—A *communication* and *perceptor-mediation* system, especially oral-centered systems developed by *man*. Based on *symbol-making*.

Link—See *communication link.*

Low-technology war—The *concept* that *war* can be limited in such a way as not to use all available *technology.*

Luddism—Antagonism to the machine in human life; advocacy of "machine-smashing" by workers. A reaction to *industrialism.*

Macrocosm—The limits of largeness that can be comprehended by *Homo sapiens.*

Man—All individuals, past, present, and future (child and adult, male and female) who belong to the genus *Homo sapiens.*

Mediating world—The *Zwischenwelt*, the sum of all cultural systems involving *perceptor-mediation* or *effector-mediation* processes.

Metaculture—A single human *culture* that would stand or already stands above specific local cultures. Its content could vary. Contrasts with *monoculture.*

Microcosm—The limits of smallness that can be comprehended by *Homo sapiens*.

Middle realm—The characteristically human world, that similar to the one in which *man* evolved in terms of complexity, pace, scale, and the like. The level of analysis at which the natural human *analysis-systems* are most effective. Intermediate between *microcosm* and *macrocosm*.

Mind—Activity of the human brain as subjectively experienced by human beings. Closely related to the use of biologically based *analysis-systems* and culturally based *symbolic-systems*. Includes both *intellect* and emotional factors.

Monoculture—The *concept* of a single cultural tradition for all of mankind. Seen by some as the inevitable result of technological processes. Contrasts with *metaculture*.

Multidirectional approach—Any developmental strategy for mankind that would accept the value of creating greater variety in human forms or in human *cultures*. Contrasts with *unidirectional approaches*.

Negative feedback—A stabilizing control system, in which the input of the senses (or some other indicator) is used to counteract and countermand the action of the system when certain pre-established limits are exceeded. See *feedback*.

Niche—The range of environmental variables within which a species can live; includes temperature, water, and food supplies, and the like.

Noncooperative links—One-directional channels of *communication,* e.g., television, in which the viewer has no way to communicate with those presenting the program.

Organism—Any living being, including plants and animals. Organisms are *goal-seeking* and make continuing adaptations and adjustments to their *environments*.

Output-facilitation—Those systems, innate and learned, which increase the effectiveness of an *organism's* ability to take action within its *environment* and to modify that environment. Includes *effector-mediation* processes. Like *input-facilitation*, it is a system for improving the effectiveness of an organism's *functional circle.*

Overspecialization—A danger in the process of *adaptation* in which an *organism* develops one feature of its anatomy to an inordinate degree or otherwise becomes so dependent on its exploitation of certain very specific features of its *environment* that its survival would be threatened by very minor environmental changes.

Perception—An *organism's* awareness and immediate discriminatory interpretation of its *Umwelt*, based on the stimulation of sense organs. By extension, can be applied to mechanisms and other inanimate systems.

Perceptor-mediation—The process by which *culture* tunes an *organism* like *man* to perceive those aspects of the *environment* which are of especial significance in the *culture* involved. Includes the linguistic aspects of the *Zwischenwelt*. See *effector-mediation*.

Phylogenetic—Pertaining to *phylogeny.* Often synonymous with "genetic," "innate," or "biologically determined."

Phylogeny—The evolutionary history of a specific type of *organism*.

Positive feedback—A destablizing control system in which perceived changes in the *environment* are used to signal an escalation of the same kind of change. See *feedback, negative feedback.*

Rationality—The process of making decisions based on all pertinent *information* and on the full use of all the *analysis-systems* that are natural to a species. Use of the *intellect.* Usually maximized when emotional factors such as *stress* and *frustration* are not excessively involved. Contrasts with *irrationality.*

Receptor system—The total *sensory system* of an *organism*; all those mechanisms that provide it with *information* on the *environment.* The *Umwelt* of a species is the result of the actions of its *receptor systems* and its *analysis-systems.*

Science—The process of accumulating highly reliable *information* about the *environment* by the systematic use of human *analysis-systems* in close association with experience. Involves observation, classification, experimental investigations, and theoretical explanation of natural phenomena by *concept-creation.* The objective of science is to minimize human *ignorance.*

Second-order consequences—Those results of human or other *telic activity* that were not sought or even foreseen when action was taken. Only in *ignorance* would an *organism* take any action with second-order consequence that would outweigh the direct benefit of the action.

Self-assertiveness—Natural tendency of an *organism* to put forward its interests, to establish its claims or comparative superiority. Not equivalent to *aggression.*

Sensory deprivation—Denial to an *organism* of the amount or variety of sensory input that is essential to its well-being. Most commonly evidenced among mammals.

Sensory overload—Receipt by an *organism* of sensory *data* in amounts or variety so great that it cannot be either effectively used or easily ignored. Contrasts with *sensory deprivation.*

Sensory systems—All aspects of an *organism's* ability to gain potentially useful *information* about its *environment.*

Sexual dimorphism—Patterns of biological difference between males and females of the same species.

Stress—A mentally or emotionally disruptive state, often the result of the necessity to deal with unnatural or unpredictable environmental factors.

Symbol—An arbitrarily chosen signal which forms part of a larger *communication* system and/or plays a role in a *perceptor-mediation* process.

Symbolic system—A *language* or other matrix of *concepts* that is capable of use for *communication* of *information* or for *perceptor-mediation.*

Symbol-making—Process of culturally extending the discriminatory power of human *analysis-systems* by arbitrarily attaching *symbols* to features of the *environment.* Used to provide the basis for *communication* between persons or for sharpening the individual's *perception* of his environment, i.e., as *perceptor-mediation.*

Technique—A skill or methodology in dealing with the *environment.* (Note: This term is often used as a synonym of *technology* in translations of Continental European studies of technology.)

Techno-industrial—Descriptive of the most recent stages of *industrialism.*

Techno-industrial man—Anyone living in a *techno-industrial* society. (Note: Not related to the *concept* of *industrial -man,* which assumes *industrial convergence.*)

Technological imperative—The idea that *man* is compelled to create and use any technological device or system that he finds he is capable of creating. The *concept* is based on identified tendencies such as *curiosity* and *diversive exploration.*

Technology—The application by any species of its biologically based *analysis-systems* in order to design and use *artifacts* (*tools* and *works-of-art*), or otherwise to modify its *environment.* Although often a form of *output-facilitation,* includes art as well. In the case of *man,* also includes those methodologies for the manipulation of persons or things which depend on the use of tools and man-made environmental features. The term is often used to refer to or to include the *technomass.*

Technomass—The total weight or bulk of all *artifacts* and other man-made environmental features present in any particular area or developed by any particular *culture.* Contrasts with *biomass.*

Telic activity—Purposive or *goal-seeking* activity.

Tool—Any *artifact* used as part of an *output-facilitation* system. Includes, but not limited to, hand-tools and weapons.

Tool-making—Process of extending the range or efficiency of an *organism's effector system* by the creation of *artifacts*. Represents part of the *output-facilitation* system.

Total-environment—All aspects of an *organism's environment,* including not only its perceived *Umwelt* but also those environmental aspects that its *sensory systems* cannot detect. Generally speaking, an organism remains in *ignorance* of those aspects of the total-environment over which it has no control.

Umwelt—The surrounding world of a species as perceived by that species. Constitutes only part of the *total-environment.*

Uneasiness—Low degree of *stress* or *frustration* within an *organism.* May be associated with a need for *diversive exploration.*

Unidirectional approach—Any developmental strategy that accepts the need to maintain the fundamental unity of the human species or to establish the unity of human *culture.*

Urbanization—The process of people gathering together to create cities; essential to *civilization.*

War—System of physical conflict between organized groups of individuals of the same species. A culturally defined form of *aggression* in *man.* Perhaps a social pathology resulting from change of *environment* occasioned by the development of *agriculture.*

What-was-to-become-man—All the forms of life that led to the genus *Homo,* from a unicellular form in the seas to the advanced *hominids.* All life-forms representing the *phylogeny* of humanity.

Work-of-art—An *artifact* which is not a *tool,* but designed for the *aesthetic effect* it produces.

Zwischenwelt—The world of *culture* interposed by *man* between his *Innenwelt* and *Umwelt*. Includes: 1) *output-facilitation* systems such as *tool-making* and other aspects of *technology* that increase the range of the human *effector systems,* and 2) *input-facilitation systems* such as the creation of *concepts* which extend the range and sensitivity of human *receptor systems.*

Index

Aborigines, Australian, 92–93, 107
Abstraction, 87–88
Adaptation, 7, 13, 59, 221; by chemical means, 200; to cold, 104, 117–20; cultural, 103–24, 143, 217; to the desert, 106–11; to the forest, 111–15; by genetic engineering, 203; to high altitudes, 121; imperfection of, 64–68; to the seas, 115–17; by surgical means, 196; to the technomass, 143, 237;
Adler, A., 212
Aesthetic pollution, 220–21, 231–32, 259
Aesthetics, 168–69, 218–26, 229–33; of scientific activity, 169; and survival, 230–32
Africa, 28–29; ethnic groups of, 7, 29, 108–14; fossil hominids of 25–26, 36–37, 41
Aggression, 28–32; and drugs, 202–3; and surgery, 197; and war, 177–81
Agriculture, 127–34, 138–39, 150– 195; and energy, 128; as unnatural, 130, 138–39; and war, 177
Ainus, 144

Airplanes, 149, 157
Alice, in *Through the Looking-glass*, 94
Alienation, 143, 160–162, 187–88, 240; and genetic engineering, 205–6
Amerindians, 34; origin of, 47, 105; ethnic groups of, 7, 114–15
Amish, 242
Ammophila, 34
Analysis-systems, 39, 78, 81–83, 238; and art, 168; limitations of, 82; and science, 166; and technology, 38–41, 133
Anomie, 5
Anti-Utopias, 228
Apes, 22–23, 25, 45–46, 90–91
Aphasia, 87–88
Applied science, 167, 169
Ardrey, R., 23, 28–29
Aristotle, 35
Art, 55, 87, 218–33, 241–42; and analysis-systems, 168; defined, 168–69; and environment, 218–33; and play, 168–69; and simplification, 75; and technology, 221
Artifacts, 89, 125, 168–69
Arunta, 93, 125
Attention span, 43,59
Australopithecus, 26, 36–37, 41–42, 86, 96

Automation, 146–47, 212–13
Aymara, 121, 133

Babbage, C., 156–46
Baboons, 19, 22, 27
Back-to-nature movements,
    209–11, 215–17
Bacteriological weapons, 182
Bates, M., 18, 61–62, 103
Bedouins, 110–11
Beecher, H. W., 144
Behavior: display, 35;
    exploratory, 16–20
Bemba, 113
Bernhardi, F. von, 177
Big game hunting, 42
Binary contrasts, 61; and
    language, 94
Biomass, 89, 165
Biosphere, 49, 151
Bipedalism, 32–33
Blanchard, 142
Brachiation, 20–21
Brain: damage, 87, 180;
    evolution of the, 21, 41–3;
    and hemispheric
    dominance, 40;
    modification, 197–99;
    size, 41, 43, 73;
    specialization, 51;
    vulnerability of, 171–72,
    241
Brzezinski, Z., 147
Burack, B., 146
Bushmen. See Kalahari
    Bushmen
Butler, S., 211

Cactospize, 34
Camayura, 113
Cambodians, 133
Capek, K., 213
Carnivora, 20, 28, 43
Carnivorous animals, 26–28;
    aggressiveness of, 29–30;
    Homo as, 32–33
Carrol, L., 94

Catastrophe, 164; theory,
    189–90
Categorization as analysis-
    system, 75, 78–79, 81,
    87–88, 95
Cats, 17–19, 28, 58, 94
Causation as an analysis-system,
    82–83, 175, 238–39
Cebus, 90
Cercopithecus, 22
Change: as analysis system:
    82–83, 175; technological,
    162, 173–74
Chemical modification of
    Homo, 200–203
Children, language
    development of, 86–87
Chimpanzees, 23, 29, 46, 58,
    90–91
China, 34, 42, 199, 200, 213–14,
    225
Chuang Chou, 72, 97–98
Cities: first, 134; industrial,
    142; perceptual form of,
    156
Civilization, 134, 198; and
    individuality, 136; and
    sexuality, 46
Climate change, 16, 27, 47, 103,
    105
Clothing, 92–93, 104–5, 108,
    110–11, 118
Clynes, M., 197
Cold environments, and Homo,
    93, 117–22
Communication, 87, 94, 142,
    153, 158–60
Communication links, 159,
    224–26
Complexity of human activity,
    75–81; planning the,
    223–30
Computers: development of,
    145; and freedom, 176
Concepts: and analysis-systems,
    78, 87; and tools, 86
Confucius, 4

Consciousness, 59, 91, 220–21, 242, 244–45
Conservation, 4, 144, 151–52, 243
Cooperative links, 159, 224, 261
Copernicus, 49
Copulation, 45–46
Craftsmanship, 98, 136, 167–68
Crisis, 171–91; and catastrophe, 188–90; leadership, 185–88
Crook, J., 178
Crossopterygians, 15
Crowding, 151, 142, 156, 173
Cultures: 84–99, 217, 218–33; conservatism of, 98, 162; origin of, 47; role of, 103, 217; tools and, 88; universality of, 89
Curiosity, 55, 81, 170, 225; in mammals, 16–17
Cyborgs, 197–98

Dart, R., 28
Data. *See* Information
Decision information ratio, 207, 241–42
Decision-making, 57, 164, 220–21; dangers in, 226–27
Depressants, 202
Deserts 106–11
Devonian era, 14–15
Dickens, C., 4
Dictionaries, 78–79
Diversity, need for cultural, 242–43
Diversive exploration, 55
Dogs, 17–20, 94, 127, 203
Dollard, J., 178
Dolphins, 60, 115
Domesday Book, 139
Dostoevsky, F., quoted, 104
Drugs, 108, 200–203, 208
Dryopithecus, 25
Dynamic circle, 66

Ecological niche, 15, 64, 73, 186

Ecology: and extinction, 3, 223; of the human mind, 39, 83, 219, 238; and the individual, 50
Economics, 224; and social collapse, 184
Ecosystems, 262
Edison, T. A., 183
Education, 17, 104
Effector-mediation processes, 38, 85
Efficiency, 156, 187
Einstein, A., 175
Electricity, 145
Electro-sociology, 198–99
Elephants, 42, 43
Eliot, T. S. 39
Ellul, J., 4, 38, 163, 165, 218–19, 228
Emerson, R. W., 136
Energy, 127–29, 140; pool, 128–29
Entities. *See* Objects
Environment: designing the, 220–23; of the open plains, 26; of the seas, 13; of the trees, 17–24
Epistemological issues, 6–7, 66–68, 70, 199–200, 206–7
Erect posture. *See* Upright posture
Eskimos, 7, 29–30, 105, 118–20, 134, 155
Estrus, 45
Eugenics, 203
Eunuchs, 199
Evolution: of early primates, 19; guided, 207–8; of hominids, 25–46; and language, 86–88, 96–97; of mammals, 16; of vertebrates, 14
Existentialism, 7
Exploratory behavior, 55
Exterogestation, 43, 96
Extinction of species, 3, 9, 64,

Extinction of species, (cont.)
234; as result of human
activities, 52, 130; possible
of Homo, 38, 59, 171–91,
232
Extrasomatic devices, 88–89,
92–93
Eyes, of primates, 19–20

Factories, 140
Fear, 175
Feedback, 57–59, 69, 160,
220–21, 232–33, 242, 244
Fetishes, 35
Fire, 42–43, 104, 113, 120
Fish, 14–15
Food, 108, 117, 127–28;
sharing, 27–28
Ford Instrument Co., 146
Forest, as environment, 17–24
111–15
Fossil fuels, 128, 140–42,
151–52
Franklin, B., 8–9, 36, 65, 148
Freud, S., 46
Frost, R., 220–21
Frustration, 183
Functional circles, 59–64, 131;
as imperfect, 65–67; and
machines, 157–58, 173;
and primitive
technology, 122–23; and
telic activity, 63–64

Galbraith, J. K., 166, 227–28
Gandhi, M. K., 213
General Electric, 146
Genetic engineering, 203–7
Genetics, 8, 150, 203–7
Geneva Convention, 182
Genocide, 183
Ghost Dance Cult, 200–201
Glandular modification, 199
"Global village," 224
Goal-directed activity, 63, 71

Goodall (van Lawick-Goodall),
J., 90
Gorillas, 23, 46, 90
Gramme, Z., 145
Gray, G., 183
"Greenhouse effect," 152
Guyana, 113, 190

Hairlessness in Homo, 33, 45
Hall, B., 211
Hallucinogens, 200
Hand, 89; evolution of the,
20–21, 33, 35–36, 40;
surgical modification of the
197–98
Hardin, G., 67
Hargreaves, J., 140
Heidegger, M., 38
Heisenberg, W., 175
Hemispheric dominance, 40
Herskovits, M. J., 98
Hierarchy as analysis-system,
76–79
Highland environments, 121
Hippias of Elis, 134–35
Hitler, A., 181, 188
Hollerith, H., 146
Hominids, 25, 40–46; and
aggression, 28–32;
evolution of, 25, 40–46
Homo, 41; erectus, 41–43;
"faber," 34; "habilis," 37;
origins of Homo sapiens,
46–48
Human nature, 222: evolution
of, 6, 41–43; limits of, 72,
221; and technology, 37–39
Humboldt, W., 85
Hunting and gathering, 27–29;
and sexual dimorphism, 46;
societies, 103–24; and
Zone four, 49
Huxley, J., 74–75

IBM, 146

Ignorance, 63, 68–69, 164, 241–42
Imput-facilitation systems, 85
India, 26, 76, 213
Industrialism, 140, 150; and the arts, 226–30; and drugs, 202–3
Industrial-man, 6, 227–28, 243
Information: genetics and, 200, 207; human need for, 42, 61–62, 73; insufficient, 53–55, 68–69; processing, 61, 76–79; and second-order consequences, 69; theory, 77
Inkeles, A., 227–28
Innenwelt (or Inner-world), 5–7, 39, 69–71, 80, 85, 91, 141, 150, 206; art and the, 218, 231; defined, 70
Inner-zone primacy, 48, 50, 63, 164, 191, 220, 241
Innovation, 69, 139, 147–48; constancy of rate of, 123–24
Insects, 13–14, 15, 60, 74, 91, 137
Institutional collapse, 174, 215–16, 240–41
Intellect: evolution of, 41–43; limits of, 6, 8–9, 66–69, 72–83; and upright posture, 33; varieties of, 207
International language, 226
Inventions, 36–37, 139
Irrationality, 173, 175, 180, 186

Java man, 41
Jhooming, 127
Johnson, A. B., 126
Jünger, F. G., 212
Jungle environments, 112–14

Kafka, F., 4
Kalahari Bushmen, 29, 107

Kennedy, J. F., 185
Kenya, 36, 41
Kuhn, T., 167

Langer, S., 146–47
Language: origin of, 39–41, 27–28, 86–87, 95–97; and perceptor mediation, 85; and sexual dimorphism, 45; and simplification, 75. 79; universality of, 96–97; and Zone two, 48–49
Lao-tze, 209
Lapps, 7
Lateralization. *See* Hemispheric dominance
Leadership, 173, 185–88
Learning, 23, 59
Leakey, R., 41
Leisure, 142, 232
Leles, 112
Lévi-Strauss, C., 77–97
Life, origins of, 13–14
Limitations on human understanding, 6
Lingula, 66
Linton, R., 137
Lobotomy, 198
Lorenz, K., 30–31, 97
Low-technology war, 181–83
LSD, 201
Luddism, 212, 216
Lynch, K., 156

Macaca, 22
Machines, 139; movements against, 211–15
Mackey, R., xi
Macrocosm, 75
Magdalenian culture, 92, 94, 104
Mammals: evolution of, 16–17; nature of, 16, 55, 157
Man. *See Homo*
March, G. P., 144

Marcuse, H., 4, 176
Marshallese, 116
Marxism, 213–14, 228
Masai, 29
McLuhan, M., 224
Mediating world, 38, 84
Megaloceros, 50
Memory, 95–96, 108; and
    civilization, 136; limits of,
    79–80
Metaculture, 226–27
Microcosm, 75
Micro-environments, 14,
    110–11, 122, 141
Micronesia, 116
Middle realm, 6–7, 74–75, 82,
    207; *Homo* as subject of,
    72–83, 239–40; modern
    technology and, 152–58;
    transcending the, 81–83
Miller, G., 77–78
Mind, relationship with
    environment, 54–55, 82–83,
    238–39
Mitcham, C., xi
Monkeys: behavior of, 18, 22;
    toolmaking by, 90
Monoculture, 224–25, 226–27
Montagu, A., 87
Mosquitos, 18, 60–61
Motion: as analysis-system, 80,
    81–82; and forest
    environment, 21
Mousterian culture, 47
Multi-directional approaches:
    in culture building, 224–25,
    242–43; in genetic
    planning, 203–7
Mussolini, B., 177
Mumford, L., 34, 87, 213
Murung, 127
Music, 56, 87, 168

Neanderthals, 47, 104
Negative feedback, 58, 220
Nehru, J., 213

Neolithic, 94
Neoteny, 33–34
Noise, 161
Non-cooperative links, 159
Notaden bennetti, 108
Number as an analysis-system,
    82–83, 238–29

Objects, 20, 34, 238–39; and
    concepts, 28, 86–87;
    manipulation of, 35–36, 73
Oceans, 13–15; environments
    for humans, 115–17
Olduvai George, 36
Olympic games, 182
Orangutans, 90
Order and symmetry, 81
Ortega y Gasset, J., quoted, 7
Orwell, G., 4, 228
Output-facilitation systems, 166
Overspecialization, 50–51
Oysters, 64

Pace of human activity, 80–81;
    in industrialism, 143, 157
Paleolithic, 92–94, 104
Parr, J. A., 161
Pascal, B., 82
Pedomorphism. *See* Neoteny
Peking Man, 42
Perception, *See* Sensory
    deprivation; Sensory
    overload
Perceptor—mediation
    processes, 39, 85, 109–10,
    116
Perpillou, A. V., 115
Pfeiffer, J., 35
Phylogeny, 38–39
Pithecanthropus erectus, 41
Planning, 43, 91, 170, 187,
    220–25
Plasticity of humans, 104;
    according to existentialism,
    7; dangers of, 150–51;
    limits on, 123

Plato, 216
Playfulness, 33–34, 170; and
    art, 55, 168–69; of
    mammals, 16–17;
    technology of toys, 34, 216
Pollution, ix, 151, 171, 222–23
Polynesians, 116–17
Population, 123–24, 132,
    152–53, 196, 240–41, 244;
    and birth control, 216; and
    innovation rate, 123; limits
    without agriculture, 215
Positive feedback, 58–59;
    dangers of, 58, 242
Posture. *See* Upright posture
Precision grip, 36
Pregnancy, period of in *Homo*,
    43–44
Preliterate cultures, 105
Priestly, J., 148
Primates, 19; learning in,
    23–24; playfulness in,
    33–34; and territoriality,
    22–23
Progress, ix–x, 174; "backward,"
    215–17
Psychology, 5–7, 160–61; of
    confinement, 54; of
    technology, 212, 240–41;
    of war, 177–81
Pygmies, Ituri, 112, 114

Quechua, 121

Races, 104–5; future, 204–7
Ramapithecus, 26
Rationality, 171, 241; and the
    analysis-systems, 171;
    attacks on, 175–76; and the
    arts, 218; and war, 180
Receptor systems. *See* Sensory
    systems
Record keeping, 136
Reich, C., 160
Reproduction in *Homo*, 14,
    43–46

Reptiles, 16
Revolution, 5
Roosevelt, T., 221
Rousseau, J. J., 4, 130, 138,
    143, 209–11
Running, in *Homo*, 32–33
Russia, 92, 115, 213–15

Scale of human activity, 74–75,
    79–80; in industrialism,
    143, 155–56; planning the,
    223–26
Schumacher, E. F., 224
Science: applied, 37–38, 133,
    167; definition of, 166–67;
    faith in, 160; limits of,
    8–9, 66–68; pure, 166;
    as simplification, 75–76,
    169, 230–31; technology
    and, 166–68
Seas, reentry into the, 205–6.
    See also Oceans
Sea otters, 115, 118
Second-order consequences, 63,
    153, 160–64, 186; control
    of, 219
Self-assertiveness, 31–32,
    179–80, 195
Sensory deprivation, 53–55, 157
Sensory limitations, 73
Sensory overload, 56–57, 157
Sensory systems, 27, 60–62,
    137; artificial improvement
    of, 197–98
Sex, 44; and genetic engineering,
    205–6; roles, 46, 112, 113,
    117, 129, 131, 135, 163,
    177–78
Sexual patterns, 44–46; and
    dimorphism, 46, 131, 163;
    unique, of *Homo*: 45–46
    of vertebrates vs. insects,
    14–15
Shakespeare, W., 210
Shannon, C., 146
Shelley, P., 144

Shelters, 93, 111, 114, 118–19
Shepard, F., 123, 210
Sherrington, C., 66
Simplification, 75–79
Simpson, G. G., 3, 237
Sinsheimer, R. L., 206
Sloths, 50, 52
Solar energy, 128
Soviet Union, 213–15, 227–28
Space: as analysis-system,
    81–82, 238–39;
    exploration, 3, 161, 222
Specialization: excessive, and
    extinction, 50, 64; of
    Homo sapiens, 46–48,
    50–52; of human brain,
    172–73, 232
Steam power, 141
Storr, A., 44, 178–79
Stress, 157–58; and war, 180–81,
    182–85
Sub-cultures, 223–26
Surgical modification of
    humanity, 196
Sweating in *Homo,* 32–33
Symbols: creation of, 39; and
    environment, 87; limits on
    number of, 75–79; and
    perception, 87–88; and
    technology, 88; unity of
    tool and, 86
Symmetry as an analysis-system,
    81

Tanzania, 36
Taoism, 225–26
Tarzan, 26, 112
Tasaday, 114
Taxonomy, 77, 81
Taylor, G. R., 211
Techniques, 142, 165
Techno-industrial man, 6, 125,
    226–29
Techno-industrial society, 25,
    56–57, 70–71, 149
Technological imperative, 164,

170, 172, 182–83
Technology: of big game
    hunting, 37; defined,
    164–66; as external factor,
    163, 186, 219, 232; as
    internal factor, 36–37, 186,
    219–21, 232, 238; and the
    Middle realm, 152–62;
    origins of, 36, 47–48,
    88–94, 169–70; philosophy
    of, 38; primitive, 36–37,
    89, 106, 119, 122–23;
    and science, 165–67
Technomass, 89, 125–26, 163,
    165, 191
Television, 56, 231
Telic activity, 63, 71
Temperature: organ, 73, 121;
    regulation, 16, 118
Territoriality, 22, 29, 173; and
    agriculture, 130–32;
    among the primates, 22–23;
    and zones of interaction,
    48–50
Thesaurus, 79
Things. *See* Objects
Third World and technology,
    214–15
Thoreau, H. D., 143, 155, 209
Time: and agriculture, 91–92,
    132–33; as analysis-system,
    42–43, 81–82, 91, 238–39;
    and attention span, 59;
    and technology, 43, 80,
    157–58
Titanic, 188
Tolstoy, 209
Tools, 92–94; animals as, 127;
    brachiation and, 21;
    making, 30, 35–39, 47–48,
    86, 165; and symbols, 86;
    use of, by animals, 34,
    90–91; using, 59, 88–94
Torres Islanders, 76
Total-environment, 68, 70, 73,
    82, 201

Toynbee, A., 144, 174, 183
Toys. *See* Playfulness
Tranquilizers, 202–3
Transportation systems, 142, 176, 216
Tuaregs, 7, 111
Turkana, Lake (formerly Lake Rudolph), 36, 41
Twain, Mark, 98

Uexküll, J. von, 60, 65–66
Umwelt, 70–71, 85, 223
Uncertainty, 175
Uneasiness, 65
Unidirectional approaches, 208; to culture, 224–26; genetic planning, 105, 204–7
Upright posture: and agriculture, 133–34; in *Homo*, 32–33; and tools, 33–89
Urbanization, x, 135–37, 155–57
Utopianism, 143, 209–10, 214

Vacca, R., 216
Vision: color, 20, 28; in primates, 19; stereoscopic, 19–20
Vocabulary, 109–10, 133; size, 77–79
Voltaire, 244–45
Von Neumann, J., 146

Wai-Wai, 113
Walking. *See* Running
Wallace, A. F. C., 81

War, ix–x, 5, 97, 135, 177–83; low-technology, 181–83
Water: management, 106–7, 108–10, 132; power, 131, 139
Watt, J., 141
Watt, K. E. F., 188
Weapons, 30, 34, 35, 90, 92–93, 112–13, 142, 153, 180, 217
Weisgerber, L., 85
Westinghouse, 146
Whales, 115
Whitney, E., 142
Wilde, O., 237
Wildlife protection, 4, 52, 243
Wilkinson, 141
Wittfogel, K. A., 131
Wordsworth, W., 158
Works of art, 168–69

Xingu, 112–13

Yahgans, 120
Yerkes laboratory, 22
Youth, 159–60

Zaire, 112, 114
Zones of interaction, 48–50, 110–11, 113–14, 117, 122–23, 130–31, 220–21
Zwischenwelt, 85, 103, 107, 112, 118–19, 125; of civilization, 135, 155; and inputs, 85, 87–88; limits of creation, 223; and outputs, 85, 88–89, 166

DATE DUE